DATE DUE

DEMCO 38-296

About Island Press

Island Press is the only nonprofit organization in the United States whose principal purpose is the publication of books on environmental issues and natural resource management. We provide solutions-oriented information to professionals, public officials, business and community leaders, and concerned citizens who are shaping responses to environmental problems.

In 2005, Island Press celebrates its twenty-first anniversary as the leading provider of timely and practical books that take a multidisciplinary approach to critical environmental concerns. Our growing list of titles reflects our commitment to bringing the best of an expanding body of literature to the environmental community throughout North America and the world.

Support for Island Press is provided by the Agua Fund, Brainerd Foundation, Geraldine R. Dodge Foundation, Doris Duke Charitable Foundation, Educational Foundation of America, The Ford Foundation, The George Gund Foundation, The William and Flora Hewlett Foundation, Henry Luce Foundation, The John D. and Catherine T. MacArthur Foundation, The Andrew W. Mellon Foundation, The Curtis and Edith Munson Foundation, National Environmental Trust, The New-Land Foundation, Oak Foundation, The Overbrook Foundation, The David and Lucile Packard Foundation, The Pew Charitable Trusts, The Rockefeller Foundation, The Winslow Foundation, and other generous donors.

The opinions expressed in this book are those of the author(s) and do not necessarily reflect the views of these foundations.

Mimicking Nature's Fire

Mimicking Nature's Fire

Restoring Fire-Prone Forests in the West

Stephen F. Arno

Carl E. Fiedler

ISLANDPRESS

Washington • Covelo • London

ISLAND PRESS is a trademark of The Center for Resource Economics.

Library of Congress Cataloging-in-Publication data.

Arno, Stephen F.
  Mimicking nature's fire : restoring fire-prone forests in the West / Stephen F. Arno, Carl E. Fiedler.
    p.   cm.
  Includes bibliographical references and index.
    ISBN 1-55963-142-2 (cloth : alk. paper) — ISBN 1-55963-143-0 (pbk. : alk. paper)
1. Forests and forestry—Fire management—West (U.S.)   2. Fire ecology—West (U.S.) 3. Reforestation—West (U.S.)   I. Fiedler, Carl E.   II. Title.
    SD387.F52A76 2005
    577.2'4'0978—dc22`   2004025493

British Cataloguing-in-Publication data available.

Printed on recycled, acid-free paper ✪

Design by Paul Hotvedt, Blue Heron Typesetters

Manufactured in the United States of America

10 9 8 7 6 5 4 3 2 1

We dedicate this book in memory of the late Vic Dupuis,
a Native American of western Montana.
Vic envisioned and practiced restoration forestry as a silviculturist
on the Lolo National Forest.

Contents

Preface   *xi*
Acknowledgments   *xvii*

1   Introduction   1

I   Fundamentals   5

2   Ecology's Role in Forest Management   7
3   Knowledge from Historical Fire Regimes   14
4   Can Fire-Prone Forests Heal Themselves?   29
5   Restoration Objectives, Techniques,
    and Economics   37

II Learning from Experience:
    Profiles of Restoration Forestry
    Projects by Forest Type   55

6   Pinyon-Juniper—The Elfin Forest   57
7   Ponderosa Pine/Fir—Research and
    Demonstration Areas   65
8   Ponderosa Pine/Fir—Forest Management on
    Public Lands   88
9   Ponderosa Pine/Fir—Privately Owned
    Conservation Reserves   108
10 Giant Sequoia/Mixed Conifer   121

11   Western Larch/Fir   131
12   Lodgepole Pine   149
13   Whitebark Pine   167
14   Restoring Aspen and Conifers across a
     Ranger District   175
15   Restoring Fire on a Wilderness Landscape   188

III Conclusions   201
16   The Restoration Imperative   203

     References   *211*
     About the Authors   *231*
     Index   *233*

Preface

A forest ecologist's experience (Stephen Arno)

After 40 years of studying forest ecology and its implications for management, I felt compelled to chronicle the achievements of the unsung innovators. The people who shared their knowledge with us for this book are applying ecosystem-based management to different kinds of forests scattered across the western United States and southwestern Canada. By explaining the rationale and workings of this "restoration forestry," I encourage others to consider similar management strategies for more of the western forests that were historically shaped by and adapted to recurring fires. I was able to enlist one of the leaders in developing ecology-based forestry, Dr. Carl Fiedler of the University of Montana, to join in this effort. The following biographical sketches help explain our passion for this initiative.

I grew up on the west side of Puget Sound in country dominated by second-growth coastal Douglas-fir that had sprung up in profusion on land logged 50–100 years earlier. The original forests of huge Douglas-fir owed their existence to great fires, as was still attested in the 1950s by charred snags of ancient trees and blackened bark on the occasional old growth trees that remained. Taking up forestry in college in the early 1960s, I was captivated by the ecological relationships found in forests. So many species of trees were adapted to slightly different conditions—to different ecological "niches"—and they combined to make up such a diverse and productive forest landscape. Clearly, fire was the historical "agent of change" that fostered the wealth of trees, other plants, and diverse wildlife in many forest ecosystems.

Certain older methods of timber harvesting and slash burning seemed to have some commonality with the natural processes of fire and successional recovery, but increasingly foresters were being led in another direction. It seemed that we were being trained to turn natural forests throughout the West into agricultural tree plantations to satisfy some all-important quest for maximizing economic returns. On national forest land this emphasis on wood production at the expense of ecological values seemed to conflict with the official "multiple use" management policy that was supposed to ensure stewardship of outdoor recreation, water, and wildlife values as well as wood. In the 1960s extensive new road systems and massive clear-cuts were promoted for managing many different kinds of forests throughout the West. Often the ground was thoroughly scraped by bulldozers and planted to the most favored timber tree.

We were told future plantations would feature genetically bred supertrees. To maximize wood production, plans called for clear-cutting the plantation at a very young age—between 40 and 80 years, depending on the productivity of the site. Terraces were gouged by bulldozers into steep south-facing slopes to make benches where planted trees could grow vigorously. Native shrubs, termed "brush," were often sprayed with herbicides to prevent them from competing with the tree crop. Insect epidemics that built up in monoculture stands could be fought with aerially sprayed DDT or other insecticides.

This type of plantation forestry seemed to be an expansion of techniques used to establish tree crops in areas of Europe where forests had been denuded by centuries of unregulated wood-cutting and pasturing. Applying such heavy-handed methods to natural forest ecosystems in western North America seemed strange and inappropriate to me and to many other foresters young and old. Increasingly, members of an environmentally conscious public became alarmed by these methods, and some eventually rejected all forms of timber harvesting on public lands.

Soon after earning a Ph.D. in forest ecology in 1970, I got the opportunity to help inject new thinking into western forestry by building the case for ecologically based management. A small group of us at the U.S. Forest Service Intermountain Research Station developed the "habitat type" land classification system, which helped thousands of employees of the Forest Service and other agencies incorporate ecological knowledge and considerations into forest management (Pfister and Arno 1980). As part of another joint effort based at the Fire Sciences Laboratory in Missoula, Montana, I worked with many different land managers to test methods for reintroducing fire and managing fuels.

The relevance of ecologically based management became inescapable when my wife and I purchased and built our home in a 60-acre tract of overly dense and stagnating second-growth ponderosa pine. In the 1970s, restoration forestry was virtually unknown, so we wound up learning how to do it ourselves—including commercial and precommercial thinning to retain and favor large vigorous trees, marketing small-diameter wood products, prescribed burning, and planting. Our two sons earned forestry degrees and have now been restoration forestry contractors for many years. They have taught me a great deal about choosing effective and economical equipment and methods for restoration.

The more I learn about western forests, the more sensible it seems to manage them based on natural processes and their effects.

A silviculturist's experience (Carl Fiedler)

Growing up in rural northern Wisconsin, it was sometimes hard distinguishing between living in and off of the forest. My brothers and I picked and sold blueberries, prince's pine, wild rice, and pine cones, peeled bark from pulpwood, fence rails, and house logs, and planted trees on cutover county lands. I soon understood the importance of perpetuating the forest that provided so much of my early earnings. Indeed, it was a forester's visit to our home when I was in third grade that cemented my decision about what I wanted to be. While other boys my age were contemplating their future as a cowboy or fireman, I had a different idea. To think that there was a job that involved being in the woods all day and learning about trees seemed too good to be true. I was going to be a forester!

An uncle's story of a place where one could catch trout by just stepping off the road led me to college in Montana. After graduate school and a stint with the Forest Service Intermountain Research Station, I started my current position at the University of Montana conducting research aimed at private land forest management. Ironically, my formal education had focused on even-aged methods (e.g., clear-cutting) that dominated public land forest management—methods that were of little interest to nonindustrial private landowners. These landowners typically cut the large valuable trees on their property and left the smaller shade-tolerant ones, a practice known as high-grading. Although high-graded stands may pass visual muster, they are ecological "accidents" waiting to happen—vulnerable to insects, disease, and fire. Surely this was not the answer either.

Since the 1970s I've spent much of my time traveling the back roads of the West—visiting and studying forests of every kind, but especially ponderosa pine. What I saw and learned led me to question the conventional view supporting even-aged management of drier forests. For example, I examined the age distribution of trees in old-growth pine stands conventionally regarded as even-aged. I found that tree ages often varied by decades and centuries. What happened in these forests in the past that resulted in trees of widely different ages? If fire visited frequently, why weren't these trees killed? Simply put, what made these stands tick? Examining hundreds of pine stands across the West—and establishing long-term research plots in some—gradually changed my thinking. Applying traditional even-aged methods somehow resembled fitting the square peg in the round hole—first choosing the silvicultural method and then "making" it work. Why not instead use methods that were complementary to or compatible with natural disturbances and species' adaptations?

Discussions with U.S. Bureau of Indian Affairs foresters further piqued my interest in uneven-aged management. However, traditional uneven-aged or "selection" methods were developed in the northeastern United States and Europe and didn't fit western conditions well. They were designed for regenerating shade-tolerant species and were too detailed for operational use.

Uneven-aged methods of some kind seemed a natural for many public and nonindustrial private forestlands where continuous forest was a primary objective and where understory fires historically perpetuated such conditions. Yet traditional uneven-aged methods needed modification for use with sun-loving western species. In 1984, in consultation with Bob Pfister (University of Montana forest ecologist, retired) and Steve Haglund (Bureau of Indian Affairs area forester, retired), I implemented an experiment on the Lubrecht Experimental Forest to test such treatments (Chapter 7). Based on what I had learned at Lubrecht, I implemented a "modified and improved" version of these treatments 8 years later as part of the Lick Creek project on the Bitterroot National Forest.

After 20 years of experiments and extensive travels in the Northern Rockies and Southwest, I've refined my view, but the basic ecological concepts that motivated the 1984 experiments are still sound today. Management based on natural disturbance processes and their effects makes sense ecologically and socially. I believe variations of the Lu-

brecht and Lick Creek approaches, along with the potpourri of examples reported in this book, hold almost unlimited promise for restoring millions of acres of western national forests.

Planning the Lick Creek project in 1991 was my first opportunity
to work with Steve Arno, and we have teamed up on numerous projects since. It has been my privilege to collaborate with him in writing
this book. We highlight real-world projects by dedicated practitioners
who overcome obstacles and organizational inertia to get things done.
We hope the diverse examples portrayed in these pages will spark the
can-do attitude that once permeated our profession. Restoration
forestry cannot succeed without it.

Acknowledgments

We are indebted to the many practitioners of restoration forestry who shared their knowledge and experience with us. Our example from the pinyon–juniper woodland in Bandelier National Monument (chapter 6) is based largely on information provided by Craig Allen and Brian Jacobs. Information on the Greater Flagstaff Demonstration Area (chapter 7) was generously supplied by Tammy Randall-Parker and Pete Fulé. Primary contacts showing us projects in ponderosa pine forests on public lands (chapter 8) were Robert Gray in the British Columbia Coast Range, Brian Tandy on the Sisters Ranger District, Paul Survis and Mike Piazza on the Wallowa Valley Ranger District, and Kathy Ramirez, Ray Eklund, and Barry Stern on the Boise National Forest. Our sources for restoration projects on privately owned conservation reserves (chapter 9) were rancher Bill Potter and neighboring forester Hank Goetz for the E Bar L Ranch; forest manager Bill Bradt, consultant forester Craig Thomas, and restoration specialist Nathan Arno for the Burnt Fork Ranch; and owner Max Watson, manager Warren Anders, and restoration specialist Matt Arno for the Rocking K Ranch. We were tutored on the long history of sequoia–mixed conifer restoration (chapter 10) by Dave Parsons, Nate Stephenson, and Tony Caprio. Principal informants for restoration in larch/fir forests (chapter 11) were Tim Love, Bruce Higgins, and Bill Oelig on the Seeley Lake Ranger District; Dennis Divoky, Carl Key, and Fred Vanhorn of Glacier National Park; Steve Wirt of the Flathead National Forest; and Mick Harrington of the U.S. Forest Service Rocky Mountain Research Station's Fire Sciences Lab. Our primary sources for the diverse restoration projects in lodgepole pine forests (chapter 12) were Jerry Chonka on the Gunnison Ranger District; Stu Lovejoy and Dave Campbell on the Bitterroot National Forest; Ward McCaughey, Colin Hardy, and Helen Smith of the Rocky Mountain

Research Station regarding the Tenderfoot project; and Cliff White and Ian Pengelly of Banff National Park. We obtained knowledge of restoration work in whitebark pine communities (chapter 13) from Robert Keane of the Rocky Mountain Research Station's Fire Sciences Lab and Diana Tomback of the University of Colorado at Denver. Ranger Bob Andrews and the staff of the Eagle Lake Ranger District generously showed us their myriad restoration projects (chapter 14), and we especially thank Al Vazquez and Tom Rickman for their extensive assistance. Byron Bonney and Bob Mutch helped us grasp and tell the story of how land managers have expanded the return of fire into the Clearwater and Salmon River backcountry (chapter 15) over the past three decades.

We are also grateful to Jim Habeck for reviewing the entire draft manuscript and to several people who reviewed parts of it and provided advice that helped improve the presentation of an often complex message. These include John Duff Bailey, James K. Brown, Pete Fulé, Peter Friederici, David Huffman, H.B. "Doc" Smith, Jane Kapler Smith, Dave Stack, Diane Vosick, and Mike Wood. Steve Robertson produced the computer visualizations used for figures 5.1, 7.2, and 11.1. Island Press executive editor Barbara Dean and contract editor John Davis greatly helped us organize and clarify our case for restoration forestry.

Chapter **1**

Introduction

Successive, widely publicized wildfires have swept through forests of western North America, beginning in 1987 in California and Oregon and 1988 in Yellowstone National Park and the Northern Rockies. During most fire seasons since, hundreds of forest homes and cabins have gone up in flames, from the mountain suburbs of Los Angeles to Kelowna, British Columbia. By now anyone interested in western forests is aware that our management and protection policies have failed to account for the historical role of fire, leaving a legacy of dense forests with sickly trees and hazardous fuels.

Since about 1990, newspapers, magazines, television news, and Congressional hearings have warned of ecological deterioration and increasing wildfire hazard in western forests. The now familiar story is that suppression of fires for nearly a century and logging of fire-resistant old growth trees spawned an overcrowded growth of smaller trees vulnerable to intense blazes and epidemics of insects and disease. Today's dense forests also lack diverse and productive grass and shrub communities needed by wildlife. Each year we channel more money, personnel, and technology into fire suppression, but uncontrollable wildfires continue to threaten forests and the homes and recreation areas within them. Despite recognizing the impending peril facing broad expanses of western forests, we remain polarized and indecisive about what to do.

After decades of studying western forests, the authors recognized that the magnificent old-growth trees that survived and depended on periodic fires disappear when deprived of this essential disturbance process. When forests of these venerable trees are managed using traditional timber harvesting methods, the features that made them famous ultimately disappear. When these forests are protected in "natural areas" that fail to restore the historical role of fire—as in the majority of parks, wilderness, and primitive areas—the big old fire-resistant trees gradually die and are replaced by thickets of small trees. Our experience revealed that long-lived trees and other important features of fire-prone forests can be restored through management that mimics the effects of historical fires. Although research studies and practical examples indicate how to restore forests and reduce potential damage from wildfires, insects, and disease, they get little play in the media. However, it is these topics—scientific findings and real-world management examples—that we bring together in this book.

This book advocates changing direction in the management of western forests and adopting an approach we call "restoration forestry" that is based on historical natural processes. Restoration forestry does not have a well-established definition. We use it to designate the practice of reinstituting an approximation of historical structure and ecological processes to tree communities that were in the past shaped by distinctive patterns of fire. The intent is not to re-create a single, distinct "historical condition" but rather a range of conditions representative of historical ecosystems (Fiedler 2000a). This is a narrower, more immediate, and more attainable goal than restoration of the entire forest ecosystem, known as "ecological restoration," and defined as "the process of assisting the recovery of an ecosystem that has been degraded, damaged, or destroyed" (Society for Ecological Restoration International: www.ser.org).

Restoration of the forest tree community (the goal of restoration forestry) triggers desired changes in the vigor and composition of undergrowth plants, large and small mammal populations, avian communities, and microfauna as well as soil, hydrologic, and biochemical processes. Thus, restoration of tree communities is the key process that initiates and facilitates the broader goal of ecological restoration. Few forest types have been studied thoroughly enough to attempt ecological restoration. One exception is the southwestern ponderosa pine forest (Friederici 2003a).

How much restoration forestry is needed? When people learn that more than one hundred million acres of fire-prone western forests harbor deteriorating conditions outside the historical range of variability, they are struck by the staggering extent of this problem. Given the difficulties of applying restoration, some may judge the situation hopeless. However, our experience suggests that *any* strategically located restoration treatments can produce noticeable benefits in reducing wildfire hazard to homes and communities and return important features of historical forests. In some areas, restoration forestry relies on returning natural fires. In others it requires cutting treatments to produce a more natural forest structure before using prescribed fire. In heavily populated areas it may rely on strategic removal of certain trees and forest fuels. In natural areas initial cultural treatments may eventually be replaced by fire. This book explains the options and considerations involved in planning restoration forestry across a range of geographical settings and ownerships. For students and others interested in more detailed information, the book cites publications that elaborate on specific topics.

How the Book Is Organized

In Part I, chapters 2–5, we examine the "nuts and bolts" underlying restoration forestry as applied to fire-dependent forests: why it is needed, how it developed, and how it is applied.

In Part II (chapters 6–15) we look "under the hood" to understand restoration projects in different forest types representing each historic fire regime and under contrasting management goals. We study notable restoration projects from Arizona to Alberta and California to Colorado. Some projects are designed to protect homes and developments. Others return natural processes to wilderness areas, enhance habitat in privately owned conservation reserves, or promote sustainability in timber-producing forests. These examples of restoration forestry represent a spectrum of vegetation types, from aspen and pinyon-juniper through the heart of the conifer forest to high-elevation whitebark pine communities.

Our examples demonstrate how diverse landowners and forest stewards designed and carried out treatments to return features and processes of historically sustainable forests, despite limited funding, smoke regulations, and many other constraints. We evaluate how well these projects have achieved restoration goals and interpret how they might be improved. The majority of these projects focus on stand-level restoration, but in chapter 14 we examine strategic restoration efforts in a large timber-producing forest, and in chapter 15 we profile a project aimed at restoring a vast wilderness landscape.

Part III concludes the book (chapter 16) by placing restoration forestry in a broad perspective and specifying factors critical for its success. We summarize how restoration forestry uses knowledge of historical natural processes as the basis for managing for different landowner goals. Restoration forestry provides for ecological sustainability of the forest and the resources and amenity values important to humans. It also allows highly developed countries to sustainably manage natural forests rather than exploiting them or those of less developed countries.

Part I

Fundamentals

Part I (chapter 2) begins by looking at some fundamentals: why traditional forestry tried to exclude fire from forests, why this attempt failed, and why foresters and ecologists now recognize the need for management based on how natural ecosystems operate. Information on fire's historic role (chapter 3) provides a foundation for designing restoration strategies. Some forests experienced an "understory fire regime," in which frequent low-intensity fires burned along the ground, consuming surface fuels, keeping the understory open, and favoring long-lived fire-resistant trees. In contrast, the "stand replacement fire regime" had infrequent high-intensity fires that killed nearly all trees but gave rise to luxuriant communities of herbs, shrubs, and tree seedlings that require fire or other major disturbance. In between was the "mixed fire regime," in which fires of varying intensities occurred at fluctuating intervals and burned in complex patterns, creating diverse tree and undergrowth plant communities and variable amounts of surviving old trees. We further examine how forest conditions have been altered in these three different fire regimes.

In chapter 4 we answer the fundamental questions posed by those challenging the premise of restoration forestry: Can't we just let nature do the restoration? If we leave the forest alone, won't it eventually return to its historical condition? Have forest environments and burning patterns changed so irrevocably that this won't work? Chapter 5 describes how management goals influence the strategies used in restoration forestry. We look at different techniques and outline the elements of a restoration management plan. Economic considerations are an integral part of any plan; consequently, we evaluate short-term and long-term costs and benefits. Lands managed with restoration forestry often don't turn a profit, but they do yield long-term benefits in aesthetics, wildlife habitat, forest protection, and where desired, timber production. We will see how the cost of restoration forestry can sometimes be offset by the value of trees removed in treatment, but that recovering this value is not the motivation for treatment.

Chapter 2

Ecology's Role in Forest Management

In 1857 Lt. Edward Beale journeyed across the high northern plateaus of what would later become the Arizona Territory with a band of camels that he dreamed would revolutionize transportation in the Southwest. He described the vast ponderosa pine (*Pinus ponderosa*) forest in glowing terms: "We came to a glorious forest of lofty pines, through which we traveled ten miles. [The ground was] covered with the finest grass. . . . The forest was perfectly open and unencumbered with brushwood" (Cooper 1960, p. 130). Similarly, pioneer journals from the 1850s described the Oregon Trail in the Blue Mountains of eastern Oregon as climbing through open groves of magnificent ponderosa pines. Pioneers extolled the lush grass beneath the trees, and almost every late summer they witnessed fires burning through the country with little effect on the trees (Evans 1990). Today dense forests and thickets of small trees blanket these landscapes, grass is sparse, and big trees are few.

Why Traditional Forestry Failed

Why didn't the methods used in traditional forestry prevent deterioration of western forests? Forestry, which predated the science of ecology, failed from the beginning to recognize the ecological importance of fire. Concepts of forestry were developed in moist regions of Europe for the purpose of reestablishing trees on land deforested centuries earlier (Arno and Allison-Bunnell 2002). Early European foresters considered fire entirely a destructive force introduced by humans. We now know that most North American forests as well as ancient forests in

Europe were shaped over thousands of years by distinctive patterns of fire (Pyne 1997).

When European-American settlements were expanding across North America in the 19th century, countless fires threatened everything from mining camps to major communities (Pyne 1982). Many fires were started accidentally by railroads, campfires, or settlers clearing land. Although a few visionaries recommended controlled burning of forests during a relatively safe season to reduce fire threats, forestry leaders, conservationists, and many landowners thought that fire should be suppressed and largely eliminated. In 1908 the U.S. Forest Service developed a primary mission funded by Congress to suppress forest fires; it also tried to prevent any use of fire as a tool to maintain forests. Over the next several decades the Forest Service led a multiagency, paramilitary-type program to eliminate forest fires.

Beginning in the 1950s clear-cut harvesting, which removes all trees from a sizeable area, was commonly applied to forests historically dominated by the mixed and stand replacement fire regimes (Clary 1986). Following harvest, the ground was usually prepared for regeneration of a new forest by scraping with bulldozers or prescribed burning. Dozer scraping displaces the productive upper soil layer, leaving a surface highly susceptible to invasion by introduced weeds. Burned clear-cuts bear some resemblance to forests in the stand replacement fire regime, except that the latter have an abundance of standing dead trees (snags). Snags cast beneficial shade and provide habitat for a variety of birds and small mammals that nest in cavities made by woodpeckers.

By the 1960s, rapidly expanding knowledge in the young science of ecology revealed that fire plays an essential role in natural forests. During the 1970s natural resource agencies changed course in response to this new knowledge and to escalating costs of fire suppression and recognized that fire should be used in forest management (Nelson 1979). However, by this time a variety of barriers had developed. An influential "fire suppression industry" had built up to serve the lucrative fire-fighting effort by providing personnel and equipment of all sorts, and it depended on continuation of the fire exclusion policy (Arno and Allison-Bunnell 2002).

Over the decades, money and other incentives were geared to putting fires out, not to using and managing fire. The public, nurtured on Smokey Bear messages, had also been convinced that all fire in the forest was bad. A host of new laws, including the Clean Air Act, Clean

Water Act, and National Environmental Protection Act, had many beneficial effects, but they also spawned regulations that hindered returning a natural disturbance process like fire. New homes and developments worth billions of dollars sprang up in dense high-hazard forests, increasing the political outcry when foresters wanted to use fire. In addition, the potential liability managers face when prescribed or natural fires go awry far outweighs any rewards they might receive for using fire successfully. Governments are accustomed to spending vast amounts to suppress fires—an effort well received by the public—but resist spending smaller amounts to reduce forest fuels and subsequent fire damage. The ability to suppress unwanted fires and to control prescribed fires remains an essential tool for managing forests. Our mistake was trying to *eliminate* fire in western forests.

Examples from different fire regimes (presented in Part II) illustrate important differences between conventional timber management and restoration treatments that include tree removal. In forests historically subject to the understory and mixed fire regimes, traditional logging removed the large fire-resistant trees and allowed saplings to proliferate and develop into thickets. Restoration treatments leave many of the large fire-resistant trees, remove more small trees and sometimes medium and large shade-tolerant trees, and often use prescribed fire to kill some of the seedlings and saplings, mimicking effects of historical fires (Fiedler 2000a). Valuable timber remains, and on some ownerships can increase and help pay for tending the stand again in the future. In place of clear-cutting in the stand replacement fire regime, restoration forestry may prescribe "variable retention harvesting," in which patches of live trees and snags are left within irregularly shaped units (Franklin and others 1999). These areas may later be prescribe burned, with treatment effects more comparable ecologically to a natural burn.

Roots of Restoration Forestry

Perhaps the earliest example of restoration forestry in America came in the 1890s when Gifford Pinchot and a German forester named Carl Schenck were hired to restore native hardwoods on the deforested Vanderbilt estate in North Carolina. However, the concept of restoring and maintaining more natural conditions in fire-prone western forests developed slowly, in tandem with the emerging disciplines of forest ecology and fire ecology. Pioneering ecologist Frederic Clements (1910) characterized the fire ecology of high-elevation lodgepole pine (*Pinus contorta* var. *latifolia*) forests and advocated using controlled fire in their management. In the 1920s research showed that when fire was withheld from longleaf pine (*Pinus palustris*) forests in the Southeast, brown-spot disease fatally attacked young pines. Soon many landowners were using fire in southern pinelands to control disease, reduce fuel buildup, and enhance habitat for quail and other wildlife (Chapman 1926, Pyne 1982).

During the early 1900s—and much to the chagrin of the U.S. Forest Service—several prominent timberland owners in northern California practiced and promoted burning beneath ponderosa pine-mixed conifer forests to reduce fuels and mimic frequent fires of the pre-settlement era (Hoxie 1910, Kitts 1919, Pyne 1982, 2001). In the 1920s and 1930s entomologist F. P. Keen linked ecological deterioration of ponderosa pine forests in Oregon to fire exclusion. Keen's revelation inspired Harold Weaver, a young forester with the U.S. Indian Service (precursor of the Bureau of Indian Affairs), to begin experimenting with fire in ponderosa pine (Weaver 1968). In 1943 Weaver penned a remarkable treatise in the *Journal of Forestry* championing fire as a silvicultural tool in ponderosa pine forests—virtual heresy in a period when fire exclusion was the official policy (Weaver 1943). Within a few years Harold Biswell, a forestry professor at the University of California, Berkeley, who had experience with burning in the Southeast, began demonstrating the use of fire in western pine forests (Biswell 1989, Carle 2002). But the voices recognizing fire's ecological value in western forests were few and the deaf ears were many. Despite decades of dedicated individual efforts to mimic natural fire in management, those in the fire exclusion camp maintained tight control over fire policy.

In the late 1940s, conservationist Aldo Leopold articulated his famous "land ethic," which advocates stewardship that "preserves the integrity, stability, and beauty of the biotic community" (Leopold 1949). Eliminating fire, like exterminating predators or clear-cutting old-growth forests, opposes the land ethic. Aldo Leopold's son Starker headed the advisory committee whose 1963 report to the Secretary of Interior recommended restoring fire to national parks (Leopold and others 1963). Soon thereafter, Sequoia and Kings Canyon national parks initiated the first program to restore natural (lightning) fires, a policy adopted in the early 1970s by Forest Service managers for use in the Selway-Bitterroot Wilderness.

The use of silvicultural cutting to restore historic structure in fire-prone forests was particularly slow to develop. The first restoration research in the West that involved both cutting and burning was initiated only in 1984. This long-term experiment on the University of Montana's Lubrecht Experimental Forest (chapter 7) was designed to evaluate modified selection cutting and prescribed burning to sustain uneven-aged ponderosa pine stands, including old-growth trees, while producing timber products.

By the 1990s environmental concerns and regulations dramatically reduced timber harvesting on public forests and forced land managers to emphasize environmental protection. In response, the Forest Service adopted a concept of ecosystem-based management aimed at restoring and maintaining natural communities of trees, other plants, and animals, commonly referred to by the term "biodiversity." Although the theory of "ecosystem management" has been publicized, evaluations of actual projects applying it are rare. Few people even know that it is being practiced, much less if it is successful.

Public interest in environmental issues increased the focus on private forestlands as well. Forest stewardship programs developed to educate landowners about environmental attributes of forests and how they can be protected and managed. Large tracts of private forests in the West have been placed under conservation easements overseen by land trusts or other conservation organizations. At first, easements often required protection from all human disturbance and fire. Now, however, recognizing the importance of natural processes, land trusts are replacing simple preservation goals with stewardship management plans that prescribe treatments to restore and maintain an approximation of natural conditions. Still, lack of awareness of restoration opportunities on private lands hampers their expansion to this significant component of the forest landscape.

Meeting Today's Needs

Restoration forestry based upon the ecological role of fire should interest anyone concerned about the long-term well-being of forests, protection of life and property, or sensible use of public funds. Federal, state, and local governments spend more and more to fight wildfires as conditions in western forests worsen and tens of thousands of new forest homes are built every year. The growing number of highly flammable structures surrounded by hazardous forest fuels makes it increasingly difficult to manage fire-prone forests, inflates the cost of controlling wildfires, and increases danger to firefighters.

Some people argue that we don't know enough about native forest ecosystems to attempt restoration and therefore should leave the forest alone. However, this simply continues the failed practices that attempt to largely exclude fire from fire-dependent forests. Biologists are wrestling with the highly complex considerations involved in restoring entire ecosystems. In contrast, we do understand the general role of fire in shaping forest structure; this knowledge serves as the basis for designing restoration forestry. The only available course for returning fire as a beneficial ecological process in western forests is through carefully planned restoration forestry, whether it employs natural fires, prescribed fires, cutting treatments, fuel removal, or some combination of these.

Today, the concept of restoration forestry is broadly accepted by federal land managers but is scarcely known to the public. Restoration forestry in its many forms is being implemented in diverse forest types on different ownerships across the West, as examples in chapters 6–15 illustrate. Present knowledge is sufficient to carry us beyond today's mostly small, isolated projects toward larger treatment areas and landscape-scale strategies. However, despite deteriorating forest conditions and unprecedented fire hazard across millions of acres, the proposition that restoration forestry is an ecological and practical imperative has not gone unchallenged.

Criticism on the one hand comes from those who believe that nature knows best, and if there are problems, nature will heal itself. These people believe that even if the alleged problems are real, they result from human interventions and that any activity aimed at restoring more natural conditions is at best misguided thinking that a second wrong (second intervention) will make it right. Nature advocates often argue that restoration forestry is a ruse for more tree cutting and forest exploitation, only this time under the veil of doing good for the forest.

Conversely, others see restoration forestry as just another in a long line of obstacles to forest management and wood production in forests where this is an established goal—a sort of "giving away the ranch" to placate environmental advocates. The perception is that restoration treatments are expensive, focus on removing only small trees, and are suitable for horse-logging hobbyists rather than trained professionals with the equipment needed to carry out treatments at a significant scale.

These antagonistic views of restoration forestry make it imperative that projects and treatments are clearly communicated using consistent terminology and that they be based on clear ecological objectives and well-defined treatments. Demonstration areas are particularly useful for this purpose. Only if objectives and treatments are well understood can the fact that restoration activities may require removing commercially valuable trees become understandable to potential detractors. Conversely, projects that require removal of only small trees to achieve restoration objectives will be better understood by skeptics who would otherwise perceive such treatments as being timid and ineffective.

Chapter **3**

Knowledge from
Historical Fire Regimes

Until the 1970s foresters and fire scientists were so absorbed in the battle against fire that they largely overlooked fire's historical role as an ecological process in maintaining different kinds of forests. Some ponderosa pine forests were known to have survived frequent low-intensity fires in the past, but many foresters assumed that such non-lethal fires were confined to a small percentage of the landscape. In August 1973, for the first time in the inland West, forest managers allowed a lightning fire to burn without attempting to suppress it (Daniels 1991, Moore 1996). Over several weeks, this ignition, the White Cap fire in the Selway–Bitterroot Wilderness of northern Idaho, grew sporadically under constantly changing weather and eventually encompassed 2,800 acres. Here at last was an opportunity to study an unsuppressed fire interacting with highly variable natural forests in rugged terrain. Inspection of this momentous burn revealed puzzling sights. For example, the fire burned through a dense stand of lodgepole pine (*Pinus contorta* var. *latifolia*) saplings, blackening their bases and charring the ground. Yet the small trees remained very much alive. This nonlethal burn was inconsistent with the conventional wisdom that fires in lodgepole pine forests kill nearly all trees.

In years that followed, several large natural fires in a few other remote areas in the West were allowed to burn for weeks at a time until extinguished by rain and snow in early fall. These free-ranging fires killed trees in a patchy pattern related to the time of burning (day or night) and to variations in fuels, weather, and topography. In some places all trees were killed, but there were also patches that escaped burning and other places where low-intensity fire spread across the surface without killing overstory trees. In some parts of the burn mosaic, fire thinned the forest, killing most small trees and thin-barked species, while large thick-barked trees survived. These observations of enormous variation and complexity of natural fires corroborated evidence from studies of historical fires whose effects were still discernible in unlogged forests as fire scars on older trees and fire-initiated age classes of younger trees. The findings suggested that historically perhaps 75 percent of western forests experienced fires that killed some trees while others survived (Arno 1980, 2000, McKelvey and others 1996, Quigley, Haynes, and Graham 1996). Most of the remaining 25 percent of forests showed evidence of ancient fires that killed nearly all of the trees and led to establishment of the existing stands. Through the centuries fires had manipulated the forest, favoring trees and entire communities of organisms that were best adapted to certain kinds of burning.

Knowledge from studying how fire interacted with forests prior to the advent of fire suppression provides insight for restoring fire-prone forests. Despite immense variability in how fires burn ("fire behavior") and in their effects, each forest type within a region historically tended to burn in similar patterns over long periods of time. In the 1990s fire scientists devised a simple classification of three *fire regimes* that encompass the different patterns of fire occurrence over long time periods. The *understory, mixed,* and *stand replacement* fire regimes provide a frame of reference for understanding how trees, other plants, animals, and soil organisms formed dynamic communities that adapted to certain frequencies and intensities of burning (Brown 2000).

Fire regimes also help us compare forests of the past and present. A few areas, probably making up less than 3 percent of western forests, are considered a *nonfire regime* because fire was so rare that it almost never had an opportunity to influence the vegetation. This includes some of the cool, humid coastal forests in western Washington, British Columbia, and Alaska; however, even many of the rain forests in Olympic National Park burned every few centuries and fit the stand replacement fire regime (Table 3.1).

Understory Fire Regime

Prior to 1900 the understory fire regime was familiar to both Native Americans and European-Americans in the West because it dominated the dry lower elevation forests that people lived in, traveled through, and used for timber, grazing, and recreation. Tinder-dry leaf litter and grass burned readily during several weeks or a few months each year. Fire swept through a given location at intervals ranging from 1 to 30 years, killing few overstory trees but scorching (and thus pruning) low branches and heavily thinning saplings and large shrubs—maintaining an open and grassy understory (as grasses quickly resprouted after a burn). The understory fire regime included an estimated 40 percent of the forest in the inland northwest and was abundant in California, Arizona, and New Mexico (Arno 2000, Paysen and others 2000, Quigley, Haynes, and Graham 1996, Gruell 2001). It was also found in forests and woodlands of western Oregon, southern Utah, southwestern Colorado, and probably in parts of the Black Hills region of South Dakota and Wyoming (Arno 2000). These sunny forests are witnessed in century-old photographs, pioneer accounts, records from the 19th century land surveys, and remaining ancient stumps of large trees with datable scars from many fires. The vast majority of forests in the understory fire regime have changed dramatically due to fire suppression and logging, but in a few places, described in Part II, living remnants of these forests are being restored.

The historical understory fire regime is commonly represented today by dense stands of small slow-growing conifers. A sleuth can reconstruct the original forest based on surveying stumps and other remnants of old-growth trees (Arno and Allison-Bunnell 2002). Stumps and old trees have sequences of scars from frequent fires reaching back as far as 500 years in ponderosa pine forests and 2,000 years on stumps of giant sequoias (*Sequoiadendron giganteum*), which also inhabited an understory fire regime (Figure 3.1) (Arno 1976, Dieterich 1980, Swetnam 1993). The pattern of frequent fires ignited by lightning and Native Americans evidently extended back a few thousand years in many areas, and this frequent burning favored trees that develop fire resistance at an early age—ponderosa and Jeffrey pines (*Pinus jeffreyi*), western larch (*Larix occidentalis*), giant sequoia, redwood (*Sequoia sempervirens*), Oregon white oak (*Quercus garryana*), and some other oaks in California and the Southwest. The open stands featured abundant grass, flowering herbs, and low shrubs that resprout readily. Leaf litter, dead wood, and ladder fuels (tall shrubs, small trees, and lower limbs of larger trees) were controlled by frequent burning.

Most studies of the understory fire regime in conifer forests show that trees regenerated as individuals or in small, scattered even-aged

Table 3.1.
Western forest types and their historical fire regimes. Abridged from Arno (2000), and pinyon-juniper from Paysen and others (2000). "M" indicates a major part of the forest type; "m" signifies a smaller representation.

Historical Forest Type	Fire Regime Type		
			Stand
	Understory	Mixed	Replacement
Avg. interval between fires (years)	*1–30*	*30–100*	*100–400*
Coastal subalpine forest			M
Douglas-fir, coastal		M	M
Douglas-fir, inland	m	M	
Giant sequoia–mixed conifer	M	m	
Hemlock–Sitka spruce			M
Lodgepole pine		M	M
Oregon white oak	M		
Pinyon–juniper	m	M	m
Ponderosa pine, east of continental divide	m	M	m
Ponderosa pine, west of continental divide	M	m	
Quaking aspen	m	M	
Redwood	M	m	
W. white pine–cedar–hemlock		M	M
Western larch		M	M
Whitebark pine		M	M

groups (Arno, Scott, and Hartwell 1995, Bonnicksen 2000, Cooper 1960, Covington and Moore 1994b). Apparently these successful new trees became established in patches where old trees were killed by bark beetles, violent winds, or fires, creating small openings with concentrations of fuel from the dead trees. Subsequent fires burned these concentrations, creating bare ground in the openings favorable for establishment and rapid growth of tree seedlings. Later fires burned lightly through the openings due to a dearth of needle litter, allowing some seedlings to survive—perhaps only one or a few per patch—and develop into a new age class of trees. The historical, open forest could regenerate itself continuously through the centuries in a fine-grained mosaic that was so subtle the forest appeared to be uniform and unchanging. Frequent fires maintained the open conditions essential for

Figure 3.1.
Giant sequoia with large old fire scars, surrounded by young fir—the Grizzly Giant, Yosemite National Park, 1971. (S. Arno photo)

developing large, long-lived trees and for perpetuating stands of shade-intolerant (sun-loving) trees. Shade-intolerant trees like ponderosa pine require relatively open conditions—especially if they must compete with shade-tolerant species. A mixed fire regime is indicated where occasional high-intensity fires occurred, along with understory fires, and killed most of the trees.

In the early 20th century foresters trained in more moist regions thought that open, frequently underburned western pine forests were understocked. They wanted more saplings to develop and therefore opposed even the "light burning" favored by some local timberland owners because it killed small trees (Weaver 1968). When fires were eliminated, the forest understory soon filled up with saplings. Eventually small trees became so thick that growth of all trees declined due to excessive competition for moisture, nutrients, and sunlight, leaving the forest vulnerable to insects, disease, and severe wildfires linked to accumulating fuel.

In recent years, huge stand-replacing firestorms have been supplanting the low-intensity surface fires that characterized the historical understory fire regime. In 1984, the 170,000-acre Hawk Creek fire exploded across the rolling ponderosa pine forests of central Montana, killing 98 percent of the trees within the fire's perimeter, including groves of trees up to 400 years old. Because heavy-seeded ponderosa pine is ill-adapted to regenerate itself more than about 150 feet from the parent tree, this landscape remains largely deforested 20 years later (Figure 3.2). In the Southwest, 50-acre crown fires in pine forests were considered large in the 1960s; by the 1970s, severe fires were burning hundreds of acres, and in 1996, the first Arizona wildfire greater than 10,000 acres was recorded (Friederici 2003a). Then in 2002 came the mother of all Southwestern fires—the 460,000-acre Rodeo-Chediski. Wildfires of such magnitude in pine forests not adapted to them have ecological consequences extending far beyond the fleeting news coverage of the events themselves. In the larger view, these changes portend the demise of magnificent ponderosa pine forests that have been a prominent feature of the western landscape.

Today's high-intensity fires in the historical understory fire regime can also damage soils, creating a heat-induced water-repellent surface that accelerates runoff and severe erosion (Arno and Allison-Bunnell 2002). The native vegetation, poorly adapted to severe fire, often recovers slowly, while introduced weeds gain a foothold and prosper (Arno 1999). By about 15 years after a stand replacement wildfire, the

Figure 3.2.
Deforestation resulting from severe wildfire: (a) ponderosa pine forest in central Montana in 1982, prior to burning; (b) nearly the same viewpoint in 1998, 14 years after the 170,000-acre Hawk Creek wildfire. (C. Fiedler photos)

dead trees have fallen, creating jackstrawed layers of old trees that can burn white hot. Heavy downed fuels that decompose slowly in a dry environment, coupled with the dense low regrowth of herbs, shrubs, and saplings, might lead to a second fire or "double burn" that is even more damaging to the soil than the previous wildfire (Arno and Allison-Bunnell 2002, Gray and Franklin 1997). One way to avoid such a degenerative cycle is to re-create and maintain relatively open, uneven-aged stands dominated by the historical fire-resistant tree species.

Mixed Fire Regime

Historically, the mixed fire regime characterized about 40 percent of the forest in broad regions of the West (Quigley, Haynes, and Graham 1996). The mixed regime generally occurred in cooler, more moist, and higher elevation forests than the understory regime. Fuel dried sufficiently to allow burning for several days or a few weeks each summer, and in any given place fires occurred at intermediate intervals, averaging about 30–100 years (Brown 2000). Individual fires ranged from low-intensity understory burns to stand replacement fires, but many were of intermediate intensity, killing most fire-susceptible trees—species with thin bark and saplings of all species—but fewer fire-resistant trees.

The mixed fire regime created great diversity within a particular forest and across the landscape due to changing weather conditions over several days or weeks of burning. In a forest developing after an individual stand replacement fire, the mixed fire regime could produce a mosaic similar to the large-scale patchwork in the stand replacement fire regime. After a series of low-intensity fires, the mixed regime might have a relatively uniform, open forest like the understory fire regime; however, the trees would be of similar age, having arisen from the occasional high-intensity fire (Arno, Scott, and Hartwell 1995, Arno, Smith, and Krebs 1997).

In areas where the mixed fire regime had many intermediate-intensity fires, the resulting forest was a crazy quilt of contrasting patches dominated by multiple age classes and species of trees. The mixed regime often produced highly variable tree mortality in forests consisting of several species with different levels of fire resistance. In moist inland forests, fires left large numbers of surviving western larch

Table 3.2.
The different levels of fire resistance for species in a mixed regime.

Species	Degree of resistance to fire
western larch	high resistance
western white pine (*Pinus monticola*), old western redcedar (*Thuja plicata*)	moderate resistance
lodgepole pine (*Pinus contorta*), grand fir (*Abies grandis*)	low resistance
western hemlock (*Tsuga heterophylla*), subalpine fir (*Abies lasiocarpa*)	no resistance

(Table 3.2), often representing different age classes that had become established after past fires. Some old white pine and redcedars survived along with occasional lodgepole pines, but hardly any hemlock or subalpine fir remained in places that actually burned. Shade-intolerant species made up much of the tree regeneration following fires. Fires also triggered production of a rich assortment of shade-intolerant deciduous trees and fruit-bearing shrubs important for wildlife, including aspen (*Populus tremuloides*), birch (*Betula*), chokecherry (*Prunus virginiana*), bittercherry (*Prunus emarginata*), hawthorn (*Crataegus*), elderberry (*Sambucus*), mountain ash (*Sorbus*), mountain maple (*Acer glabrum*), serviceberry (*Amelanchier*), *Ceanothus*, thimbleberry (*Rubus parviflorus*), huckleberries (*Vaccinium*), and currants and gooseberries (*Ribes* spp.).

A mixed fire regime created variation even in forests with only a few tree species, such as cool, dry forests in the Rocky Mountains. When fire is suppressed, these forests may grow into dense monocultures of inland Douglas-fir (*Pseudotsuga menziesii* var. *glauca*) with sparse undergrowth. In contrast, under the mixed fire regime these areas were a patchwork of fire-maintained mountain grassland, aspen groves, young stands of lodgepole pine and Douglas-fir, and groves of older Douglas-fir with open, grassy understories (Arno and Gruell 1983, 1986).

Managers are restoring the mixed fire regime in parts of several large wilderness areas and national parks by allowing some natural fires to burn and applying only limited suppression to others. In many natural areas, however, fire exclusion is still the rule and the mixed fire regime has missed one or two historical fire cycles. Fire's extended absence leads to decline and disappearance of historically dominant shade-intolerant trees such as aspen, coastal Douglas-fir (*Pseudotsuga menziesii* var. *menziesii*), ponderosa pine, sugar pine (*Pinus lambertiana*), western larch, western white pine, and whitebark pine (*Pinus albicaulis*) along with fruit-bearing shrubs and fire-maintained grasslands.

Relatively moist and productive areas in the historical mixed fire regime readily transform into dense forests of shade-tolerant trees when fire and substitute treatments are withheld. This invites more stand replacement burning when wildfires occur. Although some stand replacement was part of the historical fire pattern, the scale of stand replacement burning has increased at the expense of the intermediate-intensity fires that help produce multiple age classes and a kaleidoscope of forest vegetation diversity (Quigley, Haynes, and Graham 1996). Without restoration of a mixed fire regime, most of the large long-lived shade-intolerant trees will be lost. The continuing loss of critical features in these forests due to suppression of fire's natural role is different from but no less damaging than losses in the understory fire regime. The "ray of hope" in this bleak picture is the variety of restoration projects (reported in Part II) being conducted in the mixed fire regime using natural fires, prescribed fires, and silvicultural cutting treatments.

Stand Replacement Fire Regime

The historical stand replacement fire regime typified moist subalpine forests of the Rocky Mountains and wet temperate forests in northern Idaho and west of the Cascades from northern Oregon to southern British Columbia. This fire regime included an estimated 20 percent of the forest in the inland northwestern United States and probably a similar proportion of the forest throughout the West (Quigley, Haynes, and Graham 1996). The stand replacement regime dominated moist or cold forests where fires propagate only in summers with unusually dry weather and fuel conditions, normally in conjunction with a major regional drought (Brown 2000). Fires occurred at long intervals averaging between 100 and 400 years, and each fire killed most of the trees in large irregular patches, creating a mosaic of burned and unburned forest across the landscape. Depending on weather and fuel patterns, burned swathes might cover as little as 100 acres or as much as several thousand. In rugged mountainous terrain, the north- and east-facing slopes often had this fire regime while adjacent, drier south and west aspects supported the mixed fire regime. Individual stand replacement fires are often driven several miles in narrow finger-shaped projections by high winds (Rothermel, Hartford, and Chase 1994). Sometimes, as in the Great Idaho fire of 1910, violent winds drive stand replacement burning across a vast landscape in one or a few days (Pyne 2001).

Subalpine forests molded by the stand replacement regime contained tree species with low resistance to fire. For example, the 1988 fires in the Yellowstone National Park area burned through forests of lodgepole pine, subalpine fir, and Engelmann spruce (*Picea engelmannii*) (Knight 1996). These trees can be killed by moderate-intensity surface fire that fails to scorch the upper canopy foliage, high-intensity surface fire that scorches the canopies, or crown fire that consumes the foliage. Although these three levels of fire intensity all kill the trees, they produce different heating effects on the soil and on regenerative parts of understory plants located in the soil. The kinds and quantities of tree seedlings, shrubs, and herbaceous plants that establish after burning vary dramatically depending on the different levels of heat treatment applied to the soil (Miller 2000).

Some tree species are well adapted to stand replacement fires. Rocky Mountain lodgepole pine commonly stores seeds in closed cones that remain sealed for decades. The heat from a fire melts the resin seal, allowing the cone scales to flex open and seeds to fall into an ashy seedbed. Western larch and coastal Douglas-fir have thick protective bark and are highly fire resistant, thus a few large trees are likely to survive stand replacement fires (Miller 2000). Survivors cast seeds into the burned site, where these shade-intolerant trees can grow rapidly. Even if larch or coastal Douglas-fir are killed by fire, some green cones in the tree tops often survive and can later drop their seeds into the charred soil. In many high-elevation forests the smaller but more shade-tolerant subalpine fir slowly out-competes Engelmann spruce, but after stand replacement fires, spruce regenerates more readily than fir (Fiedler 1990, Muri 1955).

Stand replacement fires initiate a cycle of enrichment by injecting a diversity of vegetation and microorganisms in what otherwise becomes an impoverished biological community dominated by very few shade-tolerant tree and undergrowth species (Miller 2000, Stickney 1990). These fires stimulate a profusion of herbs, shrubs, and deciduous trees that provide food for wildlife and have other ecological values. Alders (*Alnus*) often proliferate after fire, and their roots add nitrogen to the soil, much like legumes used in agricultural crop rotations. Several species of shrubs (currants, gooseberries, and *Ceanothus*) and herbs (*Geranium*) and wild hollyhock (*Iliamna rivularis*) colonize burns from seeds that have lain dormant in the soil for perhaps a century since being deposited after a previous fire. Other species—fireweed (*Epilobium*), willows, and aspen—colonize by way of tiny seeds attached to downy plumes that float many miles through the air. Some seeds of fruit-bearing shrubs (elderberry, mountain ash, and bittercherry) that prosper in burned sites are brought in by birds who have eaten the berries elsewhere and pass the seeds unharmed through their digestive tracts. Still other fire-dependent plants like Scouler's willow (*Salix scouleriana*), mountain maple, or aspen may survive for more than a century as large rootstocks supporting only scant foliage above the ground, but when the forest is thoroughly burned, they sprout vigorously.

Stand replacement fires are often viewed as an unmitigated disaster to forests as well as a waste of timber. Forest scientists, however, recognize that such fires are normal in the stand replacement fire regime and part of the assortment of fire intensities found in the mixed fire regime. Stand replacement burning now accounts for perhaps twice as much area as it did historically, as a result of fuel buildup in large areas of the mixed and understory fire regimes (General Accounting Office 1999, Quigley, Haynes, and Graham 1996). Stand replacement burning could be reduced substantially by restoring forests in the mixed and understory fire regimes.

Fire suppression has had some effects in the historic stand replacement regime. Although it is very difficult to control stand replacement fires, many natural fires develop from small, smoldering burns that eventually blow up under drier conditions and strong winds (Daniels 1991). Suppression extinguishes most slow-to-intensify blazes. Moreover, fires often spread into the historical stand replacement fire regimes from adjacent drier habitats in the mixed or understory fire regimes, and this source of fire has also been greatly reduced by suppression.

In the Northwest coastal region, large stand replacement fires were once common, but now seldom occur (Agee 1993, Morris 1934). In the commercial forests here, clear-cutting on short rotations has largely replaced natural fires that used to occur at long intervals. This forestry is generally not a substitute for the natural role of fire. Wilderness and other protected areas cover a few million acres in coastal and western Cascade forests that historically experienced stand replacement fires at intervals of one to several centuries. These blazes induced nutrient cycling and deposited charcoal in the soil. They also left a temporary infusion of fire-adapted shrubs and herbs along with an enduring legacy of giant coastal Douglas-fir trees that could survive 700 years between fires. Early naturalists recognized that without fires the Douglas-fir would eventually be replaced by the shade-tolerant western hemlock (Pinchot 1899). Today natural fire is effectively suppressed, and as a result, the diverse young forest communities that arise after stand replacement fires are scarce (Hansen and others 1991). This loss of biological diversity leads to homogenized conditions across the forest landscape with unknown ecological implications.

In the historical stand replacement fire regime at upper elevations on the eastern slopes of the Cascade range and in the Rocky Mountains, large forest fires are still common, but less so than in the era before fire suppression. Suppression of fire brings on a higher proportion of old forest, with accumulated dead and down trees and live ladder fuels, and less young forest (Brown 1975, Despain 1990). Bark beetles kill extensive areas of old lodgepole pine and Engelmann spruce, and western spruce budworm (*Choristoneura occidentalis* Freeman) and root rots weaken or kill true firs (*Abies* spp.). Ladder fuels are primarily subalpine firs that proliferate after extended periods without fire. The increasing extent of old forest allows modern stand replacement fires to burn more uniformly over large areas (Agee 1998). Although the effect of fire suppression on the historical stand replacement fire regime is less obvious than in the understory and mixed fire regimes, it still constitutes a significant distortion of the ecological processes that shaped western forests.

Applying Ecological Knowledge

Each of the historical fire regimes provides a general model of forest communities and disturbance patterns that sustained them. Three ecological problems now characterize many forests that were historically shaped by the understory fire regime: increased stand density, development of ladder fuels, and replacement of shade-intolerant tree species with shade-tolerant ones. Forests characteristic of the understory fire regime can often be simulated in a general way using uneven-aged management that perpetuates a mix of trees in different age classes while maintaining an open understory. Like the historical fires, restoration treatments—silvicultural cutting, prescribed burning, or both—need to be conducted at relatively short intervals (perhaps between 10 and 35 years) to limit fuel buildup and promote success of shade-intolerant species.

In the historical mixed fire regime many forests consisted of fine-grained mosaics on the landscape with patches dominated by different age-classes of shade-intolerant trees. These patterns changed substantially through time in response to fires of varying intensities. Forests historically molded by the mixed fire regime are now often characterized by increasingly dense conditions and proliferation of shade-tolerant species. Restoration management in these forests can be designed to control the increase in shade-tolerant trees by killing or removing them in a patchy pattern while retaining shade-intolerant trees and encouraging regeneration of the herbs, shrubs, and trees that depend upon fire. Like the historical fires, restoration treatments in the mixed fire regime can be quite variable in intensity and pattern and can be conducted at longer intervals of perhaps 40–100 years.

The historical stand replacement fire regime exhibited a coarse-grained mosaic on the landscape in which irregularly shaped areas were dominated by even-aged stands of trees arising after high-intensity fire. Today, individual stands are generally within the range of historical conditions; however, because of fire suppression, old stands with an abundance of shade-tolerant trees may cover a higher than normal proportion of the landscape. This reduces habitat diversity and allows fires to burn larger contiguous areas rather than the patchy mosaics that resulted when fuel-filled old stands were fewer and farther between. It also reduces the proportion of early successional communities that are a font of biological diversity, rich in aspen and other shade-intolerant plants prized by wildlife. Restoration treatments commonly re-create even-aged stands dominated by shade-intolerant trees and the herbs, shrubs, and broad-leaved trees characteristic of recent burns. Unlike clear-cuts, restoration treatments produce irregularly shaped stands, leave some burned trees standing, and limit mechanical disturbance of the soil.

The models of historical fire regimes are substantially different from patterns created either by traditional forest management or by preservation accompanied by fire exclusion. Nevertheless, it is quite possible using a variety of treatments (in some cases employing natural fires only) to simulate important features in all three historical fire regimes. Specific decisions as to the scale, location, and objectives of restoration will vary among landowners; however, needs for restoration forestry in a given fire regime are common across ownerships.

Chapter 4

Can Fire-Prone Forests Heal Themselves?

Graphic evidence surrounds us: undesirable changes in western forests that were historically shaped by the understory or mixed fire regimes. Changes in the historical stand replacement fire regime are more subtle but may also be ecologically significant. In the understory and mixed regimes, decades of fire suppression, compounded by past logging of big, fire-resistant trees and proliferation of understory trees, has produced overcrowded forests highly susceptible to drought, severe fires, and insect and disease epidemics. Given our track record, one might ask, Why not leave the forest alone and allow natural fires to return so the forest can restore itself? Fire exclusion is widely blamed as a major cause of deteriorating forest conditions, so why not allow lightning-ignited fires to resume their historic role? With the return of fires (and if logging were prohibited), wouldn't natural processes eventually restore historical conditions? This intriguing alternative avoids the pitfalls of having humans design restoration; even the best applications of prescribed fire cannot exactly replicate the historical fire regime. Moreover, treatments directed by humans are subject to many constraints, and sometimes mistakes. But is the return of natural fires really the simple and elegant solution that it appears to be? Or is it fraught with complications and detrimental consequences because of today's fuel conditions, forest structure, possible climatic change, and political/social context? We now address these questions by considering historical fires in terms of scale, ignitions, and forest conditions.

Returning Fire to Its Historical Scale

Prior to 1900, fires burned an estimated 20 million acres per year in the conterminous western United States, about eight times the annual average of wildfires and prescribed fires today (Arno and Allison-Bunnell 2002). About 6 million acres of the historic burning was in forests and woodlands and the remaining 14 million in grassland, sagebrush, and chaparral (Barrett, Arno, and Menakis 1997). In the inland West, grass-covered valleys and plateaus served as flammable conduits for landscape-scale fire to race from one area of mountain forest to another. Pioneer geologist John Wesley Powell (1891, p. 207) portrayed the West as a region of smoke and fire: "This past season . . . I passed through South Dakota, North Dakota, Montana, Washington, Oregon, and Idaho by train. Among the valleys, with mountains on every side, during all that trip a mountain was never seen. This was because the fires in the mountains created such a smoke that the whole country was enveloped by it and hidden from view. That has been the experience [of my surveying crews] for twenty-odd years, year by year, in this region."

Could fires spread through the landscape today as they did historically? Most of the grasslands and shrublands that facilitated rapid expansion of fires have long since been grazed by livestock (removing fine fuel), cultivated, or fragmented by highways and developments. Clearly, they can no longer function in their historic role of hastening the growth of landscape-scale fires.

Returning Historical Ignitions

We do not know which areas might be restored to a historical fire regime based on lightning fires alone and in which areas Native American ignitions were an important component of the fire regime. Native peoples occupied and traversed the West for more than 10,000 years, shaping historical fire regimes in unquantifiable but likely significant ways in some areas (Stewart 2002). Explorers Meriwether Lewis and William Clark implicated Native Americans as the ignition source for seven of the ten fires they encountered while traveling across what is now Montana and Idaho in 1805 and 1806 (Gruell 1985a). Beginning in the 1820s, explorers of the Willamette and other inland valleys of western Oregon reported systematic landscape burning by Native Americans that maintained grassland and open groves of Oregon white oak across millions of acres (Boyd 1999). When European-American settlement disrupted this burning in the mid-19th century— well before fire suppression became an established practice— denser, conifer-dominated woodlands began to develop (Habeck 1961, Johannessen 1971). Evidence compiled by such disparate sources as archeologists, anthropologists, ethnographers, palynologists, historians, and ecologists indicates that Native American burning significantly shaped the drier forests and grasslands west of the Sierra Nevada and Cascade ranges as far north as southwestern British Columbia (Anderson and Moratto 1996, Boyd 1999, Greenlee and Langenheim 1990, Lewis 1973). There is also considerable evidence to support, and little reason to doubt, the conclusion that Native American burning also influenced the drier forests east of the Cascades and in the Rocky Mountains (Barrett and Arno 1982, Gruell 1985a, Shinn 1980, Stewart 2002).

The relative importance of native burning in historical fire regimes undoubtedly varied from one environment to another, but native peoples continually occupied the grassy valleys and plains that served as avenues for rapid propagation of large fires. They used fires for many purposes and their ignitions often spread freely across the land (Gruell 1985b, Lewis 1985). Native American burning practices evidently extended back more than a thousand years as a component of historical fire regimes (Anderson and Moratto 1996, Arno, Smith, and Krebs 1997, Boyd 1999, Egan and Anderson 2003, Johnson and others 1994, Swetnam 1993). We can characterize the effects of historical fire regimes in the structure of pre-1900 forests and document the process that created these forests in terms of frequencies, severities, and patterns of past fires. However, we do not know what forests would have been like without Native American ignitions.

Returning Historical Fuels

Studies of fire history and forest succession coupled with decades of experience in fire behavior and suppression show that fuels in today's forests differ markedly from those associated with the historical understory and mixed fire regimes (Arno 2000, Quigley, Haines, and

Graham 1996). In forests that used to burn frequently in understory fires, duff accumulations are now so deep that old, fire-resistant trees are killed by prolonged heating even in low-intensity fires (Covington and Moore 1994a, Harrington 2000). Tree rootlets may now be growing in the duff, whereas under historical conditions they were safely located in mineral soil. Buildups of down woody material, especially rotten wood (which becomes powder-dry and is infused with air-filled fissures), lead to more severe burning. Understory thickets now allow surface fires to torch into the main canopy in forests where crown fires were rare in the past (Cottrell 2004). The increase of forest fuels has allowed the proportion of stand replacement burning to approximately double from pre-1900 levels (Quigley, Haines, and Graham 1996). Increased stand replacement burning creates additional fuel by killing more trees. Observations and fuel modeling show that this abundant woody fuel remains flammable for up to a century in dry forests and can contribute to additional severe fires on the same site (Arno and Allison-Bunnell 2002, Brown 1975, Gray and Franklin 1997).

Returning Historical Forest Structure

Studies focused on the historical understory and mixed fire regimes commonly reveal that the structure of contemporary stands contrasts with pre-1900 conditions, with many current stands being outside the range of historical variation (Agee 1993, Arno 2000, Morgan and others 1994). This can have a major effect on the stand's response to fire. An historical stand dominated by large fire-resistant trees growing at wide spacing would likely respond to a summer lightning fire quite differently than its modern counterpart, whether that be a dense post-logging stand or the original forest now filled with understory thickets. The historical stand was much more likely to survive the average fire than either of its contemporary replacements. Under historical conditions, the large fire-resistant trees could continue to dominate the forest, whereas modern stand structures favor stand replacement burning. Absent fire, understory trees out-compete the old trees for moisture and nutrients. The old trees lose vigor and often succumb to insects, disease, or the stress imposed by burning in even low- to moderate-intensity fires (Arno, Scott, and Hartwell 1995, Biondi 1996).

In 2003 the Mineral–Primm wildfire in western Montana provided a dramatic example of differential fire behavior in adjacent stands with contrasting structures. Dense postlogging stands of pole-sized trees near Primm Meadow mostly burned in crown fire. An adjacent old-growth ponderosa pine stand with a conifer understory burned in a mixed severity pattern. However, when it reached the open, old-growth ponderosa pine stand that homesteaders had maintained for livestock grazing by removing saplings and most dead trees, the wildfire tamed to a light underburn (Arno and Fiedler 2003, unpublished observations).

Removing Political and Economic Barriers

Programs allowing return of natural (lightning) fires have been operating in a few national parks and national forest wilderness areas since the 1970s. However, only in the largest and most remote forest in the western United States—a block of more than 4 million acres in Idaho—has such a program been able to restore some semblance of the historical fire regime (see chapter 15). Even in the similarly large, greater Yellowstone National Park region, restoration efforts have been significantly constrained by the need to protect resorts and other facilities (Keane and others 2002). In the Yellowstone fires of 1988 some blazes that were initially allowed to burn as prescribed natural fires later threatened cabins and resorts. Criticism of the fire program appeared in national television newscasts, including critical comments by President Ronald Reagan.

During the same fire season 200 miles to the northwest, another prescribed natural fire broke out of the Bob Marshall Wilderness complex, burned some ranch facilities, and threatened a small town (Daniels 1991). This incident evoked disdain toward the Forest Service and its employees in the affected community and resulted in litigation to establish fault and compensate losses. A pariah image is attached to government employees who allow fire (whether of lightning or human origin) to threaten or burn homes or other private property—such as the National Park Service's prescribed fire that blew up in the spring of 2000 and burned 200 homes in Los Alamos, New Mexico (Arno and Allison-Bunnell 2002).

Because of the precedents set by government fire suppression policies since 1908, the public and its elected representatives expect valiant efforts to protect all private property and developments from forest fires. Had the government instead established a policy (as was urged by some people) of adapting to fire-prone forests, a tradition of personal responsibility for fire protection could have been fostered among landowners, as is the case today in Australia (Mutch 2001).

Some people suggest that natural fire could be allowed to return to western forests if suppression funding were shifted toward fire-proofing homes and communities. National Fire Plan funding has been available for a few years for such purposes, but little progress has been made because many homeowners are uninterested, unmotivated, or unwilling to modify their combustible roofing, siding, decks, landscaping, and hazardous vegetation within 100 feet of buildings. Even if residents were willing, comprehensive "fire-proofing" would cost tens of thousands of dollars per home site; thus, treating a million of these homes would cost tens of billions of dollars. (By comparison, fire suppression costs in the West have generally totaled $1–2 billion annually.) Moreover, crown fires in surrounding, untreated forests can loft firebrands up to a mile, and continuous vigilance and maintenance is necessary to ensure that dwellings remain largely "fire-proof." When forest residents make their homes fire-resistant, it greatly reduces their risks and allows suppression efforts to be more efficient and effective. However, even if most forest homes could be "fire-proofed," vigorous suppression would still be necessary to keep fires from damaging the vast areas of private property that border federal lands.

The reality is that national forest and national park managers do not have the administrative backing at any level to permit natural fires to burn if they might conceivably spread to private lands and developments. Most areas of public land are too small or narrow or encompass resorts or other developments. They are not sufficiently insular to have high assurance of containing a fire that might potentially burn for several weeks and be fanned by high winds. Some argue that natural fires should be allowed to develop and then, if necessary, suppressed near area boundaries. However, such action would be considered negligent because decades of fire suppression experience has established that rapid initial suppression is critical. Once a fire grows large it becomes very costly and problematic to control. Pity the fire manager who did not quench a lightning ignition while it was small and that later cost millions of dollars to control when it became a threat—or worse, overran people, homes, and other developments.

Experience from three decades of attempts by dedicated fire managers to expand natural fire programs confirms that it would not be possible to allow lightning fires to burn without suppression on most of the federal forestlands (Agee 2000, Parsons 2000, Zimmerman and Bunnell 2000). Moreover, even if such a goal could be achieved, it would fall far short of restoring the historical fire regime.

Restoring the Wrong Fire Regime

In view of the crippling constraints that prevent reestablishing an understory or even a mixed fire regime, the predictable outcome of relying on "natural" fires for restoration would perpetuate the current situation in western forestlands. Even under an emphasized program to allow lightning fires to burn, "exceptions" to the policy would be the norm, as most fires would require immediate extinguishment. There isn't enough extra funding or political will to allow any other outcome. The government's liability for court costs and fire damages alone would be staggering. The undesirable result would be continuation of the shift toward more and more stand replacement burning, an ironic consequence for a policy intended to restore natural conditions.

Excessive stand replacement burning brings landscape-scale losses of key features of the understory and mixed regimes including large, long-lived, fire-resistant trees; species-rich herbaceous and shrub communities; and the animals and other ecosystem components that depended upon those features (Gruell 2001, Keane and others 2002, Smith, in review, Thomas 2002). It diminishes forests that were characterized by large, shade-intolerant ponderosa pine, Jeffrey pine, sugar pine, western white pine, whitebark pine, or western larch trees that often survived 400 years or more through a series of lower intensity fires. The fire-dependent trees that would die out if only natural fire were allowed for restoration include craggy old inland Douglas-fir in cold, dry mountain environments such as the Yellowstone region, huge coastal Douglas-fir inhabiting mixed fire regimes, and even the giant sequoias. These magnificent trees would continue to be lost to uncontrollable wildfires or to die at an accelerating rate from the effects of unprecedented competition and insect and disease plagues.

Reality Check

The sobering reality is that we cannot rely on returning natural fires as the primary means of restoring western forests. Even if we could allow all lightning fires to burn everywhere—a practical impossibility—the landscape-scale modification and fragmentation of fuels brought about by livestock grazing, development, and roads now greatly constrain the natural spread of fire. Probably half of all western forests have missed natural fire cycles while also having been altered by logging, so lightning fires today burn hotter and cause greater mortality than fires of the past. The Nature Conservancy, Defenders of Wildlife, and the Rocky Mountain Elk Foundation are among the leading conservation organizations that recognize the need for prescribed burning and tree thinning to restore western forests (Brown 2001, Stalling 2003, Wilkinson 2001).

Recognizing that we cannot simply step aside and let nature do the restoration provides one advantage. It shifts responsibility to us to guide ecological processes to return a reasonable semblance of historical conditions. Conceding that we have long disrupted a crucial creative force in forests, we must now employ methods to mimic the effects of the historic fire regime in sustaining our forests.

Chapter 5

Restoration Objectives, Techniques, and Economics

The imperiled conditions in western forests could be compared with another cherished natural resource that once teetered on the brink of destruction, but then became the cause célèbre of a national conservation campaign and, amazingly, was restored. At the dawn of the 20th century, big game and waterfowl populations were devastated. Elk that previously numbered into the millions had been decimated by unregulated slaughter—with only a few thousand animals surviving in remote enclaves. As extinction loomed for numerous species, sportsmen, conservationists, and government agencies joined forces and within a few decades restored most western wildlife populations. Conservation and management of habitat, along with regulated harvest based on scientific recommendations, has been essential for restoring abundant free-ranging wildlife. Carefully crafted management can also provide the critical link for restoring fire-prone forests.

Objectives for treating fire-prone forests may include restoring primeval conditions in large roadless areas or wilderness, developing sustainable conditions in accessible public forestlands, or creating low-hazard, attractive environments in private forestlands and around homes. Successful restoration forestry requires that we understand the most appropriate techniques for achieving objectives that may differ by ownership, forest type, scale, and location. Silvicultural cuttings, natural fires, prescribed burning, fuel removal, and fuel alteration are the principal tools available for use. Each technique has advantages and can be used in combination with others to produce desired outcomes. This chapter investigates the nuts and bolts of restoration forestry and how to use treatments, harvest technologies, labor, and financing to achieve objectives.

Stewardship of Native Forests: The Overarching Goal

Landowner goals determine whether or how forests are managed. Goals range from exploitation for short-term gain (one form of non-management) to long-term management that emphasizes values ranging from timber production to maintaining natural ecosystems. Restoration forestry is appropriate for any form of long-term management that seeks to maintain features of the natural system. Restoration forestry modifies traditional management treatments to make them more compatible with natural processes of disturbance, regeneration, growth, and succession. It might be viewed as a modern analog of some hunter-gatherer societies that recognized their dependence on wild game, food plants, and other natural resources, and used forests in ways that contributed to sustainability. Restoration forestry promotes a concept of native forest stewardship in which people function as "high-tech hunter-gatherers," benefiting from the forest's many products and values, but only in ways and amounts that ensure their perpetuation.

People who love western forests often perceive them as unchanging, primeval nature that provides refuge from a hectic, technology-driven lifestyle. Paradoxically, ecological studies reveal that the image of a stable forest is an illusion (Botkin 1990, Cronon 1996, Nash 1973). In reality western forests developed through repeating cycles of disturbance and rejuvenation (Arno 2000, Johnson and others 1994, Foster, Knight, and Franklin 1998). Disturbances kill trees and create openings that enhance soil moisture by allowing rain and snow to reach the ground and by killing root systems that extract moisture from soil far beyond the tree's canopy. Disturbances also increase sunlight and nutrients, favoring disturbance-adapted plants and animals. Through ensuing decades the vegetation matures and transforms in structure and composition—a process called forest succession—and somewhere in this process another disturbance occurs. Fire is foremost among the ecosystem-enriching disturbances that reset succession in western forests.

Restoration foresters design and select treatments whose effects will roughly emulate the timing, scale, and intensity of natural disturbances (Fiedler 2002). Restoration forestry aims to develop a range of forest conditions that approximates those historically adapted to the fire regime, insects, diseases, and weather events common to a given area. It is not designed to achieve some discrete past condition or "snapshot in time." Instead, the objective is to emulate the size, pattern, and intensity of disturbances to approximate historical forest structures and conditions—not because they are historical, but because they are sustainable—that is, vigorous, self-perpetuating, and at low risk to biotic agents and catastrophic fire (Fiedler 2000a). Tree species have basic physiological needs in terms of reproduction, growth, and the ability to ward off damaging agents. To be effective, restoration prescriptions must recognize these needs and incorporate treatments that will address them. Specifically, treatments that decrease composition of shade-tolerant species, reduce stand density, and provide adequate light to regenerate sun-requiring (shade-intolerant) species help advance restoration goals in fire-prone forests.

Choosing Objectives and Considering Methods

Land-use intentions provide the background for establishing restoration objectives, but first, possibilities and constraints affecting management need to be identified so that objectives are realistically attainable. For example, prescribed burning is prohibited in some wildland–urban interface areas, and tree cutting may be heavily restricted. Resistance to treatments often diminishes, however, as the reasons for treatments are better understood. People remember destructive logging practices because they are visually obvious, whereas they often don't notice and therefore are unaware of carefully implemented restoration treatments. Public field trips to restoration projects in western forests usually produce favorable reactions because the participants come to understand the reasons for treatments and see good results.

The philosophy of restoration forestry seems intuitively sensible: To the extent feasible, return the vital natural fire process and its useful effects to forests that evolved under its influence. In some natural areas, restoration foresters use fire alone as the management method. In most other situations, cutting or removal of trees is a primary technique, often accompanied by prescribed burning. *The Book of Fire* (Cottrell 2004) provides general audiences with a well-illustrated description of the different forms and effects of fire in forests. Other, technical publications explain the use of prescribed fire (Kilgore and Curtis 1987, Pyne 1984, Martin 1990).

In contrast, silvicultural cutting as a component of restoration forestry has not been developed in a standardized way. Traditionally, silviculture was the art and science of managing a forest to sustain timber production and soil productivity. More recently, silviculture has focused on promoting sustainable forest conditions and maintaining ecological diversity by approximating the effects of natural processes, including fire. Before considering the silvicultural treatments available for designing a restoration prescription, it is important to understand the fundamental differences among tree removal approaches that are lumped into the term "logging." These differences are vitally important for designing forest management but are little known to nonforesters.

Comparing Exploitation, Timber Management, and Restoration Forestry

One way to illustrate differences between logging used for exploitation, timber management, and restoration is to see what each looks like when conducted in the same kind of forest. For this comparison, consider a widespread restoration problem—dense, second-growth ponderosa pine forests that arose after heavy logging a century ago. These high-hazard forests are the product of fire suppression and early "high-grade logging" that removed only valuable trees—with no concern about the future forest. Hundreds of thousands of homes and cabins now populate these forests. Fire protection agencies advise people to thin their forests and reduce fuel accumulations, but many residents are puzzled about how to accomplish this. Landowners often want the proceeds from selling some of their commercial-size trees to pay for removing excessive understory trees and other forest fuels, and some want to maximize income from logging.

Consider a typical second-growth forest in the Intermountain West supporting about 250 trees per acre (Scott 1998, Harrington 1999, Fiedler 1999). Half (125) are overstory trees of merchantable size, ranging from 9 to 17 inches in diameter, including a few widely scattered big trees (18–24 inches) that were left by early loggers because they were too small or deformed. The other half are nonmerchantable trees 1–8 inches in diameter that would cost more to remove than any revenue they would generate. (The lower size limit of merchantable trees fluctuates depending on geographic location and market conditions.) Ninety percent of the overstory trees are ponderosa pine, the historic dominant fire-dependent tree, and the remainder are Douglas-fir, white fir, or grand fir, which increase in the absence of fire. The understory

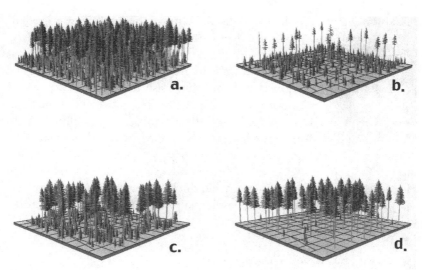

Figure 5.1.
Computer visualizations simulating effects of different treatments on stand structure: (a) untreated second-growth stand; (b) result of high-grade logging; (c) logging for timber management; (d) restoration treatment. (S. Robertson visualizations)

consists mostly of firs and includes an additional 500 seedlings per acre less than 5 feet tall. Three scenarios describe logging operations in this forest that are driven by contrasting landowner objectives: maximizing income (Figure 5.1b), managing for timber (Figure 5.1c), sustaining a vigorous forest modeled after historical conditions (Figure 5.1d).

Exploitation Logging (High-Grading)

The landowner chooses a logger whose high bid for the timber is based on removing trees rapidly at the lowest cost. He fails to check on the logger's references or examples of past work. To reduce costs, the contractor skids bundles of whole trees or logs with little concern about impact on the soil or remaining trees. All merchantable trees greater than 11 inches in diameter are removed; small or deformed merchantable trees plus all nonmerchantable ones are left standing because they cost too much to remove. Skidding large bundles of trees or logs with big equipment can badly scar the remaining trees, predisposing them to insect or disease damage. Tall spindly trees are left and may subsequently bend over or break with high winds or heavy snow.

The logger may leave skid trails in erodible condition, creating favorable sites for noxious weed invasion. Slash treatment is expensive and therefore done poorly, leaving fuel that increases wildfire hazard. Slash is bulldozed into piles along with soil and then partially burned, leaving scraped ground and large heaps of charred wood and soil. Removing the larger trees and leaving messy slash accumulations and rutted ground spoils the stand's appearance. Most of the small firs survive logging and develop into flammable thickets. Even 25 years later very little merchantable timber has developed to help pay for needed hazard-reduction treatments.

Logging for Timber Management

Wanting to take good care of the forest, the landowner hires a professional forester. Foresters are traditionally trained in managing timber for present and future yields, although many have little experience in restoring fire-prone forests. The consultant prescribes a heavy thinning, in which about 60 percent of the overstory trees are harvested to remedy the overstocked condition. About half of the understory trees are also cut or are broken off in the logging operation, and the result is an open stand of the largest overstory trees. Using appropriate harvest methods and equipment and conducting treatments on dry, snow-covered, or frozen ground prevents scarring of the remaining large trees and minimizes impacts on the soil. Success depends on choosing a reputable operator and specifying proper procedures in a contract. Frequent inspection of the ongoing work helps ensure quality. Treatment of slash is carefully planned to reduce wildfire hazard and to meet ecological needs and aesthetic concerns.

Under this approach, many of the remaining overstory trees respond with vigorous growth, and aesthetic values are maintained or improved (Scott 1998). About four hundred small firs per acre survive the logging and after about 25 years have developed into understory thickets representing significant ladder fuels. At that time, removal of a small proportion of the overstory trees will produce some revenue, but not enough to offset costs of thinning the new thickets and disposing of slash. Controlling fir thickets to reduce susceptibility to wildfire and insect and disease epidemics will be a continuing problem and expense in the future.

Logging for Restoration

The landowner retains large healthy trees and appropriate numbers and species of smaller trees as available to perpetuate desirable conditions, using historic stands as a general guide. Any revenue from merchantable trees partially offsets the cost of removing the excessive amount of small trees and perhaps burning. The landowner hires a restoration consultant after examining recent projects in similar forests. They examine tree growth rates and evidence of historical conditions. Recognizing the severe overstocking and vulnerability of this forest, they determine that a light thinning treatment would be ineffective. Thus, they jointly choose a selection cutting approach that retains about 40 percent of the most vigorous overstory trees and all of the scattered big old trees.

Commercial-size trees are harvested with a cut-to-length machine that fells, limbs, and bucks the stems into short logs in the woods. A log forwarder—an all-terrain log carrier with large rubber tires—picks up logs and transports them to an existing road. To control the fir understory, the 4- to 8-inch diameter trees are felled, cut into large pieces, and piled and burned. In some locations, these small trees could be sold for pulpwood or biomass fuel. Although the revenue derived may be below the cost of harvesting, this approach can reduce or eliminate costly piling and burning. Trees 2–3 inches in diameter (mostly firs and some stunted pine) are felled and left as surface fuel. Soon after snow melts the following spring, piles of branches and tops made by the harvesting machine are burned, followed by an underburn of the entire stand. Fire kills most of the remaining small firs, and creates a seedbed favorable for establishing vigorous pine seedlings.

In about 25 years, the next round of treatments—another selection cutting and an underburn—will further develop the desired condition of large vigorous trees with a relatively open understory. By then a new age class of pine seedlings and saplings will have developed, some of which will survive careful underburning. Overstory trees that averaged about 15 inches in diameter at the first cutting will now be 18–20 inches. Thus the general appearance of an historical forest emerges in a few decades, and during subsequent treatments some high-value timber will be removed as a byproduct of treatment.

The Restoration Forestry Prescription

Whether restoration treatments are needed or not is determined by comparing modern and historical forest conditions (Agee 1993, Arno 2000, Arno and Allison-Bunnell 2002). Three basic stand characteristics are used in these comparisons: density—the number and basal area (cross-sectional area of stems) of trees per acre; structure—the distribution of trees in different size classes per acre; and composition—the proportion of trees of different species. (Examples of these comparisons appear in chapters 7–14.) Substantial departure in one or more of these characteristics that define the "historical range of variability" may threaten sustainability and suggest remedial action (Morgan and others 1994).

Traditional silvicultural treatments defined in reference books (Smith 1997, Daniel, Helms, and Baker 1979) should form the basis or point of departure for designing treatments needed to accomplish restoration goals. This ensures that treatments can be documented and communicated accurately, so successful treatments can be differentiated from unsuccessful ones. Consistent treatment description and terminology help ensure repeatability—different practitioners, similar outcomes (Fiedler 1995).

Before implementing restoration treatments, we first need a "prescription" or plan of action, which might be an informal process on private land (McEvoy 1998). Developing the prescription provides a framework for assessing forest conditions, diagnosing problems, designing appropriate treatments, ensuring treatment implementation, and monitoring treatment effectiveness over time.

Even if followed informally, the following steps are useful. The evaluation of restoration needs begins with an *inventory*. Preferably, inventory data will come from formal sampling within the stand or area of interest but may instead come from an informal inspection. Inventory data are evaluated in the next step, *diagnosis*, to identify any ecological problems that may need treatment. *Prescription development* is the step in which different cutting and prescribed burning treatments are considered for their potential to achieve the objective, and for appearance, level of risk, and cost. *Prescription implementation* is a key step, because a well-designed prescription that is poorly applied will not achieve the objective. If the prescription includes both cutting and burning treatments, implementation may extend a year or longer. *Monitoring*, the final step in the prescription process, evaluates the stand immediately after restoration activities and periodically thereafter. It determines treatment effectiveness and the need and timing for possible follow-up treatments.

Silvicultural Treatments

Silvicultural treatments are designed or "prescribed" and implemented for "stands" ranging in size from a few acres to several hundred acres. Stands are recognizable areas of the forest that have relatively consistent characteristics of tree size, density, and composition. They are defined by topographical boundaries such as ridge tops and canyon bottoms, transitions to dissimilar forest conditions, or artificial boundaries such as changes in ownership, roads, or developments.

The two broad categories of silvicultural treatments applied to stands are differentiated by purpose and intensity. *Intermediate treatments* are of moderate intensity and make mid-course corrections during stand development. They are not intended to initiate a new stand or a new age class within a stand; they include thinning, pruning, improvement cutting, and prescribed burning. In contrast, *regeneration cuttings* are performed specifically to initiate regeneration of either a new age class or a new stand of trees. Regeneration cuttings, then, necessarily remove more trees to provide greater availability of light, nutrients, and moisture for establishment and development of young trees. Some regeneration cutting methods such as "selection cutting" retain some trees of all sizes and are designed to perpetuate *uneven-aged* stands, while others such as "clearcutting" are aimed at establishing new *even-aged* stands. These traditional methods have been modified to meet the needs of restoration forestry, and specific examples of restoration treatments are explained in chapters 6–15.

Treatment Effects on Fire Hazard

The intermediate and regeneration cutting treatments used in restoration prescriptions affect fire hazard in several important ways. For example, thinning of sapling and pole-size trees typically reduces the *torching potential*, which is the probability that a surface fire will torch into the canopy and become a crown fire (Beukema and others 2000, Cottrell 2004). Torching potential is inversely related to crown base height, which is the lowest point of a tree's crown (live or dead) that would likely carry fire upward or "torch."

Crown fire hazard is primarily influenced by canopy bulk density, which is the density of 1-hour fuels (less than 1/4-inch twigs and needles). Crown fire hazard is quantified by the *crowning index*, which is the wind speed in miles per hour necessary to maintain a crown fire once it has reached the main canopy (Beukema and others 2000, Cottrell 2004). Treatments (e.g., thinning, improvement cutting, regeneration cutting) that remove some to many of the trees from the main canopy reduce canopy bulk density and hence the crown-fire potential in a stand. Removal of only small trees, in contrast, has little effect on canopy bulk density. Comprehensive prescriptions designed to restore appropriate stand density, structure, and species composition in ponderosa pine and pine-fir forests reduce crown fire hazard much more than thinning prescriptions that remove only small trees (Fulé and others 2001a, Fiedler and others 2003, Fiedler and Keegan 2003).

Spread rate is another measure of potential fire hazard. Generally, the greater the volume of fine fuels on the ground, the faster the spread rate. For this reason, removing or burning at least some of the slash generated from the cutting treatments is an integral part of any restoration prescription.

The Restoration Management Plan

A written restoration plan for privately owned forests documents the philosophy and direction of management, as well as methods to be used. A plan establishes the credibility of the restoration objectives and may be necessary if certification will be sought for establishing a conservation easement or if forest products are to be marketed as coming from a sustainable forest ("Green Certification," see *Journal of Forestry*, February 1999, McEvoy 2004). A management plan may also be necessary to qualify for lower property tax categories, to help secure loans, or to qualify for grants from forest improvement programs offered by state and federal governments. There is no standardized format for a management plan, but important elements of such a plan are explained by Beattie, Thompson, and Levine (1983), Fazio (1987), and McEvoy (1998).

Table 5.1.
An example of historical (prior to logging circa 1900) and recent stand structures in a ponderosa pine/Douglas-fir forest. Data are trees per acre, by diameter class.

	Historical Stand		Modern Stand (second-growth)	
	Pine	D-fir	Pine	D-fir
0–4 inches	5	2	7	25
4–8	4	2	55	45
8–12	4	2	50	25
12–16	4	2	26	14
16–20	6	1	7	2
20–24	4	1	1	
24–28	3	1		
28–32				
32–36	1			
36–40	1			
Total basal area/acre =	65 sq. ft.		115 sq. ft.	
No. overstory trees				
Per acre (8+ in. diam.) =	30		125	
Avg. overstory diam. =	20		12	

The process of developing and implementing a forest restoration strategy can be compared to embarking on a long journey through unfamiliar country to reach a certain destination. The wise traveler will obtain a detailed map to use in planning and conducting the trip. Likewise, developing a restoration plan enables a forest landowner to carefully analyze alternative routes that could lead to the goal, choose the most promising course, keep track of progress, and evaluate possible midcourse adjustments. In a sense the management plan becomes a continually improving map to guide the ongoing restoration process.

The process of planning for restoration begins with examination and comparison of the forest's historical and current conditions—disturbance regime, density, structure, and species composition. The fundamental questions are: "Which species were most abundant in historical stands?" and "Which of the three fire regimes (understory, mixed, or stand replacement) was typical?" For example, comparing historical and current conditions in a pine/fir stand (Table 5.1) shows a dramatic increase in tree biomass, in Douglas-fir, and in small trees. We can interpret the trend in these data to determine which species (in this case, Douglas-fir) is likely to dominate the forest with continued exclusion of fire. If growth of the dominant trees (12–16 inch diameter) in the current stand is declining markedly, they will not attain the large sizes found in the historical stand without a treatment to reduce density.

It is important to understand the possibilities and constraints affecting forest management before setting restoration objectives. Technological feasibility of different treatments in terms of slope steepness, road access, and easements should also be considered. Two parcels of very similar forest in different locations might have contrasting possibilities and approaches for achieving restoration. It is also important to consider any regulations and liability considerations that may apply to prescribed burning in the forest. Regulations constrain tree cutting or timber harvesting in streamside zones and wetland areas in most states. Thus, it may not be feasible to restore forested streamsides that historically burned in understory or mixed fire regimes even though without treatment they are likely to eventually burn in a severe wildfire (Agee 1998, Arno and Allison-Bunnell 2002).

Economic Considerations

Restoration forestry differs from traditional forest management in that profit from forest products does not play a dominant role in formulating objectives, choosing treatments, or driving decisions such as which trees are cut and which are left. Instead, the primary objective is to nurture and perpetuate a sustainable forest by restoring a more natural range of tree density, structure, and species composition, and by reintroducing fire where appropriate. However, restoration treatments are expensive and generate large quantities of tree stems and branches that need to be recycled in some way, lest they accumulate as additional fuel. Some of this material is of high value and can more than offset the cost of transporting it to a mill (Fiedler and others 1999). Other material, such as pulpwood or firewood, might pay part of its removal cost. Thus, although economic considerations aren't the primary factors influencing restoration methods, they are used in choosing the most efficient way to carry out treatments.

Once public land managers or private forestland owners are ready to plan restoration activities, they must consider how to finance them. This is a mind-stretching exercise because restoration treatments may cost between a few hundred and a couple thousand dollars per acre. Totally unlike exploitation logging that harvests only valuable trees, restoration must commonly remove large quantities of nonmerchantable trees while leaving the most valuable ones. Still, capitalizing on opportunities to create some income—coupled with efficient operations—may reduce overall costs to a manageable level and occasionally even generate a profit.

Many public and private forestlands are viewed as long-term investments whose value as an attractive setting exceeds the potential value of the timber. The best approaches for sustaining such wildland values are those patterned after historical natural disturbances and the conditions they produced. Thus, pursuing a restoration strategy is justified to protect and enhance the land's value, and any monetary rewards from removal of excess trees, though helpful, may be of secondary importance. Still, if restoration is going to take place, we have to figure out how to pay for it. Financing options range from reducing the land's tax liability to devising efficient approaches for accomplishing treatments. Generally, several approaches must be applied in combination to achieve success.

Merchantable timber from excess or unwanted trees is potentially the most valuable byproduct of restoration treatments. Ultimately after several decades of restoration management, forests may yield a substantial flow of commercial timber as byproducts of repeated treatments. However, many forests being considered for restoration have been logged previously and retain few commercial-size trees, and most of the larger trees remaining are desired for the restored stand. Still, even previously logged forests often have some unwanted trees large enough to produce logs for a sawmill or plywood plant. Present-day western forests commonly have an excess of shade-tolerant trees such as firs and a dearth of shade-intolerant trees such as pines. Seed-bearing shade-tolerant trees may need to be removed to prevent a proliferation of their seedlings. Thus, the first restoration treatment may produce a significant volume of logs from shade-tolerant trees. If there are potential buyers for this material, it must be processed and marketed carefully to achieve maximum value and help offset treatment costs. In some areas there is a market for small trees as pulpwood (Figure 5.2) or for chipped trees and limbs—hog fuel—which are used in industrial boilers to generate steam and electricity (Northey 2002). Firewood is another beneficial product from unwanted trees that many forest landowners can use themselves, or sell, trade, or donate to others.

Figure 5.2.
Hauling byproducts of restoration treatment: a load of spindly, crooked trees headed for a pulp mill. (USDA Forest Service photo)

The initial restoration treatment often produces 20 or more tons per acre of stems not usable for lumber and perhaps 10 tons of limbs and tops. Selling or using some of this material reduces the cost of piling and burning it. Waist-high slash constitutes a fire hazard, a barrier to animal movement, and a visual eyesore.

A virtual smorgasbord of technology is available for accomplishing restoration treatments, ranging from inexpensive devices that increase the productivity of manual labor to sophisticated high-output machines that eliminate physical labor. The size or scale of the proposed project affects the choices available for implementing treatments. Treating 5 acres around a home may limit choices to a restoration contractor who specializes in small parcels or to hand labor by the owner. As the scale of the treatment area expands, the use of high-production or sophisticated equipment becomes more feasible and necessary. Per-acre treatment costs are very high for small tracts and home sites because there isn't enough area involved to justify use of high-efficiency equipment. Treatments conducted on steep ground (slopes exceeding 40 percent) generally require cable-harvesting systems or helicopters, also resulting in high costs.

Manual labor can be prohibitively expensive in forests that require thinning and removal or burning of numerous nonmerchantable trees. Public land managers may be able to get help from sources such as youth corps, conservation jobs programs, or firefighters during slack periods. In contrast, individual landowners may find family members to be the best source of labor for restoration activities. Anyone involved in restoration work should follow safety procedures outlined in publications available through state forestry Cooperative Extension offices. A thinning contractor may be a better alternative than using unskilled labor because the contractor should be an experienced, efficient worker with appropriate equipment. A specific written contract for such work is advisable, and before cutting begins the landowner may want to approve marking of trees to remain ("leave trees") (McEvoy 1998).

Conservation easements can provide private landowners with financial advantages for conducting sustainable forestry (McEvoy 2004). The landowner in return gives up future development rights. The U.S. Forest Service's Forest Legacy Program, state wildlife and parks departments, The Nature Conservancy, the Rocky Mountain Elk Foundation, and numerous regional or local land trusts can help landowners establish conservation easements. Land trusts are often most interested in protecting forestlands that provide key wildlife habitat, ecological diversity, or open space near cities and major suburban areas. Conversely, small forested tracts in rural areas typically have little appeal for easements.

Federally funded programs have traditionally provided partial reimbursement for a wide range of forest management activities that contribute to sustainable forests. These programs change frequently but are commonly administered by or known to state service foresters. Cost share funding to help private landowners treat hazardous fuels has been available through national forest offices and some state and local forest fire protection agencies as a component of the National Fire Plan (www.fireplan.gov).

Scheduling

The ecological and financial success of treatments may depend on careful scheduling that interacts favorably with economic, environmental, and biological conditions. People often embark on a project when they feel the urge to do it, even though the timing might be disastrously wrong. Treatments should be preplanned and their execution delayed until conditions are favorable. For example, markets for small sawlogs are sometimes poor and restricted to relatively large minimum diameters; whereas at other times high prices are offered and small diameters are accepted.

Managers and landowners need to pay attention to seasonal weather changes. Heavy equipment should be kept off water-saturated or thawing ground to prevent soil compaction, rutting, and erosion. Trees shouldn't be cut during seasonal periods when bark beetles can breed in felled trees or "green" slash and their offspring can attack remaining live trees. Operating in extreme weather conditions may be unproductive or hazardous for machinery and workers and degrade the quality of work.

Safe and efficient use of fire requires thoughtful scheduling. Burning slash piles might be done with low risk of escape soon after heavy precipitation and when hot windy weather is unlikely to return soon. In a forest that has missed several natural fire cycles, the initial understory burn may need to be done when the mineral soil and lower part of the organic layer (humus and lower duff) is still wet. Suitable conditions may occur for only a day or two in early spring after the snowpack melts or in autumn after a few dry days follow a soaking rain. The right conditions may develop on a weekend and it may take special arrangements to capitalize on the opportunity.

Phenology, the annual cycle of vegetation activity, should be considered when scheduling treatments. Prescribed burning during the period of active growth in spring or early summer can stress trees and other plants. Sequencing of treatments is also important. In areas where prescribed burning is planned, it is often best to thin first to create more open conditions for burning and to avoid having to harvest charred trees. It may be favorable to delay underburning for a full year after thinning so that slash can cure and leave trees can gain vigor.

Financing vs. Investing

For more than a century western forests were viewed primarily as a source for commodities. In contrast, a large proportion of today's public considers noncommodity uses like wildlife habitat and a place for enjoying nature to be the most important forest values. By the dawn of the 21st century people were commonly paying more than $50,000 to acquire a small tract of forest where they could build a home or cabin, with no intention of selling timber or developing the land for profit. Homeowners in suburban areas expect to make significant investments to maintain their property, yet forest owners have historically been reluctant to do so. However, because scenic and forest property values can be devastated by a wildfire or an epidemic that kills trees, landowner perspectives are changing.

The bottom line is that a century of fire exclusion coupled with past timber harvesting now requires an investment in corrective action to restore and perpetuate attractive, low-hazard forest conditions. Costs can be reduced by carefully crafting treatments that remove unwanted trees efficiently and by taking advantage of available markets and cooperative programs. However, constantly changing markets and technology require nimbleness to find viable methods for achieving restoration objectives.

Part II

Learning from Experience: Profiles of Restoration Forestry Projects by Forest Type

Chapters 6–15 describe restoration forestry projects from diverse areas and situations in the West (Table 6.1). Many examples come from the U.S. Northern Rocky Mountains because they were easier to track down and possibly more numerous. Most restoration forestry projects are known primarily to the people involved and are not well publicized. We have visited all of the areas described except for the Gunnison Ranger District in Colorado (in chapter 12), where we relied on a publication by colleagues (Zimmerman and Omi 1998) and information, interviews, and review provided by the project's founder.

Varied kinds and levels of documentation are available regarding these projects—much of it informal. Thus, our write-ups do not consistently report the same depth of information. Instead, we sketch why and how the project is being conducted, profile forest conditions, describe methods of treatment, report what has been accomplished, identify obstacles to restoration, and offer our candid but understanding evaluation. These accounts include some basic measurements, in English units, that compare stand structures before and after restoration treatments. (Descriptions of two projects in Canada include metric equivalents in parentheses.)

We could not identify or cover all of the worthy restoration forestry projects in the West, but we chronicle some notable ones and hope others will add to this list of pioneering efforts. Meanwhile, we offer this sampler to demonstrate the promise that expanded restoration holds for advancing conservation of fire-prone forests.

Table 6.1.
Annotated list of restoration projects described in chapters 6–15 (NF = National Forest).

Restoration Projects by Primary Forest Type	Management Purpose		Primary Treatments		
	Sustainable Forest	Natural Area	Natural Fire	Rx Fire	Cutting Treatmts
Pinyon-Juniper					
Bandelier National Monument		X			X
Ponderosa Pine					
Greater Flagstaff Forest Partnership	X			X	X
Ponderosa Pine-Fir					
Bitterroot NF; Lubrecht Experimental Forest	X			X	X
Squamish Provincial District; Deschutes NF	X			X	X
Wallowa–Whitman NF; Boise NF	X			X	X
E Bar L Ranch	X				X
Burnt Fork Ranch; Rocking-K Ranch	X			X	X
Sequoia-Mixed Conifer					
Sequoia-Kings Canyon National Parks		X		X	
Western Larch-Fir					
Seeley Lake Recreational Corridor	X			X	X
Bob Marshall Wilderness; Glacier National Park		X	X		
Lolo NF Old-growth Remnant		X		X	X
Lodgepole Pine					
Gunnison NF		X		X	
Bitterroot NF	X			X	X
Tenderfoot Experimental Forest	X			X	X
Banff National Park		X		X	
Whitebark Pine					
National Forests in Northern Rocky Mts.		X	X	X	X
Landscape Scale—Several Forest Types					
Lassen NF	X			X	X
Central Idaho Wilderness & Primitive Areas		X	X	X	

Chapter 6

Pinyon-Juniper—
The Elfin Forest

The American West evokes images of wide open spaces, where an occasional sheepherder's wagon is the only hint of civilization amidst a sea of sagebrush and small trees that runs to the horizon. This "elfin" forest of small pinyon pine and juniper trees, or "PJ" as the locals like to call it, occupies tens of million of acres across the Intermountain West, primarily in the Great Basin and Southwest.

In California and Nevada, the pinyon pine is usually single-leaf pinyon (*Pinus monophylla*), while eastward it is typically Colorado pinyon (*P. edulis*). The junipers include several species: alligator (*Juniperus deppeana*) and one-seed junipers (*J. monosperma*) in the Southwest, Utah juniper (*J. osteosperma*) further north, and western juniper (*J. occidentalis*) in California. Although pinyon and juniper commonly occur together, juniper also grows in pure stands on millions of acres in the northern and drier parts of its range. Juniper's leathery, scale-like leaves provide superior moisture retention, allowing it to survive on sites too dry for pinyon or ponderosa pine.

Despite its timeless appearance, this is a landscape in transition. Pinyon-juniper woodlands are in some places marching upward into dry ponderosa pine forests and in others downward into shrub and grassland communities (Allen and Breshears 1998, Jacobs, Gatewood, and Allen 2002, Gottfried and others 1995). Fire suppression, livestock grazing, and climatic shifts are viewed as the primary factors behind expansion of the PJ woodland type (Gottfried and others 1995). Enhanced atmospheric carbon dioxide (CO_2) may also contribute, as elevated CO_2 levels appear to favor growth of woody species over herbaceous ones (Polley and others 1997).

Pinyon and juniper have been staples of Southwestern life for centuries, providing pine nuts, firewood, and building materials for native peoples, and more recently, fence posts, mine props, and raw material for specialty products such as furniture, clocks, lamps, and assorted decorative items. Given these many values and uses, one might ask "So what's the problem with having more PJ?" As we shall soon see, this question is not a simple one.

Pinyon–juniper woodlands are not only dramatically expanding their range, some are also becoming more dense. Overgrazing and fire suppression are seen as key factors allowing densification to occur. Drier sites may be considered pinyon–juniper dominated once they exceed a mere 20 percent canopy cover. These bushy trees have spreading root systems that extend into intercanopy openings and compete with native grasses for moisture. Stands supporting no more than 40 percent canopy cover may be moisture stressed, with "natural" reestablishment of herbaceous cover a near impossibility.

Pinyon–juniper woodlands vary greatly in structure, composition, and dominant fire regime across their range and in the degree of departure from historical conditions. For this reason, Romme, Floyd-Hanna, and Hanna (2003) propose classifying PJ woodlands into three types: pinyon–juniper grass savanna, pinyon–juniper shrub woodland, and pinyon–juniper forest. The pinyon–juniper grass savanna type is typically found on sites characterized by fine-textured soils, gentle terrain, and abundant summer moisture. Frequent, low–intensity fires characterize the fire regime. The pinyon–juniper shrub woodland type features a well-developed shrub layer and occurs on deep soils in areas dominated by winter precipitation. Mixed-intensity and stand replacement fires at intervals of several years to several decades (but < 100 years) typify the fire regime. The third type, pinyon–juniper forest, is found on combinations of soils and topography that protect stands from frequent fires. Soils may be too shallow or rocky to support continuous herbaceous cover, or the terrain so rugged and broken that it provides natural barriers to fire spread. Stands in this type may escape fire for centuries but typically support stand replacement fires when they do burn (Romme, Floyd-Hanna, and Hanna 2003).

A century of change in the PJ grass savanna and PJ shrub woodland types has brought unforeseen ecological impacts and sparked interest in restoration. Three deteriorating conditions in PJ woodlands warrant special attention. One is dense, low-vigor stands in which pinyon is vulnerable to bark beetle attack. The Ips beetle (*Ips confusus*) epidemic that started killing pinyon pine in the 1990s still rages across parts of eastern Arizona and northern New Mexico. A severe regional drought in recent years either initiated or magnified the beetle outbreak. The second condition is the displacement of native grassland species by aggressive nonnatives. The most outstanding example is cheatgrass (*Bromus tectorum*), an invasive plant that is overwhelming the diversity of native herbaceous communities and fueling a volatile new fire regime in Great Basin woodlands. Cheatgrass is a short-lived annual that creates copious quantities of fine fuel. The third condition involves massive soil erosion within some PJ stands due to loss of herbaceous cover. Severe declines in herbaceous cover are caused by overgrazing, increasing tree canopy cover, or both. This condition has the most profound and debilitating long-term implications and is the one we will feature here.

The restoration of pinyon-juniper grass savannas provides a striking contrast to that of most other forest types. Restoration activities in this type are designed to reduce the amount of PJ from current levels and favor species other than pinyon and juniper. Treatments are aimed at reestablishing sustainable watershed conditions and herbaceous communities, rather than restoring stand structure per se (Jacobs, Gatewood, and Allen 2002, Sydoriak, Allen, and Jacobs 2000).

Our restoration example comes from the heart of PJ country in northern New Mexico. The setting is dense pinyon-juniper woodlands covering magnificently rugged terrain within Bandelier National Monument. Pinyon-juniper occurs on a wide range of conditions within this 33,000-acre monument, but restoration activities are focused on the PJ grass savanna type occupying highly erosive soils.

The Bandelier story does not start with restoration of the pinyon-juniper type, although its prominent role in this drama becomes evident soon enough. Indeed, Craig Allen—research ecologist at Bandelier—and his associates have been applying prescribed fire to restore the monument's mixed conifer and ponderosa pine forests since the 1980s. Bandelier was dedicated by President Woodrow Wilson in 1916 to preserve Pueblo Indian ruins and contains one of the highest concentrations of ancient structures and archeological sites of any unit in the national park system. However, these relics do not occur in a vacuum, but instead are embedded in a dynamic—and in many cases deteriorating—forest, woodland, or grassland environment. Formal monument designation has not provided the full and permanent protection of cultural remains that was envisioned with Bandelier's creation in 1916. In particular, it cannot insulate ruins and artifacts from unforeseen threats related to deteriorating ecological conditions.

The pinyon-juniper influence in this story begins more than 800 years ago, when the Anasazi people gradually relocated eastward from the Colorado Plateau to north-central New Mexico. The Anasazis, ancestors of the Puebloan peoples, were intensively farming their new environs by the late 12th century (Allen 2002). They raised their crops within open pinyon-juniper woodlands in the northern Rio Grande valley and foothills of the Jemez Mountains, including present-day Bandelier National Monument. Pinyon and juniper trees were harvested for domestic and agricultural uses, reducing already sparse tree cover while favoring grasses and forbs. The herbaceous layer dried readily and provided fuel for surface fires. It also recovered quickly, supporting sufficient fuels just a few years after burning to again carry a fire. The pattern and interval of surface fires are not well documented (Baker and Shinneman 2004) but likely helped maintain pinyon-juniper and ponderosa pine grass savannas for centuries (Gottfried and others 1995, Touchan, Allen, and Swetnam 1996).

But change was in the wind. Spanish explorers arrived in the 1530s and established the nearby colony of Santa Fe in 1610 (Allen 2002). The Spaniards introduced horses and sheep to the Southwest, and both animals were readily assimilated into the Puebloan culture. Sheep grazing likely disrupted burning patterns locally, but impacts on fire regimes were not believed to be at the landscape scale (Allen 2002). European-American settlers arrived on the scene in the 19th century, and the cattle they brought further increased grazing impacts. But it was not until completion of the southern route of the transcontinental railroad in 1881, and the access to large markets it provided, that livestock populations erupted. An astonishingly large herd of cattle and an estimated five million sheep grazed New Mexico by the late 1800s (Wooton 1908). Unrestricted grazing and associated trampling from millions of hooves diminished the herbaceous cover, pine needles, and litter that historically fueled surface fires. These grazing effects, coupled with organized fire suppression beginning in about 1910, reduced the frequency and extent of fire on the landscape (Allen 2002, Pyne 1982, Swetnam 1990).

Aldo Leopold first documented this phenomenon—livestock grazing changing fire regimes—in southern Arizona in the 1920s (Leopold 1924). Severe drought in the 1950s further reduced herbaceous cover

Figure 6.1.
Surface soil (sheet) erosion in a pinyon–juniper stand in Northern New Mexico. Larger trees are beetle-killed pinyon pine. (C. Fiedler photo)

and decimated ponderosa pine growing in lower elevation savannas (Allen and Breshears 1998), allowing establishment of more drought-hardy pinyon and juniper at densities unprecedented for the previous 800 years (Allen 2001). This wave of expanding PJ woodland brought strong competition for soil moisture, further reducing herbaceous ground cover. The result was a fundamental shift from grassland- to woodland-dominated vegetation in little more than a century (late 1800s–2000). Although this change is troubling in itself, the erosion that accompanies it is an ecological calamity in the making (Figure 6.1).

Craig Allen knows the ecology and cultural history of north-central New Mexico like few others. Allen has spent the better part of two decades studying Native American history, culture, and land use on the Pajarito Plateau, which encompasses both Bandelier National Monument and the community of Los Alamos. Severe soil erosion occurring at Bandelier and the associated displacement or loss of embedded cultural artifacts profoundly disturb him. These deteriorating conditions inspired Allen and plant ecologist Brian Jacobs to design studies to quantify soil losses and evaluate the potential of restoration treatments to reestablish herbaceous cover. Because the objectives of managing the monument are culture-based, the restoration of pinyon–juniper grass savannas here is focused on influencing processes rather than woodland structure. The most pressing objective is to dramatically reduce current woodland erosion rates that average about one-half inch of soil loss per decade (Wilcox and others 1996, Wilcox, Breshears, and Allen 2003).

A functioning pinyon–juniper ecosystem is able to maintain the stability and productivity of the soil mantle upon which it develops. Broken into its fundamental parts, a pinyon–juniper stand consists of three kinds of patches—tree canopies, herbaceous plants, and bare soil (Davenport and others 1998). In terms of their potential to absorb water (percolation theory), these patches are viewed as either "on" or "off." In a functioning system, canopy patches and herbaceous patches are both "on" and can store moisture, whereas patches of bare soil are "off" and generate runoff (Davenport and others 1998). The herbaceous patches are really the glue that holds the system together. If herbaceous cover is gradually out-competed for light and moisture by expanding tree canopies and root systems or converted to bare soil through heavy grazing or trampling, the system approaches a threshold. If this threshold is exceeded, and the "off" cells (bare soil patches) become interconnected, erosion ensues and the system unravels.

To better understand the erosional disintegration of the pinyon–juniper stands at Bandelier, Allen and Jacobs have constructed catchments as part of a paired watershed experiment to monitor soil loss. An untreated (control) drainage is paired with an adjacent drainage where the pinyon–juniper stands have received restoration treatments. The objective is to compare erosion between the drainages and relate soil loss to the amount and timing of precipitation. Early results have sometimes been shocking—a single precipitation event caused the off-site movement of more than 1,000 cultural artifacts in the untreated drainage (Allen, unpublished data).

A second facet of the Bandelier research is evaluating ways to reduce pinyon–juniper density and reestablish herbaceous plant cover. Several treatments are being tested. Trees were thinned with chainsaws and then (1) removed from the site, (2) left where they landed, or (3) cut in pieces and dispersed across the intercanopy openings.

A comparison of the different approaches shows that thinning and then distributing the slash is a highly effective approach for slowing erosion and establishing native species. Scattering the thinning slash into openings increased infiltration and soil moisture and created hospitable sites for regeneration of herbaceous species. Grasses and forbs increased sharply in the treated areas (Hastings, Smith, and Jacobs 2003, Jacobs, Gatewood, and Allen 2002), and erosion declined dramatically as herbaceous species cover approached a mere 15–20 percent.

Allen and Jacobs have conducted dozens of field trips to their restoration site for groups and individuals representing all sides of the preservation versus restoration debate. Because restoration activities have been focused within a portion of the monument designated as wilderness adds further controversy to this undertaking (Sydoriak, Allen, and Jacobs 2001). Whatever their prior opinions, most visitors— including environmental advocates—come away as supporters of these well thought out and carefully implemented restoration treatments.

Differences in vegetation between untreated and treated areas are striking. The plant community in the untreated area remains dominated by trees (42 percent canopy cover). Herbaceous cover is sparse and erosion continues unabated. The treated area, in contrast, is dominated by a robust herbaceous layer, with only scattered pinyon and juniper trees (9 percent canopy cover) remaining after treatment. Herbaceous cover (grass + forbs) increased from about 7 percent before treatment to 30 percent 3 years after treatment. Patches of bare soil are scattered and largely unconnected, which has reduced erosion dramatically. The final management activity proposed for the treated area is a broadcast burn sometime in the next 5–10 years—after the slash has decayed enough to allow low-intensity burning. After that, no treatments are planned in the foreseeable future other than to let the age-old tug-of-war between succession and disturbance play out over the landscape.

The potentially devastating unwinding of the woodland/soil system at Bandelier has a silver lining. The threat to the monument's cultural remains has rallied restoration efforts in a vegetation type that is rapidly changing across much of the West and is often overlooked by conservationists. The Bandelier story demonstrates that attempts to "preserve" dynamic ecosystems may not produce the desired results. The take-home point is that some protected areas may also require restoration if they are to sustain the resources and values they were created to perpetuate.

The Bandelier restoration site and associated fire regime historically supported a pinyon-juniper grass savanna. A century of fire exclusion

allowed dramatic increases in tree density and associated loss of herbaceous cover, so the restoration treatments prescribed by Allen and Jacobs directly addressed these changed conditions. However, such
treatments are not necessarily appropriate for other sites or woodland
types and for dense pinyon–juniper woodlands in general. Recent work
by Baker and Shinneman (2004) suggests that stands classified as
pinyon–juniper forest commonly went for centuries between stand replacement fires, and current dense stand conditions with old-growth
trees are probably not outside their historic range of variability in stand
structure, fire frequency, or potential fire behavior.

The highly variable disturbance regimes associated with the different pinyon–juniper types emphasize the importance of understanding
local vegetation/disturbance relationships before deciding what restoration strategy is needed, if any. Knowledge of woodland dynamics is limited relative to that of other forest types. The role of climate (especially
episodic drought) versus that of grazing or fire exclusion on woodland
change is not well understood, arguing for a cautious approach to
restoration in this type. Given these uncertainties, an adaptive management approach is recommended, with small-scale trials to observe
results and modify treatments. Successful approaches can then be used
in operational-scale restoration efforts.

Chapter 7

Ponderosa Pine/Fir—Research and Demonstration Areas

The long history of attempting to manage ponderosa pine forests without accounting for fire's ecological role eventually led to restoration forestry. In a few ponderosa pine forests with unique histories, forest managers, scientists, and citizens looked to develop a different kind of management to address deteriorating conditions. They agreed that management treatments should in some way be patterned after the historical fire regime that helped produce forests of beautiful, long-lived trees in semiarid environments.

We profile three research and demonstration areas central to the development of restoration forestry. At the first area, a dozen photo points established in 1909 and rephotographed periodically illustrate the effects of excluding understory fires from pine forests. In the second area, an unusual citizen's appeal in the 1930s eventually led to the first scientific study of restoration cutting and burning treatments. In the third example, residents, scientists, and land managers joined forces to find workable approaches for sustaining the ponderosa pine forest that encompasses their city.

Lick Creek Demonstration Area

In 1906 the Lick Creek area southwest of Hamilton, Montana, was a hub of activity, befitting its status as one of the first large national forest timber sales in the country. Like millions of acres of virgin ponderosa pine forest elsewhere in the West, the original forest at Lick Creek was dominated by old-growth pine ranging from 200 to more than 400 years old. These "yellow pines" were mostly open-grown—

often only 30–40 trees per acre—with trunks averaging more than 30 feet apart (Arno, Scott, and Hartwell 1995, Leiberg 1899, Smith and Arno 1999). Old-growth stands were interspersed with scattered individuals and patches of younger pines and saplings. About 10 percent of the overstory trees were inland Douglas-fir, most abundant on north-facing slopes and in swales. Early photographs (Smith and Arno 1999) depict large pines with smooth, fire-pruned trunks extending high above the ground and an open, grassy understory—a visually striking structure groomed for centuries by low-intensity fires. Fire scars on living trees and stumps of logged trees show that fires occurred at intervals averaging about 7 years between 1600 and 1895. On one stump the sequence of scars from frequent fires was traced back to about 1545.

The 1906 sale was meant to initiate an era of sustainable timber management. [The following account is condensed from Smith and Arno (1999).] This first attempt at active management of the national forest lacked today's emphasis on nontimber values such as perpetuating large old trees for wildlife habitat and aesthetics. Eventually, nearly all trees would be harvested when they reached financial maturity and their growth began to slow at age 100 years or so. The 1906 sale involved selective cutting that left from 5 to 50 percent of the original volume to continue growing and be available for future harvests. Elers Koch (1998) recounts a visit to Lick Creek by Gifford Pinchot, founder of the U.S. Forest Service, while he and his crew were marking the stand for harvest. Pinchot thought that too many trees were being marked for cut, so had the crew go back and adjust their marking. Tree markers were instructed to leave thrifty pines with good crown form and to mark to cut all Douglas-fir more than 10 inches in diameter. Foresters worried that allowing Douglas-fir to increase would correspondingly increase damage from dwarf mistletoe, a parasitic plant that infects this species. Some clumps of small (nonmerchantable) pines were also thinned. This large sale (massive by today's standards) produced 37.6 million board feet of timber from 2,135 acres and took 5 years to complete. Branches and tops (slash) from the harvested trees were piled by hand and burned, a practice the purchaser considered unnecessary. However, fires were no longer allowed to spread through the forest as they had in the past.

The original harvest was completed in 1911, and during the following decades the remaining trees grew vigorously. By 1946 the timber volume of overstory trees had increased 60 percent, to about 6,100 board feet per acre. Within 20 years after the sale, pine and Douglas-fir seedlings and saplings established throughout the area. Much of the Douglas-fir regenerated after the last understory fire in the 1890s but before logging began in 1907, giving it a head start over the shade-intolerant pine that regenerated mostly in openings created by logging.

Between 1953 and 1981 several additional cuttings took place on different portions of the original sale area. These removed some of the dominant trees from crowded groups, damaged trees, and those with poor crowns—including slow-growing old trees. Saplings and pole-size trees were also thinned throughout much of the area and left to decay where they fell. A prescribed underburn was conducted in one small part of the area in the 1980s; otherwise, fire was excluded from this forest until restoration treatments began in the 1990s.

A Forest Service photographer captured several views of the Lick Creek forest in 1909. The camera positions for these scenes were relocated and permanently marked during the 1920s. They were rephotographed every decade throughout the 20th century. Wildlife biologist George Gruell and his colleagues at the U.S. Forest Service Intermountain Research Station examined vegetation changes between 1909 and 1979 as depicted in the photo series and interpreted their probable causes (Gruell and others 1982). They also analyzed data on tree growth and regeneration over the decades and evaluated effectiveness of the timber management activities for perpetuating a healthy uneven-aged ponderosa pine forest. The 1909 scenes were photographed after logging had begun, so the stumps of harvested trees were visible, as were tops and branches in unburned piles. The understory vegetation was only lightly disturbed by the skidding operations. Thus, conditions prior to tree removal can be inferred. One prelogging photograph from Lick Creek and others from nearby ponderosa pine forests show similar stands of large trees with open, grassy understories (Leiberg 1899, Smith and Arno 1999).

The 1907–1911 logging operations created openings in the forest, and skidding and pile burning removed litter, duff, and understory vegetation in spots. The 1920s and 1930s photos show that postlogging conditions encouraged conifer regeneration and establishment of vigorous Scouler willow and bitterbrush (*Purshia tridentata*) shrubs, whose young twigs provide important forage (browse) for deer, elk, and moose on winter range. By the 1950s, absence of understory fire was allowing

Figure 7.1
Photo sequence from a camera point at Lick Creek showing change in forest structure following elimination of the understory fire regime and selective harvesting in 1907 or 1908. (a) In 1909 the stand is nearly pure ponderosa pine with an open understory. Stumps indicate the relatively few trees that were removed. (b) By 1948 a dense Douglas-fir understory had developed. (USDA Forest Service photos)

young conifers to form thickets (Figure 7.1). Thickets increased through time, despite some scattered thinning that added slash to the buildup of pine needle litter. Even though many Douglas-fir trees were removed in the early 1900s logging, the proportion of young firs kept increasing in the absence of fire. Pine saplings survive understory fires better than Douglas-fir because they have shorter crowns and develop protective corky bark more rapidly. Repeated selective harvests between 1953 and 1981 removed many of the remaining large trees, but competition from increasing numbers of small and medium-size trees diminished the abundance and vigor of willow and bitterbrush shrubs.

Gruell and his colleagues (1982) concluded that 70 years of carefully guided selective cutting and thinning failed to substitute for historical fires in controlling the proliferation of understory trees and accumulation of fuels. They contended that the shift toward dense stands and greater Douglas-fir composition would increase susceptibility to bark beetles, western spruce budworm, dwarf mistletoe, and root rot. To reverse these trends, they recommended reintroducing low-intensity prescribed burning in conjunction with thinning and improvement cutting that retained the most vigorous pines of different ages.

In 1987, the Bitterroot National Forest's first forest plan suggested that management take into account natural ecological processes. Soon afterward, the Darby Ranger District conducted an integrated resource analysis for the Lick Creek area, obtaining recommendations from a range of citizens and natural resource specialists. This process produced a description of the "desired future condition" and a list of management activities that would begin guiding the forest toward that goal. Recognizing that the historical photo series and early silvicultural cutting and growth records were a unique asset, the district ranger designated Lick Creek as a formal demonstration/research area.

Historically, frequent understory fires perpetuated the uneven-aged pine stands at Lick Creek. By the 1980s, despite decades of selective cutting and thinning to promote vigorous pine, the forest at Lick Creek exhibited increasing vulnerability to insects, disease, and crown fire, and decreasing aesthetic values and wildlife forage production. A primary goal coming out of the Lick Creek planning meetings was to guide management toward more sustainable stand structures, while improving wildlife habitat, aesthetics, and tree growth.

In 1991 the Intermountain Research Station and the University of Montana's School of Forestry agreed to cooperative studies with the Bitterroot National Forest to provide a basis for restoration management at Lick Creek and in similar forests elsewhere. The collaborators agreed to develop stands having large, medium, and small diameter pines in proper proportions to maintain a large-tree component in perpetuity. This would require adapting the traditional "shelterwood" and "selection" silvicultural systems because neither was designed to perpetuate large old trees as a major component of a managed forest. The modified silvicultural system would need to remove excess small, medium, and large trees every 25–30 years or so, while retaining enough vigorous trees in each size class to perpetuate an uneven-aged, pine-dominated forest. Each of these silvicultural cuttings would remove enough trees to induce regeneration of a new age class of ponderosa pine. Stands that started with just one age class would attain an uneven-aged structure after two or more cutting treatments (entries).

The collaborators agreed that prescribed fire should be used as a substitute for the historical underburns. Low-intensity fires would be scheduled in conjunction with each silvicultural cutting to reduce logging slash, duff, and litter, recycle nutrients, and control conifer regeneration, especially Douglas-fir and the shade-tolerant grand fir found on moist sites. These fires would also stimulate herbs and shrubs valuable for wildlife.

Reducing overall stand density and the glut of small trees was necessary to allow safer use of prescribed fire. In 1991 no markets existed for small trees; only trees greater than 8 inches in diameter could be removed and sold for products. Thinned trees less than 8 inches were cut into pieces and left in the woods. Harvesting had to generate revenue to pay for timber sale preparation, tree marking, and prescribed burning. Reintroducing fire for the first time after a long period of fire exclusion might stress the remaining trees and invite bark beetle attacks. However, if the largest and most vigorous trees were retained, thinning might improve their vigor before fire was applied.

Three kinds of ponderosa pine/Douglas-fir stands covered contiguous areas large enough (> 100 acres) to accommodate the multiple treatment units or "replications" needed for research experiments. Douglas-fir comprised less than 20 percent of the overstory in all stands, but Douglas-fir seedlings and saplings were abundant in many areas.

The youngest stand was about 70 years old and occupied a dry, moderately steep south-facing slope. This stand had a tree basal area of 85–100 square feet per acre; here a commercial thinning treatment was prescribed to reduce basal area to about 50 square feet. The intermediate stand, located on a more moderate south-facing slope, was 80–85 years old and supported about 120 square feet of basal area per acre. A modified shelterwood cutting was prescribed to reduce basal area in this stand to about 40–45 square feet per acre. The third stand occupied a moderate southwest aspect and contained pines of many ages—including some very large, old trees—and averaged about 110 square feet of basal area per acre. A modified selection cutting was prescribed to reduce basal area to an average of 50 square feet per acre. This stand was leave-tree marked to retain pines across the full range of diameters. Snags and potential snags were retained at about one per acre. The most vigorous trees were retained in all three stands, and small openings were created in the shelterwood and selection treatments to induce a new age class of pine. The ranger district implemented similar treatments in areas surrounding the experimental stands, for a total treatment area of about 530 acres.

The entire area was managed under a conventional timber sale that produced 1.5 million board feet of sawlogs and plywood peelers. Harvesting was conducted in 1992 using manual felling with chain saws. Felled trees were winch-yarded to designated skid trails and skidded to an existing road with a crawler tractor. By the late 1990s, low-impact, cut-to-length harvesting machines and log forwarders were commonly used for this kind of treatment.

To reduce the amount of slash left in the units, loggers skidded commercial-size trees to roadside landings with limbs still attached. Limbs were then removed, piled, and burned at the landings. The tree-tops—cut at about 6 inches in diameter outside the bark—were left where they fell to recycle nutrients and woody debris to the soil. Prescribed fires consumed the smaller branches but not the green wood in the tops. Stands in the research study were divided into units, including (1) unharvested "controls," (2) harvested areas left unburned, (3) harvested areas receiving a "wet" burn, (4) "dry" burn, (5) spring burn, or (6) fall burn. A "wet burn" was applied early in the spring, when the lower duff and large woody fuels were still moist. The collaborators also needed to test a "dry burn" prescription, several days later in spring, to expand the window of opportunity for using fire successfully. A successful burn consumed some of the fuel bed while causing little damage to the overstory trees.

Treatments were compared in terms of fuel reduction, tree mortality and growth response, undergrowth species response, tree regeneration, and soil nutrients. Other studies measured the public's visual preferences for different treatments, and the comparative quality for wildlife habitat of snags killed by fire or mechanical girdling.

The harvested, unburned treatments left most of the existing Douglas-fir saplings in place, allowing them to dominate the understory of the future stand unless they are later removed by thinning or improvement cutting. The different burn treatments killed most of the small firs and significantly reduced litter and woody fuels while damaging few overstory trees. Even the dry burns were followed by modest and acceptable levels of overstory tree mortality. In contrast, all burn treatments killed an average of about 65 percent of the small trees (less than 7 inches in diameter) that had survived the harvesting operations. Killing small trees was an objective of burning in the thinning and shelterwood treatments, because few were healthy pine saplings likely to develop into large trees. Conversely, the goal of underburning in the modified selection treatments was to allow most of the smaller pine (averaging 4 inches in diameter) to survive, and about 80 percent of them did. Overall, the different burn treatments spanned and defined a range of burning conditions that are broadly applicable in similar restoration projects.

The cutting and burning treatments at Lick Creek released a flush of nitrogen into the soil. Some was taken up by the postburn vegetation, which was then heavily grazed by deer, elk, and moose. Resprouting willow was browsed so heavily that it has been unable to grow vertically except where protected in wire cages. With so little of this lower elevation forest available in thinned and burned condition, the high elk and deer populations in the area congregate on the few areas where nutritious forage is available.

The experience at Lick Creek demonstrates that coupled with appropriate cutting treatments, prescribed fire can control excessive numbers of saplings and reduce surface fuels, recycle nutrients in a semblance of natural processes, and reduce severe wildfire hazard. However, it also exposes challenges in restoring a fire-dependent forest that has missed several natural fire cycles. Heavy fuel accumulations, coupled with low tree vigor and presence of fine roots close to the surface, leave trees vulnerable to fire damage. Trees are almost universally stressed, and even moderate fire injury may increase their susceptibility to beetle attack. Invasive, nonnative plants were already established at Lick Creek, and their coverage increased with cutting and burning treatments. However, soil disturbance could be greatly reduced with winter logging and somewhat reduced using cut-to-length harvesting systems. Alternatively, leaving deteriorating forest conditions and fuel buildups untreated leaves them vulnerable to far greater soil disturbance and weed invasion when wildfires inevitably occur.

The coordinated effort at Lick Creek among managers, researchers, educators, and the public helped gain acceptance within and outside the Forest Service for new approaches to forest management. Most people came to recognize that management based on natural disturbance processes could meet both ecological and social needs in an area heavily used for recreation, sight-seeing, hunting, and timber resources. Because the Lick Creek study area parallels a loop road near the popular Lake Como Recreation Area and is part of a self-guided auto tour, it will continue to provide an example of restoration forestry's potential for perpetuating ponderosa pine forests.

Lubrecht Experimental Forest

It was the middle of the Great Depression, and Ma Potter—proprietor of a guest ranch in western Montana—was beside herself. Her angst was not for lack of business. In fact, business was surprisingly good, as guests to the ranch hailed either from back east or Europe and had deep pockets. What vexed her soul was the proposed cutting of magnificent old-growth ponderosa pine trees bordering the dirt road (now Montana Highway 200) used to transport guests from the train station in Missoula. The land was owned by the powerful Anaconda Copper and Mining Company, and the company was logging to feed its sawmill some 15 miles west at the mouth of the Big Blackfoot River. Ma Potter pleaded with the logging foreman to spare the splendid yellow pines, and her perseverance finally carried the day. A few years later the company donated nearly 20,000 acres of mostly cutover land, including the scenic highway corridor, to the University of Montana (UM). In 1937, these lands became the UM Lubrecht Experimental Forest. Little did Ma Potter know that nearly a half-century later her intervention would provide raw material for a pioneering research project.

The first restoration experiment in ponderosa pine forests in the West was implemented in 1984 on the Lubrecht Forest (on Ma Potter's contested strip of land), with another replication on the nearby guest ranch. This project featured a modified form of selection cutting along with prescribed underburning and focused on the density and sizes of trees to *leave* rather than to cut—radical concepts at the time. But first a larger story needs to be told about the "identity crisis" that gripped forestry in the years leading up to this historic experiment.

Turmoil in the Trenches

In the wake of the Watergate scandal and Vietnam War, virtually all institutions and norms were being challenged in 1970s America, and forestry was no exception. In forestry, a battle was waging between the prevailing management philosophy that focused on wood production versus an emerging philosophy that also recognized the ecological and amenity values of forests. Significant advances in the understanding of ecological relationships also occurred, such as development of the "habitat type" system for classifying forest sites (Pfister and others 1977). This expanding knowledge raised questions about the one-size-fits-all application of even-aged treatments, particularly clearcutting.

This was also a time of introspection for the authors, although we were not the only ones. Our change in understanding didn't happen overnight but was fundamental enough to be a professional epiphany. Consideration of individual species' adaptations to different site conditions (e.g., dry, warm, cold, or wet) and disturbance regimes (e.g., low-intensity, mixed-intensity, or stand replacement) led us to question the appropriateness of applying even-aged management nearly everywhere. Nowhere was our change in view more profound than in forests historically dominated by ponderosa pine.

Countless hours spent measuring tree diameters in ponderosa pine stands to determine size-class structure, extracting increment cores to determine age-class structure, and analyzing fire scars to determine fire histories provided insights that textbooks and conventional wisdom could not. Fire scar analyses showed low-intensity fires historically occurring at 5–30-year intervals within most old-growth stands, and age-class determinations typically showed trees establishing not only in different decades within a century, but also in different centuries. Remarkably, in this natural uneven-aged system the shade-intolerant pine had continued to dominate and prosper despite the presence of more shade-tolerant Douglas-fir. How revealing it was to find that the large pines in a stand that looked reasonably alike and were assumed by many to be similar in age were in fact quite different. For example, imagine four trees in an old-growth stand that were found to be 225, 275, 325, and 475 years old in the year 2000. Now turn back the clock to the year 1775. These same trees were a first-year seedling, a 50-year-old pole-size tree, a 100-year-old medium-size tree, and a 250-year-old old-growth tree. This broad age range suggests a low-intensity disturbance regime in which regeneration occurred some years and not others and in which occasional surface fires killed most trees while they were small, but a few survived the gauntlet of repeated fires to reach large size and old age.

Ponderosa pine's unique architecture provides further evidence of its adaptation to low-intensity disturbances. Pines have deep roots, thick bark, open crowns, large fleshy buds, and long needles arrayed to deflect rising heat—characteristics that allow them to survive a surface fire regime but confer no protection or advantage in crown fires. Ponderosa pine also has heavy seeds (~12,000 per pound) that typically disperse within about 150 feet of the parent tree. This attribute reflects a species adapted to regenerating in small openings created by low intensity fire, pockets of beetle-kill, or occasional lightning strikes—not in the expansive openings created by stand replacement fires or other large-scale disturbances. The question then arises, what kind or combination of silvicultural treatments might emulate the disturbances that sustained ponderosa pine forests for centuries, and to which the species is so admirably adapted? And could these treatments perpetuate uneven-aged forests with large old pines, and their associated ecological and scenic values, while also yielding some timber products?

The answer to these questions lies in the treatments being evaluated as part of the Lubrecht restoration project. Although hindsight suggests that the treatments implemented in 1984 would be applied a bit differently today, they did address the critical components of a restoration prescription—density, structure, and species composition of the reserve stand. Two treatments—a combined improvement/selection cutting to a reserve density of 60 square feet per acre, and that same cutting in combination with prescribed underburning—were compared to a no-treatment control. Selection cutting methods were chosen as most appropriate for accomplishing the study objectives of maintaining some trees of all sizes in the stand, especially large trees, and regenerating a new age class of ponderosa pine. Improvement cutting removed pole-size and larger Douglas-fir to prevent conversion to this more shade-tolerant species in the future, and underburning was prescribed to kill most Douglas-fir seedlings and saplings. The prescription that involved both cutting and underburning was hypothesized to best emulate the kind and intensity of disturbances that historically sustained ponderosa pine forests.

Proponents of traditional timber management leveled a litany of criticisms at the selection cutting treatments being tested at Lubrecht, even though the treatments were experimental rather than operational. Critics contended that shade-intolerant ponderosa pine could not be regenerated under the partial overstory of uneven-aged stands, whereas shade-tolerant Douglas-fir would regenerate profusely, resulting in conversion to fir. They believed the treatments cost too much and produced too little timber. They also thought the methods were too complex for operational use and that logging would significantly damage the smaller trees retained in uneven-aged stands. Critics argued that prescribed underburning was inappropriate because it would kill the small trees deliberately left to develop into large trees in the future. Finally, some detractors noted that the system was incompatible with the record-keeping methods used by federal agencies.

Although there was some substance to most of these criticisms, experience since 1984 shows that the problems raised can be reduced or neutralized using well-designed treatments and streamlined implementation methods (Becker 1995, Fiedler 1995). Years earlier fire ecologists such as Weaver (1943) and Biswell and others (1973) provided strong conceptual support for uneven-aged management of ponderosa pine based on historical fire regimes. The focus here should not be on whether the treatments implemented at Lubrecht have shortcomings—they do. The more important question is whether this and other restoration approaches now being tried throughout the West are more appropriate than previous ones for developing sustainable, productive, and attractive pine forests adapted to natural disturbances.

The passionate opposition to the Lubrecht treatments is understandable given the context of the times. Forest management was coming out of an era when timber was king and economic efficiency and manipulation of site conditions were considered all-important. Clearcutting was the dominant regeneration cutting method of the time: it was the easiest to layout; it was the cheapest to implement; it produced the most volume; it provided the ample light needed by preferred species such as ponderosa pine, western larch, and Engelmann spruce; and it initiated a single-aged "tree crop" tailor-made for maximizing production of timber in short rotations. Following clearcutting, the site was typically scraped to bare soil with a bulldozer to remove potential competition from herbaceous vegetation or shrubs. The nutritionally valuable organic layer atop the soil was also scraped into piles or windrows in the process. Clearcuts on steep slopes were sometimes "terraced" with bulldozers to minimize vegetative competition, provide a level surface for planting, and create favorable conditions for seedling growth. These treatments often achieved their narrow objective, which was to secure regeneration of a new stand—but little regard was given to either their appearance or ecological side effects. Public reaction to large clearcuts and terraced mountainsides ranged from anger to disgust and helped fuel a growing environmental movement. Forestry circled the wagons, unwilling to concede deficiencies in its ubiquitous application of clearcutting or to consider an unconventional alternative like that being demonstrated at Lubrecht.

Modifying a European Approach to Meet Western Needs

The kind of selection cutting that appears to best emulate the effects of historical disturbances on forest structure is a considerably modified version of the selection cutting method described in textbooks. Selection cutting has its roots in Europe and was typically applied in stands of shade-tolerant species like fir and spruce where fire was not a dominant disturbance process. Individual trees were cut here and there in a given harvest entry, hence the name single-tree selection. Furthermore, the high value of wood relative to the cost of labor to remove it allowed stands to be reentered every several years, and sometimes annually, with few trees per acre removed in each entry. Little additional light or moisture was freed up within the stand, and the shaded conditions that remained after cutting favored regeneration of shade-tolerant species.

Selection cutting for the purpose of perpetuating shade-intolerant ponderosa pine stands required some fundamental modifications. One primary change is the focus on trees to leave rather than cut. This approach allows the marker to focus on leaving the number, species, size, and juxtaposition of trees in the existing stand that make the most progress toward the desired stand of the future. Perhaps most importantly, only leave-tree marking can ensure that desired density levels are achieved. Regenerating pine requires that basal area density be reduced to low levels—40–60 square feet per acre—so that adequate light and moisture is available to induce pine regeneration (Fiedler, Becker, and Haglund 1988). Establishing regeneration in conditions where it can grow vigorously is critical to sustaining uneven-aged pine forests (Fiedler 1995). Although ponderosa pine requires only moderate light levels for seedlings to survive and linger for years in a sickly, light-starved form, nearly full sunlight is necessary for trees to grow out of the seedling/sapling stage. Leaving density too high following treatment is likely the most common shortcoming in attempts to restore uneven-aged pine forests. Similarly, pole- and medium-size trees require low stand densities to achieve large size.

Finally, old trees need relatively open conditions to maintain modest growth rates and survive several hundred years. Some may question the importance of maintaining growth in old-growth trees. What difference does it really make if a 2-foot-thick old-growth tree grows an inch in diameter or hardly at all over the next 20 years? The answer to this question might be phrased "better living through chemistry." Trees have the ability to manufacture defensive chemicals to survive most insect and disease attacks, but this process takes lower priority than growth (Waring and Pitman 1985). Hence, low-vigor trees—as evidenced by low growth rates—are unable to marshal enough resources to manufacture adequate chemicals for their defense. Large old trees growing among a dense layer of smaller trees are especially vulnerable to attack, underscoring the importance of maintaining reasonable growth rates.

Implementing Treatments

The modified selection cutting prescription developed for the Lubrecht study involved leave-tree marking across the full range of tree sizes, from 2 to 36 inches. Tree marking guidelines focused on keeping healthy pine of all sizes with crown ratios (crown length/total tree height) greater than 35 percent, not to exceed an average of 60 square feet per acre. Approximately half of the reserve basal area was in trees larger than 16 inches. The prescription specified that no Douglas-fir be retained, presuming that this species would gradually seed in from surrounding areas.

All cutting associated with treatment implementation occurred in August. Trees smaller than 14 inches in diameter were felled with a mechanical clipper, while larger trees were hand-felled by chainsaw. All cut trees larger than 4 inches were skidded whole (tops and limbs intact) to a landing using a grapple skidder. Trees larger than 10 inches diameter were processed into sawlogs at the landing. Smaller cut trees and limbs and tops of sawlog-size trees were ground into hog fuel and transported to the local pulp mill. A modest number of small saplings (several dozen per acre) were cut, slashed, and left where they fell to augment the fuel bed for prescribed underburning in early October.

Lessons Learned

Two decades of monitoring the restoration treatments at the Lubrecht Forest and nearby guest ranch confirm the importance of low densities for achieving restoration goals. Nowhere is this more telling than when comparing differences among treatments in the growth and survival of mature trees (greater than 16 inches in diameter). Large trees in the two selection cutting treatments are growing nearly three times faster on average than those in the control, while four times as many large trees have died in the control as compared to the treated areas (Fiedler 2000b). Sapling-, pole-, and medium-size trees are also growing considerably faster in the treated areas, indicating that large-tree recruitment will likely continue well into the future. The system of perpetuating attractive, uneven-aged pine forests through time will work only if many of the large old trees can survive nature's vicissitudes, medium- and pole-size trees are developing into large old trees, and pine seedlings and saplings are establishing and growing well enough to replace today's big trees sometime in the distant future.

The numbers and kinds of seedlings being recruited also differ dramatically between the treated areas and the control. In the two treated areas ponderosa pine seedlings outnumber Douglas-fir approximately 20:1, while in the control plots Douglas-fir seedlings outnumber pine by more than 2:1 (Fiedler 2000b). Despite the encouraging number and proportion of pine seedlings that have established since treatment, their height growth is disappointing and not adequate to ensure development into sapling size in a reasonable time frame. Similar results at both the Lubrecht Forest and guest ranch locations suggest that the 60 square feet per acre reserve basal area is too high for adequate development of small trees. The restoration experiments at Lick Creek, discussed earlier in this chapter, and long-term monitoring on the

Flathead Indian Reservation in Montana, show that reserve densities of 45–50 square feet per acre do provide suitable conditions for pine regeneration and early development.

Regardless of ecological benefits, restoration treatments will not be accepted for broader application if people dislike their appearance. The fishbowl setting of both the Lubrecht and guest ranch restoration sites provides a stiff test of their aesthetic appeal. The Lubrecht Forest site borders the scenic Blackfoot highway—a popular travel route for locals and tourists alike. Over the 20-year life of the project, Lubrecht Forest director Hank Goetz has received countless compliments but not a single complaint about the appearance of the treatments. Scores of field trips to the treatment areas with students, citizens, and professionals have produced similar responses.

At the guest ranch, a popular riding trail winds through all three experimental units, exposing guests on horseback to a 360° view of the restoration treatments. Ma Potter's son, Bill, frequently asks guests for their opinions of the experimental treatments. Responses are both positive and inquisitive, giving Potter a chance to expound on one of his favorite topics—good forest stewardship. Support for the treatments becomes even stronger when people understand the compelling need behind them.

One purpose of research—whether in medicine, agriculture, or forestry—is to identify both positive and negative implications of treatments before they are widely applied. Results from 20 years of intensive tree-level measurements and observations at the Lubrecht Forest and guest ranch sites can provide guidance for others who wish to develop restoration projects in similar forests. Although the 60 square feet per acre reserve basal area evaluated in this experiment was sufficiently low to spur diameter growth of trees of all sizes, significantly increase survival of large trees, and induce regeneration of ponderosa pine, it was too high to allow the small-tree height growth that is critical to perpetuate uneven-aged pine forests.

Another potential problem is developing at the two sites—one that has implications in all pine forests that contain shade-tolerant trees. Both study sites supported hundreds of Douglas-fir seedlings per acre prior to treatment. In the selection cutting treatment that received underburning, nearly all Douglas-fir seedlings were killed (Kalabokidis and Wakimoto 1992). However, small fir in the unburned selection cutting treatment remained unscathed, and their height growth has exploded. Many of these Douglas-fir are now sapling-size and will need to be cut at the next harvest entry in 5 or 10 years to prevent them from crowding out the pine seedlings that have established since treatment. Prescribed underburning is an especially effective means of killing the fire-vulnerable Douglas-fir and true firs when they are small, but many landowners, especially private ones, are unwilling to take the risk of burning. This problem becomes more difficult and costly to deal with as trees become sapling-size and larger, but it must be addressed to achieve sustainable pine forests.

The Lubrecht Forest–guest ranch experiment was the first of its kind to evaluate the effects of selection cutting and underburning for restoring ponderosa pine forests. The immediate objectives were to restore environmental conditions that increase tree vigor, induce regeneration of ponderosa pine, reduce fire hazard, and reintroduce fire as an ecological process. The broader objective was to demonstrate restoration treatments for managers to learn from or critique and to provide a frame of reference for refining restoration techniques in the future.

Greater Flagstaff Forests Partnership

The open, fire-sculpted forests of stately ponderosa pine that greeted the first Euro-American visitors to the Southwest no longer exist (Cooper 1960, Covington and Moore 1994a, b). Today, these forests retain only scattered old yellow pines enveloped in thickets of sapling- and pole-size trees. Huge wildfires are damaging out-of-balance pine ecosystems and continue to threaten the region's forests and the humans and property within them. Despite ample media coverage, little has been done to confront this looming problem. One notable exception, however, is a community-based project in northern Arizona called the Greater Flagstaff Forests Partnership (GFFP) (Friederici 2003b). The GFFP encompasses 100,000 acres of the Coconino National Forest and private lands surrounding the city of Flagstaff (population 53,000). The beauty of this setting, a 7,000-foot-high plateau covered with ponderosa pine forest, scattered meadows, and small aspen groves near the foot of the towering 12,000-foot San Francisco Peaks, may lead the casual observer to conclude that all is well with nature. However, a visit with Pete Fulé, professor of forest ecology at Northern Arizona University (NAU), soon dispels such an idyllic notion.

Fulé knows this landscape well and has found most of the surrounding forests overloaded with trees—especially small- and medium-
size ones (Fulé and others 2001b). Most trees in these dense forests are
less than a century old, having regenerated in heavily logged areas following the prodigious 1919 ponderosa pine seed crop (Pearson 1923).
Past overgrazing, coupled with too many trees competing for too few
resources, has taken its toll on native grasses that once flourished under
parklike stands of magnificent yellow pines. Today's crowded trees—
often 10 times denser than historically (Covington and Moore
1994a)—have lost the vigor needed to ward off insects and diseases.
Weakened trees are easy targets for bark beetle (*Dendroctonus ponderosae*)
and engraver beetle (*Ips pini*) attack because they are unable to produce
enough gummy resin to inundate or "pitch out" the boring insects.

Driving into the Flagstaff area, one sees patches of ponderosa pines
with rust-red foliage everywhere—grim evidence of trees unable to
resist the beetle onslaught. When conditions allow beetle populations
to explode to epidemic proportions, even vigorous green trees can be
killed. Considering the current tree-killing binge by beetles, one wonders
how the trees in the renowned old-growth pine forests that used to blanket this landscape ever managed to develop large size and great age.

In recent years severe forest fires have engulfed well more than a
million acres of southwestern ponderosa pine forests. In 2000, the
Cerro Grande wildfire scorched its way to more than $600 million of
damage in and around the unprepared city of Los Alamos. Two years
later, 467 homes and summer cabins went up in smoke in the 460,000-
acre Rodeo-Chediski firestorm in the Heber/Overgaard area of Arizona. The threat of a similar holocaust sweeping across the Flagstaff area
sparked community-wide interest in restoring more fire-resistant, sustainable forests. Area residents recognize that unless they take action to
reduce the forest fuels problem, newspaper headlines could soon trum-
pet "Flagstaff Burns!"

Wally Covington, a professor of forest ecology at NAU and the driving force behind the university's Ecological Restoration Institute,
knows this threat all too well. For years he has championed a vision
to reduce the size and intensity of wildfires through management designed to restore declining ecological conditions in the Southwest's
pine forests (Covington 1995). Based on his experience, Covington has
proposed restoration treatments based on historical numbers and patterns of trees—conditions described and photographed by explorers
and early settlers.

Thus was sown the seed for the GFFP, a cooperative effort involving managers of public lands, NAU, private landowners, and environmental organizations, some of whom previously opposed tree cutting or prescribed burning. Initially, GFFP focused on the 10,000-acre Fort Valley area northwest of the city, about two-thirds of which is proposed for treatment. Acting district ranger Tammy Randall Parker of the Coconino National Forest has been a leader in bringing the unlikely partners together. A wildlife biologist by training, Parker helped guide GFFP participants to find common ground where little existed before, including development of an ecological vision:

"Within 20 years, the Flagstaff wildland/urban interface will be a mosaic of open, parklike forests containing scattered timber stands with higher densities, interspersed with natural parks which approximate—although do not duplicate—conditions present before Euro-American settlement. Forests and woodlands will be dominated by open growing clumps of large old trees in a matrix of native bunchgrasses, wildflowers, and shrubs. Parks will be dominated by native grasses and wildflowers. Periodic low-intensity fires will maintain open habitats, cycle nutrients, and keep wildland fuel levels low, reducing the hazard of catastrophic crown fires. The presence of introduced species will be greatly diminished and native wildlife species will occupy their original niches within the ecosystem, moving freely through established wildlife corridors. A broad spectrum of uses—based upon science and adaptive ecosystem management principles—will be enjoyed by Northern Arizona residents and visitors. Although the majority of the landscape will be restored to more natural conditions, management practices will vary to address specific, well-defined management goals." (http://www.gffp.org/about_gffp/guide.htm#ecological)

Parker and the GFFP steering committee encouraged broad participation in the Fort Valley project by allowing participants to submit for evaluation their preferred restoration approach. Although there is no consensus on what comprises an appropriate restoration treatment, participants have agreed to evaluate proposed treatments and to apply and monitor those that show promise in achieving fuels reduction and restoration goals.

The NAU Ecological Restoration Institute (ERI), U.S. Forest Service, and Southwest Forest Alliance, an environmental organization, provided the restoration treatment alternatives being evaluated at Fort Valley (Figure 7.2; Table 7.1). The *ERI approach* uses the historic forest structure from remaining old-growth trees and identifiable stumps to guide the selection of trees to leave. This "historical reconstruction"

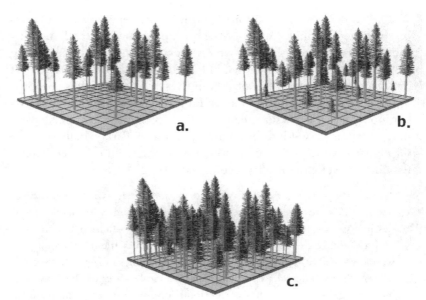

Figure 7.2.
Computer visualizations of the three restoration alternatives being demonstrated in the Greater Flagstaff Forest Partnership Project: (a) Ecological Restoration Institute alternative; (b) U.S. Forest Service alternative; (c) Southwest Forest Alliance alternative. (S. Robertson visualizations)

or "presettlement forest" approach simulates the structure and pattern of original forests as closely as possible. The premise here is that historic forests consisted of specific fine-grained patterns for a reason, perhaps linked to patterns of soil moisture or nutrients. All remaining old-growth trees are retained. In addition, medium- to large-size post-settlement trees are retained to replace "missing" old-growth trees as evidenced by old stumps, snags, downed trees, or stump holes. If potential replacement trees are larger than 16 inches in diameter, 1.5–3 trees are retained near the location of each missing old-growth tree. If replacement trees are less than 16 inches, 3–6 are retained as old-growth recruits for the future. Re-creating historical old-growth tree locations and patterns is an integral part of this restoration philosophy.

Research forester Carl Edminster and John Bailey, NAU professor of silviculture, designed the *Forest Service alternative*, which involves marking leave trees to approximate the numbers and sizes of trees in

Table 7.1.

Number of ponderosa pine trees per acre that remain after implementing the Ecological Restoration Institute and U.S. Forest Service restoration alternatives (comparative numbers were not available from the Southwest Forest Alliance). Note: these numbers are averages from a specific project; tree sizes and numbers vary widely from acre to acre throughout the area. The NAU numbers reflect the full restoration approach of 1.5 large- or 3 medium-size postsettlement trees retained for each "missing" old tree, which comes closest to emulating historical forest structure.

Diameter (inches)	Control (untreated)	Ecological Restoration Institute	U.S. Forest Service	Southwest Forest Alliance
	Average number of ponderosa pine trees per acre			
0–4	229	1	11	--
5–8	107	4	12	--
9–12	72	18	11	--
13–16	53	18	7	--
17–20	13	8	7	--
21–24	4	4	4	--
24+	3	3	3	--
Basal area (sq. feet/acre)	(164)	(68)	(51)	--

historical uneven-aged stands. The *Forest Service alternative* is an experimental prescription, not a standard agency approach. Maintaining stands with trees of many different sizes and ages, and creating conditions that allow for regeneration of a new age class and replacement of harvested trees, requires a major density reduction. In many stands, basal area needs to be reduced by half or more to approximate the desired density. The long-term objective is to perpetuate clumpy stands with a wide range of tree sizes, with slightly fewer trees in each successively larger diameter class. This approach follows the concept of a "selection system," allowing for some mortality or cutting of smaller trees so that the remaining trees can develop and replace the larger trees that die or are harvested. It also creates conditions suitable for regenerating shade-intolerant ponderosa pine following cuttings at about 20-year intervals.

The restoration approach taken by the *Southwest Forest Alliance* focuses on removing small trees and could be termed "thinning-from-below" or "low thinning." Most trees less than 9 inches in diameter are cut along with a modest number between 9 and 12 inches, and a few between 12 and 16 inches. This approach also attempts to maintain or recreate the clumpy nature of historic stands.

No trees larger than 16 inches were cut under any of the alternatives outside the study plots. This constraint was placed on all proposed treatments because of the assumption that postsettlement pines larger than 16 inches will become old-growth trees relatively soon and the concern that removal of some larger trees at Fort Valley may be extrapolated to other places in the Southwest where such trees are scarce.

The three restoration approaches were implemented on more than 4,000 acres by autumn of 2002. When the alternative treatments are viewed side-by-side at Fort Valley, differences are apparent if not striking. Stands treated under the ERI approach (historical reconstruction) appear fairly open and dominated by old growth, with virtually no remaining trees less than 12 inches in diameter. Although old-growth trees also stand out in areas treated under the Forest Service alternative (selection system), perhaps the most notable feature is the broad range of tree sizes. Stands treated under the Southwest Forest Alliance approach (thinning-from-below) exhibit greater density despite the relatively few small trees remaining. Following cutting, all harvested areas will either be broadcast burned or pile burned to reduce the hazard associated with logging slash. Ecological effects of burning, such as recycling nutrients and stimulating response of certain undergrowth plants, are other important objectives of broadcast burning.

When asked how the effectiveness of the restoration alternatives is being evaluated, Pete Fulé identified three criteria—two ecological and one social. The first is whether the grasses, forbs, and shrubs in the undergrowth are returning to historical levels in terms of cover and composition. For example, success would likely be indicated by a dramatic increase in native species, such as Arizona fescue (*Festuca arizonica*). Second, are old-growth trees surviving well? Success would be indicated by low mortality rates in old-growth trees and gradual recovery from symptoms of stress such as sparse crowns, yellow-green needles, and dying branch tips. Lastly, is the treatment gaining broad public acceptance? This question will be answered affirmatively if the GFFP gets community approval for similar treatments in the Kachina Village area southwest of Flagstaff, the proposed second phase of this long-term restoration project.

Initial response to the three restoration treatments at Fort Valley has been generally positive. Nearly all involved agree that this project is better than the alternative of doing nothing about deteriorating forest conditions and threatening fuels.

The Southwest has been a focal point for research aimed at understanding historic ponderosa pine forests (Cooper 1960, Pearson 1933, White 1985) and for restoring them (Allen and others 2002, Covington 1995, Fiedler and Cully 1995, Friederici 2003a, Fulé and others 2001b, Lynch, Romme, and Floyd 2000). Recent research has focused on responses of trees, undergrowth plants, soils, vertebrates, and endangered animals and plants to restoration treatments. This growing knowledge base provides a firm foundation for the much-expanded practice of restoration that is needed. The GFFP provides a specific example for others as they consider the social challenges and ecological benefits of practicing restoration in places where humans and forests meet.

Chapter 8

Ponderosa Pine/Fir—Forest Management on Public Lands

M anagers of public lands that have not attracted special attention (such as for research) sometimes proceed on their own into
restoration forestry. Breaking new ground in management becomes
compelling in ponderosa pine forests where elimination of understory
fires has triggered a conversion to firs, with profound ecological effects.
However, many challenges await those who seek to innovate, even if
for recognized ecological benefits. We describe forest districts in southwestern British Columbia, Oregon, and southern Idaho where foresters
have forged ahead to re-create key features of the understory fire
regime on a broader scale.

British Columbia Coast Range

British Columbia's Coast Range is a place where misty fjord-like in-
lets are lined with rain forests and rocky cliffs, with glacier-draped
mountains looming high overhead. This seems a most unlikely place
to find fire-maintained groves of ponderosa pine. Nevertheless, about
100 miles (160 km) north of the city of Vancouver and just a few miles
inland from ice-covered peaks lies a dry, rain-shadow zone where
open-grown ponderosa pine and inland Douglas-fir inhabit the mountain canyons. Prior to 1900, venerable trees with broad, spreading
canopies stood sprinkled among bunchgrass communities on sunny
south- and west-facing slopes. By the mid-20th century, much of this
old-growth forest had been selectively logged. Whether logged or not,
however, by the 1990s these semiarid sites were densely packed with
small slow-growing Douglas-fir. The original undergrowth of grass and

forbs (flowering herbs) was replaced by litter, duff, moss, and only a few scattered shade-tolerant plants. After studying this deteriorating forest, ecologist Robert Gray and provincial forester Jim Gilliam took action to return more desirable conditions patterned after the historic structure and fire regime.

The rain-shadow forests on the leeward side of the Coast Range cover slopes perched above deep glacial valleys extending north and east from the town of Pemberton. Annual rainfall is only 20–25 inches (50–62 cm), and summers are hot and dry, with an average July temperature of nearly 75°F (23.7°C)—warmer than Spokane, Washington, and Flagstaff, Arizona. Soils on these sunny exposures become parched and drought-stricken between May and September.

Dry lightning storms are infrequent in the Coast Range, so the potential for lightning fires is relatively low. However, this area is the historic homeland of a large population of Lillooet First Nations, an Interior Salish tribe that employed fire extensively to promote plants used for food, fiber, and animal forage. For instance, the Lillooets burned to propagate huckleberry (*Vaccinium membranaceum*), wild raspberry (*Rubus idaeus*), glacier lily (*Erythronium grandiflorum*), wild onion (*Allium cernuum*), spring beauty (*Claytonia lanceolata*), buffaloberry (*Shepherdia canadensis*), and serviceberry (*Amelanchier alnifolia*), as well as to enhance forage for mule deer (Turner 1999, Turner and others 1990).

Robert Gray studied the fire history of the dry Coast Range forests and found scars from as many as 18 different fires on a single tree. Fire scar sequences show that at least as early as the 16th century, low intensity fires swept these stands at intervals averaging between 5 and 10 years (Gray 2001, Gray and Blackwell in press, a). Gray also found that the cessation of frequent burning in the early 20th century led to an astonishing change in forest structure. Without continuing fires, the open stands and savannas of old-growth ponderosa pine and Douglas-fir numbering between 5 and 40 trees per acre (12 and 100 per ha) filled in with thickets of small conifers, often numbering 500 per acre (1,200 per ha). Stands that were selectively logged in the 1940s are now so crowded with stems and lower branches of young Douglas-fir that it is difficult to walk through them.

Open-grown conditions in historical stands prevented crown fires from developing, but abundant ladder and canopy fuels now allow wildfires to "crown out" and kill trees over large areas (Gray 2001). The sparse fuels in historic pine stands also allowed interspersed patches of moist-site forest to survive fires because flames were not intense. The moist areas, characterized by western redcedar and paper birch, supported many shrub and herbaceous species valuable to wildlife. Surviving moist-site patches added habitat diversity on the landscape, while today's wild-fires are likely to kill the trees in both dry and moist habitats.

Foresters recognize that the drastic departure from historical conditions portends additional problems such as increasingly stressed trees, reduced wildlife forage, and loss of large trees as habitat. Pathological studies and Gray's observations suggest that open-grown trees in historic stands were resistant to root disease epidemics that can now spread readily through the interlocking root systems of today's crowded stands (Byler, Marsden, and Hagle 1990, Filip 1994, Monnig and Byler 1992).

In 1997 the Squamish District of the British Columbia Forest Service initiated restoration in the dry forests north of Pemberton. Their objective was to develop operational methods for reducing the threat of wildfire and restoring forest and undergrowth structure similar to historic conditions. About 1,100 acres (450 ha) were treated between 1999 and spring 2003, mostly with thinning or shelterwood cutting treatments followed by prescribed burning. Restoration treatments would rejuvenate wildlife habitat and food plants used by Lillooet First Nations and maintain visual quality and other resources and values. Treatment goals included retaining the scattered old ponderosa pine and Douglas-fir trees and reducing competition by thinning the young trees surrounding them. Other goals included creating a mosaic of different stand densities, returning tree composition closer to the historical range of conditions, and retaining snags and some large-diameter down wood (coarse woody debris).

The Squamish District also established a Terrestrial Ecosystem Restoration Program to design and test treatments for common dry forest types, including old growth with understory conifers, crowded 60-year-old Douglas-fir, and dense postwildfire saplings (Gray and Blackwell in press, b). Treatments include prescribed burning only; thin and burn; thin, mulch, and burn; and thin, remove, and burn. Tree basal areas averaged about 190 and 162 square feet per acre (44 and 37 square m per ha), respectively, in the old-growth and 60-year-old stands, and thinning reduced these to about 100 square feet per acre (23 square m per ha). Gray and his colleagues are monitoring growth response and tree mortality (Gray and Blackwell in press, a). Treatments are aimed at reducing stress in old-growth ponderosa pine stands linked to fatal attacks by western pine beetles (*Dendroctonus brevicomus*). Measurements of undergrowth response to treatments show major increases in production and nutrition of shrub forage and in the quantity and diversity of undergrowth species.

Researchers are also assessing how treatments affect surface and ladder fuels (Gray and Blackwell in press, b). Untreated stands may have up to 45 tons per acre (10 kg per square meter) of duff, litter, and branch wood, several times the historic levels. Despite these heavy accumulations, fire treatments carefully applied in early spring or fall reduced surface fuels much closer to their historic range. Gray has also raked surface fuels away from old ponderosa pine and Douglas-fir trees and wrapped the bases of snags and old fire-scarred trees with the fire-resistant fabric used for firefighter shelters (Gray and Blackwell in press, a). He found these techniques helpful, but very expensive—$21 Canadian per tree.

District forester Gilliam pointed out before the Kelowna wildfires occurred that decades of fire suppression had inadvertently transformed the interior dry forests' structure into highly flammable conditions (McGinnis 2002). His assessment was tragically borne out during the summer of 2003 when catastrophic fires swept 660,000 acres (266,000 ha) of British Columbia, mostly in the dry southern interior's Douglas-fir and ponderosa pine forests. Flames destroyed 334 homes and a $70 million sawmill, while 50,000 people evacuated their homes as fire threatened suburbs of Kelowna and nearby communities. The government commissioned an independent, postfire review to recommend remedial actions for reducing risk to life and property. A prescient editorial in the *Vancouver Sun* (2002) recognized the Squamish District's restoration efforts and argued for expanding them: ". . . government must tackle the problem with a significant program. . . . The alternative is to wait until public policy is driven by a crisis. If we do that, we'll have a fierce debate characterized by opportunism and overreaction—like the one currently raging in the United States—after our forests have burned."

Oregon's Eastern Cascades

A worst-case scenario for disintegrating, fire-dependent forests is taking place on the east slope of the Cascade Range in central Oregon.

Here, prior to 1900, frequent low- to moderate-intensity fires created relatively open mixed-conifer forests. These were dominated by large old fire-resistant trees—shade-intolerant ponderosa pine and sometimes sugar pine, western white pine, or western larch, along with coastal Douglas-fir, which is intermediate in shade tolerance. Frequent fires held the competing, shade-tolerant "white fir" [actually a natural hybrid of white and grand firs (*Abies concolor* × *A. grandis*)]—and sometimes other true firs or hemlocks—in check. Early selective logging removed many of the big trees, and fire exclusion allowed white fir to proliferate. This new fir-dominated community was more vulnerable to drought stress, root disease, insect attacks, and fire than the original forest (Fitzgerald 2002).

The altered, unstable forest was colonized by the northern spotted owl (*Strix occidentalis caurina*) because the dense, layered fir canopies provided security from predators that the original forest did not (Everett and others 1997). In the late 1980s and early 1990s, drought, a budworm epidemic, and a buildup of root disease and bark beetles killed most firs. Bark beetles also killed many large pines. Dead trees covered the mountainsides, fueling a series of costly, property-threatening wildfires, including the 91,000-acre B and B fires in 2003.

The Sisters Ranger District of the Deschutes National Forest covers 324,000 acres on the east slope of the Cascades northwest of Bend. About half of the district is a pure ("climax") ponderosa pine type on "high desert" sites, and nearly as much (46 percent) is in the more moist mixed-conifer forest. To help restore historical open-grown ponderosa pine cover type to some of today's mixed-conifer stands, the district staff has used combinations of sanitation/salvage cutting, low thinning, retention shelterwood, group selection, slash removal, piling and burning, and underburning. However, treatment implementation involves first navigating lengthy planning procedures (including public involvement) and a labyrinth of frequently changing rules and guidelines. Projects must survive repeated opportunities for administrative appeals and, finally, lawsuits brought by organizations that want the forest left alone.

Much of this conundrum is rooted in the Northwest Forest Plan's protective measures aimed at benefiting animals that depend on old-growth forests (USDA-USDI 1994). The plan established extensive late successional reserves (LSRs), where old-growth habitats are designated for protection and where it is difficult to conduct active management other than suppressing fires. When forest treatments are proposed within an LSR—and when the proposal is challenged in court—the overriding view is that in the presence of uncertainty, active management should be deferred (Thomas 2002). It is difficult to prove that management action will not have negative effects, whereas prohibiting all tree cutting and fire is given de facto approval without having to verify potential effects of no action.

Despite the forest calamity and the regulatory conundrum, staff of the Sisters Ranger District are attempting a significant restoration effort. The district staff developed, modeled, and demonstrated strategies and tactics designed to transform the deteriorating mixed-conifer forest in LSRs into sustainable spotted owl habitat (Maffei and Tandy 2002, Sisters Ranger District 2001). The best spotted owl habitat consists of large, long-lived shade-intolerant trees coupled with a dense, midlevel fir canopy. The district's broad strategy consists of "rotating" owl habitat on the landscape by surrounding habitat areas with stands at low risk to severe fires, insects, and disease. The low-risk stands can develop into owl habitat within a fairly short time frame; thus, existing habitat areas could be replaced before they deteriorate. This strategy is based on biological evidence that spotted owl habitat in the eastern Cascades is inherently unstable and vulnerable to disturbance and that shade-intolerant trees must initially have open growing conditions to attain large size.

Tactically, the area would be managed by mimicking the processes that created the large trees and heavy midlevel canopy, thereby creating nesting and roosting habitat for owls. The suitable habitat would be rotated in a shifting mosaic throughout the LSR. The understory fires that historically created open-grown, large-tree dominated forests would be simulated using a combination of thinning and prescribed burning at 20- to 30-year intervals. Once this forest developed, owl habitat could be created by allowing in-growth of firs. At any given time, the amount of suitable habitat and different stages of developing habitat would be appropriate for long-term sustainability. Suitable habitat and important features like large trees would rarely be at high risk to severe fires or epidemics.

In October 2001, the forest supervisor approved the district's Mc-Cache Vegetation Management Project, which includes restoration treatments covering 5,000 acres within a 15,000-acre LSR. In May 2004, after having prevailed in administrative appeals and a lawsuit, the district was able to begin implementing the project (*Oregonian* 2003). The McCache Project breaks new ground by incorporating both short- and long-term habitat considerations into proposed alternatives, including the "no action" alternative. The analysis demonstrates that managing to restore an historical forest structure is more beneficial to forest-dependent wildlife in the long run than attempting to preserve a damaged and unstable forest (Sisters Ranger District 2001). The budworm epidemic and wildfires have destroyed more than half of the district's suitable spotted owl habitat since the 1980s (Figure 8.1). Also, failing to implement forest restoration harms sensitive species such as the flammulated owl and white-headed woodpecker that require open forests.

The 5,000-acre portion of the LSR that will be treated in the Mc-Cache Project is currently unsuitable for spotted owl habitat but can be managed to provide sustainable habitat in the future (Sisters Ranger District 2001). The project reduces the risk of losing late-successional habitat by creating low-hazard stands in a pattern that facilitates wildfire control. It will also gradually restore healthy, late-successional habitat conditions in damaged older stands and treat young stands so they can develop late-successional attributes in the future. The treatments include mowing 700 acres of large, flammable shrubs—principally green-leaf manzanita (*Arctostaphylos patula*) and evergreen ceanothus (*Ceanothus velutinus*). Precommercial thinning, slash disposal, and underburning treatments are scheduled for conifer plantations on old clear-cuts to reduce wildfire hazard and promote large-tree development. The project also includes 1,500 acres of noncommercial thinning (trees less than 8 inches in diameter), 700 acres of commercial low thinning, and more than 4,000 acres of underburning and burning concentrations of slash.

The centerpiece and most controversial part of the McCache Project is 1,865 acres of "Ponderosa Pine Restoration." This prescription was developed for mixed-conifer stands suffering heavy insect and disease mortality. Treatments include disposing of dead trees to reduce hazardous fuels, removing white fir to release pine from competition, and creating openings for pine regeneration. The objective is to first restore the long-lived ponderosa pine component of the forest and then facilitate development of large pines that could be part of suitable owl habitat in the future. The goal is to grow big trees like those in historic stands. Silviculturist Brian Tandy explains that once these composi-

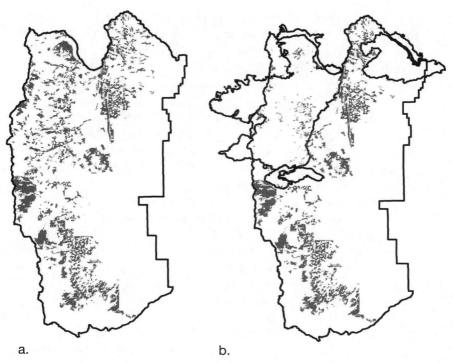

a.   b.

Figure 8.1.
Maps of northern spotted owl habitat on the Sisters Ranger District: (a) district outline with nesting-roosting-foraging habitat (shaded) in 2001; (b) remaining owl habitat after four large wildfires (enclosed in solid lines) in 2002 and 2003. (From U.S. Forest Service)

tional and structural goals are achieved, managers will have more options. For example, prescribed fire or even lightning fires might be used to maintain the LSR.

One stand type that will be treated in the Ponderosa Pine Restoration consists of widely scattered, old-growth pine towering above thickets of white fir—much of it dead. Except for occasional open patches, the stand has more than 200 living and dead stems per acre exceeding 5 inches in diameter. About 90 percent of these are white fir, and two-thirds of them are dead. The living white fir is infected with dwarf mistletoe (*Arceuthobium*), root diseases *Armillaria* and *Fomes annosus,* Indian paint fungus (*Echinodontium tinctorium*), and fir engraver beetle (*Scolytus ventralis*). Ponderosa pine and occasional coastal Douglas-fir, lodgepole pine, or larch are mostly still alive and substantially less affected by diseases, but number only 5–30 trees per acre. The need to maintain relatively heavy canopy cover because of LSR regulations constrains the restoration prescription. Desired basal area for the stand is 90–120 square feet per acre, but the preferred seral species (mostly large ponderosa pine) make up only 20–50 square feet. A marking guide specifies which trees will be retained, including all individuals of the desired species, and then only as much white fir as needed to reach a total of 30–40 square feet per acre. Additionally, the district has chosen to retain trees of all species that are 21 inches or more in diameter, which includes many white fir that are only 60–100 years old. Otherwise, the marking guide specifies removal of white fir adjacent to the desired species. White fir that are retained should be the healthiest and largest ones available. Most dead trees will be removed to reduce fire hazard. If sound, dead trees will be used for pulpwood; if decayed, they will be piled and burned. Four to thirteen standing dead trees per acre will be left to meet wildlife needs. The district has also chosen to leave all 20-inch and larger snags.

Live trees will be harvested down to 5–7 inches in diameter at breast height, depending on markets. The resulting open stands with insufficient natural regeneration of ponderosa pine will be planted. In areas with high levels of dwarf mistletoe infection in ponderosa pine, other seral species such as coastal Douglas-fir or larch will be planted. Restoration will be accomplished using timber sales, stewardship contracts, Forest Service crews, and partnerships with alternative labor forces such as from the Department of Corrections. Approximately 10 million board feet of sawtimber and a similar quantity of pulpwood will be harvested in the ponderosa pine restoration treatments.

The district's proposal to conduct large-scale active management in an LSR has attracted media attention, including an article in Oregon's largest newspaper entitled "Spotted owl complicates solutions to fires in forests" (Milstein 2000). Large wildfires in central Oregon have proven very costly for suppression, rehabilitation to prevent erosion, repair and replacement of damaged roads, facilities, and burned residences in the wildland interface (Fitzgerald 2002). In July 2002, the Cache Mountain fire roared through the canopy of untreated forests heading toward a wildland residential area north of Sisters. When the wall of flames hit thinned stands with the slash removed, it dropped to the ground and became a surface fire that firefighters could control.

This and similar incidents of wildfires that calmed down when they encountered treated stands have enhanced public support for treating broader areas of the national forest. By December 2003, the district had conducted about 6,500 acres of small tree thinning, 2,900 acres of shrub mowing, and 1,700 acres of underburning, often as multiple treatments on the same acreage. Much of the thinning and hand-piling have been accomplished by volunteer crews from Oregon detention facilities.

The district has cooperated with the Friends of the Metolius, a local conservation organization, to assuage public concerns about impacts of thinning and burning. Together, they have established a series of 11 demonstration plots lined up along a major road. Treatments include restoration of a historic stand structure, various types of thinning, and burning with and without shrub mowing. The Friends of the Metolius helped decide which treatments to demonstrate and helped develop educational signboards. Tandy believes this cooperative exercise has improved relations between district staff and citizens and enhanced public understanding of forest ecology and management alternatives.

It seems ironic that environmental regulations linked to the Endangered Species Act (ESA) hinder restoration of historical ecological processes (Thomas 2002). However, the ESA (1973) and many other environmental statutes were developed in an era when fire exclusion was widely accepted as critical for maintaining natural ecosystems. We now recognize this fallacy but do not have mechanisms for revising environmental policy to reflect the real needs of fire-dependent habitats. Jack Ward Thomas—wildlife biologist and former U.S. Forest Service chief who helped develop the Northwest Forest Plan (1994)— later reviewed the plan's effects on national forest management (Barnard 2003). He concluded that it had impeded necessary treatments in fire-prone forests. Tandy and his colleagues on the Sisters Ranger District hope their efforts in the McCache Project will break this impasse and serve as a beacon to guide management of LSRs.

The Blue Mountains

After months of plodding across inhospitable plains and desert and suffering shortages of drinking water, firewood, and forage for their livestock, pioneers on the Oregon Trail struggled up the steep, stony path climbing into the Blue Mountains. Here, bone-weary pilgrims discovered clear streams, green meadows, and open forests of huge ponderosa pine and other conifers (Evans 1990, Wickman 1992). Often they observed fires burning beneath the trees. One member of an 1853 wagon train, Rebecca Ketcham, wrote (Evans 1990, p. 238), "our road has been nearly the whole day through the woods, that is, if beautiful groves of [ponderosa] pine trees can be called woods. . . . The country all through is burnt over, so often there is not the least underbrush, but the grass grows thick and beautiful."

The Blue Mountains are a 100-mile-wide, 200-mile-long section of the Columbia Plateau stretching from central to northeastern Oregon and extending a short distance into Washington (Hunt 1967). This high, rolling plateau is incised by deep, semiarid canyons, and isolated mountain ranges project above it here and there. The gorges and dry plateaus support mostly grassland. However, with increasing soil moisture, grassland gives way to groves of ponderosa pine and then to mixed-conifer forest, which ascends the mountain slopes to about 6,000 feet in elevation. Prior to 1900, fires at intervals averaging between 10 and 35 years kept most of the mixed forest relatively open and dominated by large old ponderosa pine, western larch, and inland Douglas-fir trees. There were also patches of younger trees, including lodgepole pine, grand fir, and aspen, numerous openings, and a luxuriant growth of shrubs and herbs (Evans 1990, Hall 1976, Wickman 1992).

In the 1990s the Blue Mountains remained a beautiful, spacious rural landscape, but a closer look revealed forests in dramatic decline and very different from historic conditions. The mixed-conifer forest was packed with a thousand or more small Douglas-fir and grand fir per acre, with only sparse representation of herbs and shrubs. The Blue Mountains forest had become a poster child demonstrating the disastrous consequences of land use and management that defy natural processes (Langston 1996, Mutch and others 1993, Wickman 1992). Epidemics of spruce budworm and other insects and diseases along with wildfires killed large expanses of forest, creating a landscape often more gray than green. This massive mortality degraded wildlife habitat, stream quality, scenery, public safety, and timber values.

The "unraveling" of a fire-prone ecosystem was traced to heavy livestock grazing, logging of large trees, and exclusion of the frequent fires that promote shade-intolerant species and open stands (Mutch et al. 1993). When prolonged drought struck the region in the 1980s, the crowded forests became easy prey for insect and disease attacks. Like the old saying that everyone complains about bad weather but nobody does anything about it, people debated the problem of forest decline, but public skepticism that land managers could improve conditions precluded treatment. Recently, however, concern has translated into action to restore areas on the Wallowa-Whitman National Forest.

Much of the mixed-conifer forest on the Wallowa Valley Ranger District north of Enterprise, Oregon, consisted of large old ponderosa pine, Douglas-fir, and larch that were harvested in the early 1900s using a network of temporary railroads. By 2000, the postlogging forest had become dense mixed stands of 80-year-old, pole-size trees with an understory of younger grand fir. Between 1994 and 2002 the district commercially thinned about 20,000 acres of these second-growth forests. However, conventional timber sale contracts used for thinning were not designed to achieve restoration forestry objectives like removing nonmerchantable firs. Remaining firs rapidly fill in the space created by thinning, counteracting efforts to develop large-diameter trees. Thinning also creates enough space for grand fir and Douglas-fir to regenerate, but too little for shade-intolerant pine and larch seedlings.

In 2000 the Wallowa Valley District embarked on a new kind of project that permitted greater discretion to achieve restoration goals. The district won authority from Congress to proceed on a Stewardship Pilot Project designed to restore the large-tree attributes of the historical forests, increase the proportion of ponderosa pine and larch, lower forest density, reduce wildfire hazard, and provide wood fiber to benefit local economies. Stewardship authority was granted for the Buck Vegetation Management Project covering 880 acres of forest about 25 miles north of Enterprise. Stewardship authority allows all forestry and roadwork in an area to be handled under one contract. Activities that cost money and those that generate profit are under the same contract, and the Forest Service is able to select a bidder based on the best proposal for achieving desired results, such as protecting the soil while using equipment to remove trees. The district staff describe the soil and stand conditions they want to achieve, then select the proposal that most efficiently and effectively addresses those needs.

The Buck Vegetation Management Project was originally planned as a timber sale but was reworked to try out stewardship contracting as a means of returning more sustainable conditions to the mixed-conifer forest. The project used a service contract that included commercial and precommercial thinning of dense stands; reconstruction, maintenance, and closure of roads; and harvest of nearly 3 million board feet of small logs as well as 700,000 board feet of pulpwood. The selected contractor proficiently performed the cutting treatments, with minimal impact on the soil and remaining trees.

Stands in the Buck Project area consist of pole-size Douglas-fir and ponderosa pine along with smaller grand fir. Stands averaged 290 trees per acre of stems at least 5 inches in diameter. Basal area averaged 130 square feet per acre. Thinning from below reduced this to about 80 trees and 70 square feet of basal area per acre. Meanwhile, the removal of smaller trees increased the average tree diameter from 9 inches before thinning to 13 inches after. District silviculturist Paul Survis explained that low thinning will spur diameter growth in the remaining trees, allowing them to attain sizes not possible under existing conditions.

Excess or damaged trees up to a maximum size of 20 inches in diameter were harvested and sold as sawlogs or pulpwood. Logs as small as 4 inches in diameter and 8.5 feet long were also sent to sawmills, generating net income. Trees as small as 5 inches in diameter were harvested, with nonmerchantable stems and branches sold as pulpwood and hog fuel to partially offset the cost of removal. The district plans to underburn much of the treated area to reduce remaining fuels, kill some of the remaining small understory firs, recycle nutrients, and enhance habitat diversity.

Past harvesting compacted the soil, degrading site productivity by reducing soil porosity and air and water movement within the rooting zone. Compacted conditions in old skid trails take years to ameliorate as soils freeze and thaw, plant root systems expand, and burrowing animals and invertebrates work the soil. Based on research and monitoring of soil conditions, the district has established several measures for minimizing compaction from harvesting operations (Wallowa Valley Ranger District 2000). Stands on sensitive soils are only thinned when there is a substantial snow cover or if cut-to-length harvesters and log forwarders are used over a layer of slash.

Recognizing that the Buck Project is only a first step toward restoration, Survis and timber sale administrator Mike Piazza are considering options for follow-up treatments that can achieve longer term goals. They would like to remove the understory firs that remain after treatment. Prescribed fire can kill many of the small firs, but moderately intense burns have triggered bark beetle attacks in the overstory Douglas-fir, which have been overcrowded and weakened for years.

Ponderosa pine tolerates moderate scorch damage, but Douglas-fir is more abundant in modern stands. Felling the understory firs before or after prescribed burning may be the most effective way to remove this problem.

Ecological studies demonstrate that ponderosa pine and larch could not have dominated historical stands in association with grand fir unless periodic fires kept density low. The district has successfully planted and naturally regenerated ponderosa pine on moderately open burned sites, but few such sites exist. The district has created a few "group-selection openings" in the dense grand fir stands near Billy Meadows Guard Station. All of the scattered old ponderosa pine and larch were retained in these openings, plus a few large firs. Then openings were underburned to create a favorable seedbed for pine and larch. These regeneration treatments, added to thinning strategies like those in the Buck Project, provide the springboard to perhaps a century-long effort to reestablish the forests so admired by the Oregon Trail pioneers. However, forest preservation activists have fought the district's use of group-selection cuttings. Consequently, successful demonstration areas and educational outreach are key steps to gain support for expanded restoration efforts in the Blue Mountains.

Boise National Forest

The Boise National Forest was one of the first in the national forest system to recognize and articulate that something was wrong in the woods. As early as 1992, the forest supervisor released a pamphlet outlining the acute forest health problems on the Boise and a three-pronged approach for addressing them. An article titled "The Boise Quickstep" (McLean 1993) was published in *American Forests* magazine a year later, providing national exposure for these concerns. In 1998, three ecologists from the Boise presented a paper titled "We will not wait: Why prescribed fire must be implemented on the Boise National Forest" (Barbouletos, Morelan, and Carroll 1998). These examples bolster the Boise's reputation for seeing problems early on and doing something about them. But before we go further, let's turn the clock back to the Civil War era and learn about events that led to today's degraded forest conditions in southwestern Idaho and the actions being taken to address them.

It was the mid-1860s, and the earth around the territorial capital—Idaho City—was being turned upside down. Gold had been discovered in the Boise Basin in 1862, and in the next few years, Idaho City mushroomed into the largest city in the Northwest—larger even than Portland. Splendid old-growth ponderosa pine forests on the valley floor and surrounding hillsides were largely stripped away to allow placer mining of gold deposits—the value of which exceeded the Klondike gold strike. Heavy cutting continued, even as the mining boom itself waned. Logging provided the wood needed for settlement and development, including that of Boise, the bustling frontier town located 30 miles to the southwest. The young stands that established in the decades that followed comprise today's dense, 100- to 120-year-old ponderosa pine forests. Recent severe wildfires (1989, 1992, 1994, 2000, and 2003) have taken their toll, however (Figure 8.2). Approximately two-thirds of the Idaho City Ranger District's pine forests have burned in the last 20 years. Fortuitously, the community of Idaho City, with its many historic wooden buildings, has thus far been spared.

Personnel on the Idaho City Ranger District have documented locations of fire starts since 1956 and know that wildfires in the area typically move from southwest to northeast. One of the last contiguous chunks of unburned forest that remains on the Idaho City district—the Warm Springs Ridge area—lies southwest of the city, the direction from which the prevailing winds blow. Both lightning- and human-caused fires are more frequent here than on other parts of the district. Thunderstorms that enter the Boise Basin commonly move up two major drainages in the Warm Springs Ridge area, and isolated residences, rural subdivisions, and Highway 21 provide numerous human-related ignition sources. Although district personnel had been keenly aware of fire for years, it wasn't until they witnessed the proximity and explosiveness of the 1994 wildfires that they really "got religion." The next fire might take out the town.

With the motivation that impending wildfire can bring, the district began analyzing conditions and treatment possibilities for Warm Springs Ridge. This approximately 20,000-acre landscape consists of three general components—the Highway 21 corridor, the wildland-urban interface, and the surrounding wildland forest. Although current forest conditions vary widely among these components, the long-term management objective does not. The intent of management treatments is to create conditions that reduce the risk of high-intensity fire, allow

Figure 8.2.
Deforestation and erosion from severe wildfire in a historically ponderosa pine–dominated forest, Boise National Forest, Idaho. (Photo by Ravi Miro Fry for the Boise National Forest.)

reintroduction of low-intensity fire, and improve overall resiliency to natural disturbances.

Because forests in the highway corridor and interface are visible to one and all, any management activity—whether cutting or burning—is potentially controversial. Several other factors complicate matters. Much of the forested area occupies slopes too steep for ground-based tractor logging, requiring more expensive cable or helicopter systems. In addition, thousands of acres of plantations were established in the early 1960s to reclaim brushfields that took over after wildfires in the 1930s. These plantations are now densely stocked with limby, 6- to 12-inch-diameter trees. The smaller trees that would be removed in thinning are costly to handle and too small for commercial sawlog products. What, then, to do?

The urgency and apparent intractability of the Warm Springs Ridge situation only heightened the resolve of district personnel to get something done, despite the obstacles. They were gratified by the strong support for action they received from the local Resource Advisory Committee, a mix of county government officials, environmental groups, ranchers, loggers, and local residents. The committee backed activities aimed at fuel reduction, watershed restoration, and potential economic development.

The district's first attempt to reduce fuel loading on Warm Springs Ridge involved placing a proposed 700-acre treatment area (called the Casner Project) under a traditional timber sale contract—an attempt that failed. Failure was at least partially attributable to the closing of three sawmills in southwestern Idaho in 2001. Ray Eklund, district silviculturist, along with Kathy Ramirez, timber sale contracting officer, soon recognized that business as usual would not suffice. To make things happen, they would need to employ some creative approaches to contracting, financing, and implementing treatments on the ground.

Their second attempt at implementing the Casner Project involved a hybrid strategy. They crafted a service contract, with an embedded timber sale, as the administrative vehicle for accomplishing the first phase of vegetation treatment. This approach allowed them a means of transferring title to the material (stumpage) to be removed, in exchange for the contractor performing all of the required treatments (harvesting commercial-size trees, thinning small trees, and piling slash to reduce fuel loadings so that prescribed burning could occur later).

The next challenge came in financing the project, since there was no single source of money large enough to pay for the work they hoped to accomplish. Their solution was to combine funds from their district budget appropriated for timber management/stand improvement activities with funds from the National Fire Plan designated for fuel reduction. Treatments were completed in fall 2003—an impressive timetable of accomplishment for a project on federal lands.

Another even larger effort, the 3,000-acre Glide Project, was developed about the same time and approved for Pilot Stewardship Authority in 2001. Specifically, this new authority allows the Forest Service to enter into pilot projects to test more efficient and flexible ways of conducting management activities, including noncommercial treatments. The Glide contract was awarded in 2002, and the project is proving a valuable test area for trying nontraditional contract authorities. The project is 30 percent complete and on track for completion in 2005, considerably faster than the 8–10 years that would be needed under traditional authorities.

Different challenges are posed by the thousands of acres of pine plantations in the Warm Springs Ridge area, including the steepness of some proposed treatment areas, the relatively small size of most trees to be removed, and the high visibility of many areas considered for treatment. The district is employing a couple of novel approaches to get the job done. Hand-thinning with chain saws is being used to reduce existing plantation densities of 100–150 square feet per acre down to 50–75 square feet per acre by removing every other tree or every third tree in each row. In areas along the Highway 21 corridor, a helicopter was used to transport the submerchantable 6- to 10-inch-diameter thinned trees to landing areas outside the stand. Although helicopter yarding is expensive, it was potentially cheaper than alternatives, given the visually sensitive setting and the fact that it obviated the need to build roads. Because thinned trees are transported to the landing intact, limbs and tops are removed from the site, which eliminates the costly step of piling and burning them within the stand. In plantations located away from travel corridors and interface areas, small stationary machines called "mini-yarders" use a cable system to pull or "yard" thinned trees to existing roads or trails along ridges. The district has hired crews from the Southern Idaho Correctional Institution to do the thinning and yarding. This arrangement affords them a low-cost labor force while providing inmates productive work and the opportunity for rehabilitation. Trees yarded to the landing are either purchased by firewood contractors or removed by locals for personal use.

Barry Stern, forest silviculturist, notes that there is an ironic twist to the story behind the large number of 40- to 50-year-old plantations on the Boise. Most planting was done to reclaim brushfields that established after wildfires burned through slash left over from early-1900s logging. The brushfields weren't regenerating naturally, so they were either contour plowed or terraced with a dozer and then planted. Unfortunately, many of the 35,000 "reclaimed" acres on the forest were planted with trees of unknown origin. The Boise is currently evaluating the "pedigree" of these plantations to determine which come from locally adapted seed and which do not. Those of uncertain heritage pose a sort of ecological roulette in terms of sustainability. Maladapted trees are particularly vulnerable to extreme weather events, a weakness that may not manifest itself for years until such events occur. Furthermore, as these off-site trees mature they will likely interbreed with surrounding indigenous trees. At some point, restoration of these acres will have to go backward before it can go forward. True restoration can be accomplished only by removing the dubious trees, replacing them with seedlings from a locally adapted seed source, gradually developing a sustainable, disturbance-resistant structure, and then reintroducing appropriate fire.

The district is using a bit different approach to restore the extensive natural stands that came in after heavy mining- and settlement-related logging, such as in the Casner area. These pine-dominated forests, now more than 100 years old, have never been thinned by either fire or ax. Stand densities are typically in the 140–160 square feet per acre range, making them highly vulnerable to both crown fire and bark beetles. Low thinning and improvement cutting in the 700-acre Casner treatment area, for example, is reducing densities to the 70–80 square foot range. Although these densities are too high for regeneration and vigorous early development of shade-intolerant pine, that was not the objective of treatment. Densities are low enough to significantly reduce susceptibility to beetles, increase growth and vigor of the 12- to 30-inch-diameter leave trees, and provide favorable conditions for the follow-up broadcast burning that is an integral part of the overall treatment prescription. The highest priority stands for treatment are those paralleling roads, both to create low-hazard travel corridors and to accelerate development of the "old-growth" look.

Now several years into the Warm Springs Ridge project, Ray Eklund and Kathy Ramirez are proud of what the district has accomplished. Indeed, the Boise experience shows that creativity and tenacity can overcome most obstacles to restoration, even in the difficult operating environment of the national forest system. This yeoman's effort at restoration on the Boise was featured on the December 3, 2002 Morning Edition program of National Public Radio (NPR). NPR reporter Elizabeth Arnold noted that the Idaho Conservation League, a major environmental group that often opposes Forest Service projects, had nothing but praise for the work around Idaho City. The League attributes its support to the fact that the district solicited and responded to outside concerns from the outset, that harvesting was conducted off of existing roads or by helicopter, and that while some large trees were cut, even larger ones were left. Closer to home, when Ray Eklund is asked what he has learned from the Warm Springs Ridge experience, he responds that he now sees how much more there is to do—"We've only scratched the surface," he says.

Chapter 9

Ponderosa Pine/Fir—Privately Owned Conservation Reserves

The stereotypic western ranch consists of grass and sagebrush running to the horizon, a scene broken only by scattered mesas or coulees and herds of cattle. In reality, thousands of ranches from the plateaus and mountains of the Southwest to the inland valleys of British Columbia feature extensive areas of forest. Until recently, ranchers looked somewhat askance at their timbered property, seeing it as less productive for livestock grazing than adjacent grasslands. In the early 1990s prices paid for logging rights ("stumpage") jumped by 400–500 percent. To help make ends meet, financially strapped ranchers eagerly engaged contractors to log some of the commercial-size trees on their property. By the late 1990s, however, many ranches with forestland were being purchased by people who aspired to enjoy and protect the natural environment and the wildlife it supports, rather than to raise livestock for income. By this time, many long-time ranchers as well as new ranch owners had come to recognize that carefully crafted management, not just exploitation or protection, would be necessary to sustain and enhance their forestland.

We will examine three Montana ranches now being managed as private conservation reserves. Historically, understory and mixed fire regimes maintained large-tree-dominated forests on these ranches, interspersed with grassy openings, patches of aspen, and shrubs near streams. Logging most of the larger trees and excluding fire left forests overcrowded with saplings and pole-size trees that were weakened from competition and pathogens and vulnerable to wildfire. The ranch owners, old and new, recognized that these deteriorating conditions threatened their goals. In our first example—the E Bar L guest ranch—the long-time owner worried that the scenery and wildlife critical to his horseback-riding clientele were under siege to bark beetle attacks and wildfire threats. The other two ranches had traditionally depended on raising cattle to make a living, and secondarily on cutting timber. In the 1990s both ranches were acquired by new owners whose goals were stewardship, scenery, and wildlife habitat. The three ranches represent a gradient of increasing financial costs of restoration as terrain gets steeper and as timber productivity declines. Nevertheless, the owners are convinced that restoring more open forests with big, vigorous, disturbance-resistant trees is the right thing to do.

E Bar L Ranch

Bill Potter, patriarch of the E Bar L, gazes out across his ranch in Montana's Blackfoot Valley with a sense of relief, despite some lingering concerns. (The E Bar L guest ranch is embedded within the larger Potter Ranch, but because the combined entity is also commonly referred to as the E Bar L, we will use that name throughout.) Potter has worked 70 long years here and weathered all kinds of conditions, a period in which he has developed an uncommon bond with the land. The sprawling, 4,000-acre E Bar L—the oldest family-owned guest ranch in Montana—is what the "Ponderosa" ranch from the 1960s TV series *Bonanza* could only hope to be. The E Bar L is bounded on the north and west by nearly 3 miles of the Big Blackfoot River, now widely known from the movie *A River Runs Through It*. It features a rustic lodge flanked by homey log cabins, expansive meadows speckled with horses, miles of riding trails, buckskin-barked ponderosa pine savannas, and foothills blanketed with pine/Douglas-fir forests. At the far end of the ranch lies the "old-growth" section, which features stands of old-growth pine, Douglas-fir, and western larch. Not surprisingly, guests return year-after-year to unwind and ride in the glorious natural setting that is the E Bar L.

Despite the panoramic views and genuine Old-West feel, all was not well on the E Bar L leading up to 1998. Uncertainty as to the future of the ranch had gnawed at Potter and his wife Betty for years. They worried that heirs might subdivide their cherished ranch into 10-acre ranchettes, or, if it was left intact, that they would either liquidate the forests for quick cash or do no management at all—options that were equally offensive to the Potters.

They especially agonized over what would happen to the nearly 3,000 acres of forest that they had worked so hard to restore. Bill Potter's goal was a forest of the future much like that of the distant past, and he had worked to achieve that vision since the 1970s. He had been gradually moving the existing dense pine/fir forests with only scattered large trees toward a more open, uneven-aged forest dominated by large, old-growth pine. The restored conditions would be attractive to visitors, but even more importantly they would be resistant to bark beetles and wildfire. Potter has learned firsthand how thinning can reduce bark beetle damage, as evidenced by his pithy observation, "If you don't manage pine forests, the bugs will do it for you."

Circumstances appeared to be conspiring against him, however. Potter, born in 1917, had made only modest headway toward his goal, and time was not on his side. Given the sheer size of the ranch, he looked to stabilize stands by applying a light cutting that he calls a "3-D" treatment—removing dead, dying, and deformed trees. Much time was spent "chasing beetles" rather than making substantial headway toward his long-term goal. Stands were growing denser, and shade-tolerant firs were gradually encroaching under maturing pine. Despite his vigilance and best efforts, he was barely holding the line. It demoralized Potter to think what would happen when he could no longer do this work himself, and he saw his vision slipping away.

But help was on the way from neighbors Hank Goetz, director of the nearby University of Montana's (UM) Lubrecht Experimental Forest, and Land Lindbergh, son of pioneer aviator Charles Lindbergh and long-time Blackfoot Valley rancher. Both men have a strong land ethic, and both had gained Potter's trust over the years—every bit of which would be needed as they collectively pondered long-term options for the E Bar L. The upshot of countless conversations around Potter's kitchen table was that a conservation easement would likely be the best option for ensuring that the E Bar L would remain a working ranch with a thriving forest in perpetuity.

Conservation easements are a means for private landowners to conserve rural and wildland landscapes, while deriving tax benefits. Easements have become especially popular as a means of keeping western ranches intact and preventing their subdivision. In the West, however, these easements initially did not address long-term forest sustainability. To the extent forest ecosystems were addressed, the approach was hands-off, attempting to "freeze in time" what are inherently dynamic systems. This approach furthered the myth of the static forest that could be preserved if protected from fire and human manipulation. In 1998, The Nature Conservancy broke rank with the prevailing view and proposed ecosystem-based management of forested lands within the easement framework, under the premise that "conservation across entire landscapes—working landscapes—is the only way to protect enough habitat to sustain biodiversity" (Reid 1998). The prototypical easement that Potter, Goetz, and Lindbergh had envisioned for the E Bar L fit this newly articulated philosophy to a tee. Later in 1998, the E Bar L signed an agreement conveying a conservation easement to The Nature Conservancy based on these principles (Kappel 2002).

But this would not be just any easement. It would lay out the overall vision or purpose of the easement, define long-term forest management goals, and provide principles and guidelines to meet those goals. As Hank Goetz wryly noted, the wording related to treatment guidelines would have to be sufficiently detailed to serve as Potter's "long arm out of the grave," ensuring that his vision for the ranch would someday be realized. Yet the wording had to be flexible enough to allow for new knowledge, unforeseen changes in climate and markets, heretofore unknown insects or diseases, and new technologies.

The wording of the easement captures Potter's vision "to enhance, restore, and perpetuate the old-growth, uneven-aged forest communities and the processes needed to perpetuate them." It is under "Consistent Uses of Property" where the conservation easement for the E Bar L broke new ground: "To actively engage in selection cutting, prescribed burning, thinning, and other forest management activities for the purpose of developing or perpetuating old-growth, uneven-aged stands, controlling threat of insects and disease, reducing the hazard of wildfire, and providing a continuous and perpetual flow of commercial wood products from the property." Not only is forest management allowed under this easement, it is *required* (Figure 9.1).

Forestry terminology and silvicultural treatments are defined in the easement, and prescriptions are presented for each of the five types of stands (tree species/structure combinations) identified on the ranch: (1) even-aged ponderosa pine, (2) uneven-aged ponderosa pine, (3) old-growth ponderosa pine, (4) even-aged Douglas-fir/western larch, and (5) old-growth Douglas-fir/western larch. These generic prescriptions identify the silvicultural methods to be used for maintaining and regenerating each kind of stand, but leave details on harvest levels and

Figure 9.1.
Ponderosa pine stand managed using restoration forestry on the E Bar L Ranch. (C. Fiedler photo)

timing of treatments to be determined when the prescription for a specific stand is developed. The specific treatment prescriptions developed for individual stands or projects must be approved by the partners (The Nature Conservancy, the Potter family, and the UM School of Forestry) before any management activity can be initiated on the ground. Under the agreement, the Potter family will continue to own and manage the ranch in the future.

An integral part of the E Bar L agreement is that the partners meet each fall and plan management activities for the coming year. The agreement also specifies that The Nature Conservancy contract with the UM's Montana Forest and Conservation Experiment Station to oversee these activities.

Handing over the reins to the ranch, especially to a governmental entity, is not as unlikely as it might first seem. As a neighboring landowner to the Lubrecht Experimental Forest, Potter for years had made his land available to Forest personnel and UM faculty for a variety of research and demonstration projects. He derives great pleasure in pointing out exceptions to conventional forestry wisdom and watching visiting managers and researchers squirm while they search for explanations. Such insights, coupled with an innate curiosity about the natural world, make him a veritable scientist in a John Deere cap. Potter's great hope is that this partnership will help focus work on several knotty management problems that have tormented him for years. Foremost among these is at what stage of development sapling-size pine thickets should be thinned. Thin them too soon, and they become limby trees as they mature. Thin them too late, and they become vulnerable to bending and breakage from wet snows. Another concern is how to go about opening up previously unthinned pine stands consisting of 6–12 inch diameter trees. If they are thinned too lightly, they remain vulnerable to bark beetles. Conversely, if they are thinned more heavily based on silvicultural guidelines to promote individual tree growth, they suffer substantial breakage from heavy wet snow.

Another unique aspect of the E Bar L easement is the creation of a Forest Management Stewardship Fund. The fund, managed by The Nature Conservancy, is supported with gross proceeds from the sale of timber or timber products. The fund is used to rent or lease equipment to carry out management activities and to pay those doing the work. Revenues from products are also used to conduct nonrevenue-producing activities in stands where harvesting has occurred, such as precommercial thinning, slash treatment, or prescribed burning. The fund can also be used to maintain existing research and demonstration areas or support new projects.

Five years after the signing, the conservation easement on the E Bar L could be defined as a work in progress. To date, annual management activities have been of three kinds: low thinnings, which remove the smaller trees in even-aged pine stands; improvement cuttings, which remove Douglas-fir and poorly formed or low-vigor pine from even- and uneven-aged pine stands; and sanitation-salvage cuttings, which remove beetle-infested or killed trees or clumps from pine stands in general.

Two primary questions remain in weighing the potential for long-term restoration success on the E Bar L. The first question or concern is whether restoration cutting treatments will proceed quickly enough and aggressively enough to preempt growing hazards from bark beetles and wildfire. Density reductions are needed over large areas of the ranch to defuse this impending threat. Light thinning or improvement cutting in scattered stands will not suffice.

The second question is what role prescribed fire will play in the restoration effort at the E Bar L. Currently, the only use of fire is to incinerate thinning slash in permanently dedicated "burn pits." Although prescribed burning to achieve ecological goals is allowed under the easement, Bill Potter's concerns reflect those of many private landowners. Their discomfort with the use of fire is palpable—the risk of loss if something goes wrong outweighs the perceived benefits of burning when things go right. Purists may argue that restoration prescriptions that do not include fire are missing a key component and therefore are not worth doing. Restoration pragmatists see this glass as half full, where many objectives still get accomplished. Stand density is reduced, which promotes large-tree development and induces regeneration of sun-loving seral species. Wildfire hazard—particularly that of crown fires—is substantially reduced, as is vulnerability to bark beetle attack. From the pragmatist's viewpoint, half a loaf is better than no loaf at all.

The conservation easement developed for the E Bar L provides one example of how this instrument can be used to further forest restoration on private lands and guarantee that forest stewardship goals receive priority in the future. The E Bar L example also demonstrates the flexibility now available in adapting conservation easements to a variety of situations and needs, including active restoration. It may also inspire other private landowners to look into that considerable opportunity for themselves.

Burnt Fork Ranch

The Burnt Fork Ranch covers about 6,000 acres of the narrow valley defined by Burnt Fork Creek east of Stevensville, Montana, extending upward to the 6,000-foot level on the surrounding ridges of the Sapphire Range. The ranch has a 3,000-acre conservation easement from the Rocky Mountain Elk Foundation, and another similar easement is pending (Stalling 2003). The easement precludes subdivision and development but allows forestry and other management activities that are compatible with goals to protect, restore, and sustain wildlife habitat. The property features luxuriant streamside habitat, irrigated hay meadows, mountain grasslands, and about 2,000 acres of ponderosa pine and Douglas-fir forest extending down the ridges. More than 150 elk and mule deer winter here, utilizing critical habitat that is increasingly being converted to rural subdivisions.

The shared goal of ranch owners Randy and Kay Creech and the ranch's manager Bill Bradt is to restore the native vegetation using natural ecological processes as a guide. A retired forester, Bradt's goal for the forest is to eventually return the historical dominance of large, well-spaced ponderosa pine by greatly reducing excessive numbers of small Douglas-fir. Thinning and prescribed fire are used to reduce fir and rejuvenate the herbaceous plants, shrubs, and patches of aspen favored by elk. However, most fir thickets on north-facing slopes are retained for wildlife cover.

Achieving the first stage of Bradt's vision required removing about 75 percent of the 400-plus trees per acre greater than 4 inches in diameter, few of which were merchantable. This ambitious operation involved thinning from below, cutting damaged and mistletoe-infected trees, and removing limbs and tops. The largest, most vigorous trees were retained, with little scarring or other damage from the harvesting operation. Cutting about 75 percent of the mostly smaller trees reduced tree biomass about half. On the average, about 13 tons of small sawlogs were harvested per acre and 24 tons of nonmerchantable stems and branches were chipped at landings in the woods.

An impressive 800 acres of this intensive thinning was accomplished in the first year and a half. Over the entire area, the sawlog revenue offset much of the cost of harvesting and processing small trees and slash into hog fuel and then transporting it. These activities averaged about $500 per acre. Improving the road access needed for this kind of harvesting further increased costs, but Bradt regards the road network as part of the ranch infrastructure useful for continuing management of forests and grasslands.

Forester Chuck Seeley from Smurfit-Stone Container Corporation, the local pulp mill that uses hog-fuel chips to generate electric power, took the lead in selecting stands for thinning. Craig Thomas, a forester working for Johnson Brothers Contracting, arranged and directed operations on the ground. After making an inventory and assessment of the needs and costs of treating different stands, the contractors, Bradt, and the landowners agreed to treat the dense stands that had relatively good road access. Then, Thomas faced the challenge of locating landings large enough to pile trees and also accommodate a mechanical chipper and the 55-foot-long semitrailer vans used for hauling chips. Semitrailers are seldom used on mountainous logging roads because unlike logging trucks, they have low ground clearance, require broad radial clearance for turning, and are easily damaged. Nevertheless, Thomas and Bradt were able to upgrade the ranch's road system to allow the low-slung semitrailers to reach strategically located landings. To limit road construction, trees were skidded uphill or longer than normal distances to the landings.

The trees were harvested by track-mounted feller-bunchers, and bunches of trees were pulled to the landings using a grapple skidder. Thomas and Bradt trained the operators to recognize which trees to harvest and which to leave and worked with them to develop efficient methods of harvesting, skidding, sorting, delimbing, and grinding trees—some less than 10 feet tall. The small trees and piles of limbs and tops from commercial-size trees were fed into a large chipper using a grapple loader. The chips were hauled about 50 miles to the pulp mill.

Higher tree densities were left on exposed ridge tops to prevent wind and snow damage. After 5–10 years, when tree root systems and stems have grown sturdy, Thomas and Bradt expect to be able to conduct a second thinning on these sites. Uphill skidding caused soil rutting in some places; consequently, Bradt and the contractors are studying other options such as cut-to-length harvesters and log forwarders for future operations. These would allow low-impact harvesting from the existing, sparse network of low-standard roads.

In May 2003, a local contractor, Firewise Forest Landscaping, underburned 110 acres of the thinned stands for about $80 per acre. This was a "remedial" burn intended to help restore a forest structure that would be conducive to maintenance burning in the future. In places, troublesome ladder fuels remained in the thinned stands. Many trees also retained branches near the ground due to fire's long absence, and patches of old, highly flammable sagebrush were intermixed with the trees. Therefore, the burning crew carefully ignited forest fuels in a pattern designed to reduce torching of trees and occasionally sprayed water from a tanker truck to prevent it.

Complete removal of thinned trees had left too little fuel to support continuous burning across the forest floor. To facilitate returning fire for ecological purposes, future thinning could leave branches and treetops scattered across the ground, allowing more uniform coverage by a spring or fall burn. Despite the underburn's low intensity, patchy bark beetle mortality occurred afterward, suggesting that future burning be delayed a full year or two after thinning to allow trees to gain vigor from newly available soil moisture and nutrients.

During August 2003, large wildfires were burning in the Sapphire Range just a few miles north and south of the ranch when lightning ignited a fire near the ranch boundary. At first the blaze torched trees and grew rapidly in untreated forest, but soon encountered the thinned and prescribed burned stands. Suddenly the flames died down, becoming an easily suppressed surface fire.

Thomas and Bradt regularly host tours of this restoration project in hopes of expanding the application of similar treatments to other private and public forestland. Some environmental advocates agree with this kind of management when they see it on the ground. Thomas observes that significant areas of the Lolo and Bitterroot national forests are already accessed and close to hog-fuel or wood-pellet mills. He argues these areas could be treated at a profit, because the large volume of excess timber needing removal would offset costs of chipping and hauling biomass. In forests near communities, such treatment could create a forested fuel break without prescribed burning, thereby freeing up some of the limited burning days each year for use at other areas needing prescribed fire.

Rocking K Ranch

The Rocking K Ranch extends across more than 5,000 acres of mountainous forest and grassland in the upper Rock Creek drainage west of Philipsburg, Montana. Elevations range from 5,200 feet in the narrow valley along Rock Creek to 6,200 feet on the nearby forested ridges. Located on the eastern slope of the Sapphire Mountain Range, the Rocking K is situated in the cold, dry climatic zone that encompasses the high country along both sides of the Continental Divide. The harsh climate clearly affects the forest. Ponderosa pine, so abundant on the west side of the Sapphire Range, including Burnt Fork Ranch, is sparse at best in the upper Rock Creek basin, likely because of the brief frost-free season. About half of the Rocking K is forested, while much of the remainder is dry grassland. Wet meadows dot the property, and cottonwood-willow communities line Rock Creek, a blue-ribbon trout stream.

In the 1990s when Max and Kay Watson purchased the ranch, short, limby Douglas-fir dominated the dense forests. Some north slopes and moist sites supported patches of lodgepole pine and a sprinkling of Engelmann spruce. Fir was encroaching into many old aspen groves. The dense fir forest had scant undergrowth, and lingering "skeletons" of sagebrush shrubs (which cannot compete with dense conifers) provided silent witness that these areas had once been open and grassy (Arno and Gruell 1986). The original open-grown firs—some 3–4 feet in diameter—were selectively logged two or three times during the 20th century, and fire scar sequences reveal that fire visited at about 30-year intervals prior to the early 1900s (Arno and Gruell 1983, 1986).

Subsistence ranching has always been difficult in this rugged, dry country, and it commonly leads to heavy use of both grass and timber. Max Watson, a successful businessman, didn't need to make income from this property. Instead, he relished the prospect of restoring the forest, aspen groves, grassland, and meadows. He believed that stewardship would be a source of satisfaction and a good investment, considering the high value placed on well cared for property in a scenic setting. Watson hired a conservation-minded ranch manager and an environmental consulting firm, Land and Water Consulting, to identify suitable restoration techniques. Warren Anders, the ranch manager, uses cattle as a tool for beneficial disturbance by carefully rotating grazing in both time and place (Savory and Butterfield 1999). The ranch hands also installed more efficient irrigation systems and restored water sources to help rejuvenate meadow areas. They planted willows and other depleted shrubs in streamside areas and improved fencing to meet management needs.

Restoring the forest was like entering terra incognita. The consultants were able to identify general concepts based upon historic fire-maintained forests and their associated grasslands and aspen groves (Arno and Gruell 1986, Gruell 1983, Gruell, Brown, and Bushey 1986). However, no one had carried out a comprehensive restoration program in similar forests. The consultants recommended a contractor, Woodland Restoration, Inc., who helped Watson and Anders define their forest stewardship goals, which were to reduce wildfire hazard while restoring biodiversity, tree vigor, and wildlife habitat. They also wanted to improve scenic values by creating more open conditions featuring large trees and aspen groves.

Consulting closely with Anders, Woodland Restoration began applying and adapting restoration treatments on the ground. Woodland Restoration soon discovered that a moderate-size, cut-to-length harvester on steel tracks with a self-leveling cab was necessary to efficiently thin the crowded fir stands. A skilled operator using this equipment could do the work without significantly damaging the remaining trees or the soil. They used an all-terrain, rubber-tired forwarder to pick up the logs and carry them—sometimes half a mile—to a site accessible to a self-loading log truck. The forwarder hauls about one-third of a log-truck load per trip. They operated this equipment mix on the moderately steep slopes (up to 45 percent inclination) that characterize much of the ranch's forest. The steepest terrain was thinned using a line machine (cable yarder), with special care taken to avoid damaging leave trees or creating obvious harvest strips.

The cut-to-length harvester and log forwarder allowed restoration to proceed without expanding the ranch's existing sparse network of narrow, single-lane roads or having to construct landings for limbing, sorting, and loading logs. This eliminated the costs and impacts of building more roads. The cut-to-length system also negotiated the ranch's rough topography with minimal impact on soils or damage to leave trees. Thinning and harvesting with cut-to-length equipment left limbs and small nonmerchantable trees dispersed on the ground as a fuel bed that could be burned in the spring, prior to the wildfire season. By May 2004, Woodland Restoration had conducted thinning (removing primarily smaller trees) and improvement cutting on nearly 500 acres of the Douglas-fir stands and had underburned much of that area. A more expensive alternative to burning slash *in situ* would be to transport it by forwarder to landings for chipping into hog fuel or burning in large piles.

Basal area before treatment typically ranges from 150 to 220 square feet per acre, and treatment lowers it to around 80 square feet. A thinning crew fells the smallest nonmerchantable trees and leaves them on the ground for burning. The harvesting machine operator then fells and processes trees more than about 5 inches in diameter, which are removed. The operator is highly trained to select and retain the largest, most vigorous trees in a well-spaced distribution, eliminating the need for tree marking. The basal area is typically reduced by removing 60–80 percent of the smaller trees, plus broken-topped or otherwise damaged larger trees.

Woodland Restoration co-owner Matt Arno estimates net costs of the thinning and burning treatments range between $300 and $800 per acre. This reflects cost offsets from selling small logs to a stud mill that specializes in processing 2 × 4- and 2 × 6-inch lumber from small trees. Trees too small for sawn products are used in whatever way they can to help remove excess fuels at moderate cost. Some are sold to a pulp mill, used or given away for firewood, or converted into jackleg fencing to protect aspen groves, springs, and other sensitive sites from grazing.

In 2003, Woodland Restoration invited a Forest Service entomologist to inspect the Douglas-fir bark beetle outbreak that was killing trees on adjacent, unthinned Deerlodge National Forest land. He advised that the best protection for adjoining ranch forests could be achieved by continuing to treat them with the methods already in use. In stands near the beetle attack, he suggested waiting 1 or 2 years before prescribed burning to allow leave trees to regain vigor before subjecting them to stress from scorch damage.

Two years after thinning and underburning, fewer than 5 percent of the retained trees have died. The luxuriant undergrowth in thinned areas provides a sharp contrast to the sparse plant cover beneath untreated stands. Livestock were kept out of treated areas, resulting in a profusion of native bunchgrasses, pinegrass (*Calamagrostis rubescens*), and forbs such as heart-leaf arnica (*Arnica cordifolia*). Shrubs such as snowberry (*Symphoricarpos albus*) are sprouting vigorously, and early successional species such as aspen sprouts, wild raspberry, and a showy native, *Phacelia*, are abundant. Treatment has clearly reinvigorated the native vegetation and wildlife forage long-suppressed in these fire-protected forests.

Ranch manager Anders points out that transects reveal a virtual explosion of forage following treatments. He and other ranch hands have seen a jump in the number of mule deer and wintering elk—about 140 of the latter during the winter of 2002–2003. Wildlife and livestock impacts on aspen sprouts and grasses have also diminished, which Anders attributes to much improved plant vigor resulting from thinning, prescribed burning, and carefully regulated grazing. Watson feels restoration work on the Rocking K makes sense and looks good; he has personally shown these treatments to two members of Congress. He sees it as a potent example of what could be done to economically and effectively restore fire-prone forests on public lands.

Chapter 10

Giant Sequoia/Mixed Conifer

In 1891 a young adventurer named Gifford Pinchot, who would later become the first chief of the U.S. Forest Service, was exploring forests in the western United States. He wended his way on horseback up the long western slope of the southern Sierra Nevada Range rising high above California's Central Valley. Ascending past the 5,000-foot level, Pinchot came upon the remains of the deep winter snowpack that helped nurture a magnificent forest of sugar pine, ponderosa pine, white fir, and other species. Many of the trees exceeded 5 feet in diameter and 200 feet in height. Then, he encountered the giant sequoia, a species that dwarfs all others. Despite its unmatched size, Pinchot was struck by the sequoia's beauty: "When the black marks of fire are sprinkled on the wonderfully deep richer [sic] ocher of the bark, the effect is brilliant beyond words" (Pinchot 1947, p. 44). Recent settlers tried to impress Pinchot with their stories of saving sequoias from wildfires, yet he wondered how these people thought the giant trees had survived fires during the previous 3,000 years of their lives.

Naturalists have long recognized that frequent fires were an intrinsic part of the giant sequoia's existence. Virtually all these "big trees" retain char from past fires on their massive trunks, insulated with fibrous bark that ranges up to a foot or two thick. Past fires also leave small scars in places among the sequoia's root buttresses near ground line where the bark is thin (Caprio, ecologist, Sequoia and Kings Canyon National Parks, pers. comm. 2003). Early caretakers of Sequoia National Park wanted to burn fuel accumulations around the big trees, and during the 1920s the park's superintendent provoked the Forest Service by advocating light burning to maintain the forest (Kilgore 1970, Pyne 1982). Finally in the 1960s, growing recognition of fire's ecological importance allowed the Sierra national parks to pioneer a program using prescribed burning and lightning fires to restore fire-prone forests.

In 1963 Secretary of Interior Stewart Udall endorsed the management recommendations of a prestigious advisory committee headed by A. Starker Leopold (Aldo Leopold's son) of the University of California. The committee's report advised that large western national parks be maintained "as nearly as possible in the condition that prevailed when the area was first visited by white man" (Leopold and others 1963, p. 32). The report pointed out that "much of the west slope [of the Sierra Nevada] is a dog-hair thicket of young pines, white fir, incense-cedar, and mature brush—a direct function of over-protection from natural ground fires" (Leopold and others 1963, p. 33). The Leopold committee emphasized that to achieve a semblance of the historical conditions, park managers must restore the fire process that helped create them.

The ink was hardly dry on the Leopold report before two studies focusing on the relationship of fire to giant sequoia were underway in Sequoia and Kings Canyon National Parks (SEKI), which lie adjacent to each other in the southern Sierra (Pyne 1982). One study revealed the ecological importance of fire to sequoia regeneration and the other found alarming quantities of fuel in sequoia groves (Biswell 1968, Hartesveldt and Harvey 1968). Both led to recommendations for prescribed burning. SEKI started experimental burning in its sequoia groves in 1965 and began a prescribed burning program for them in 1969. Soon, SEKI extended burning operations to include the much broader mixed-conifer forest surrounding the scattered sequoia groves. Fire managers also began to allow some lightning fires to burn as "prescribed natural fires" in the parks' high country. Within a few years the spectacular jewel of the Sierra Nevada, Yosemite National Park, instituted similar burning practices.

A 2,000-year record of fire etched on stumps of giant sequoias shows that these enormous trees were scarred by fire every 5–25 years (Swetnam 1993). Most fires burned along the ground surface with low flames, but occasionally a more intense blaze would torch into the crowns and kill patches of tall trees, especially the accompanying fir and incense-cedar. In 1297 A.D., after a 5-year drought, a fire in the Mountain Home Grove apparently killed most trees, including many sequoias (Caprio and others 1994). Surviving sequoias dramatically increased ring growth after competing trees died, and a multitude of sequoia saplings arose in the burn. Studies that determine age of trees within sequoia groves commonly identify clusters of sequoia regeneration encircling the charred remains of a monarch that died, burned hot, and created a gap in the stand (Caprio, pers. comm. 2003).

Sequoia benefits by being more fire-resistant than any of its competitors. Also, sequoia seedlings are highly shade-intolerant, requiring sunlit openings like those created by fire to regenerate. Fire is also needed to remove most of the duff layer and allow the tiny roots of sequoia seedlings to reach mineral soil before they die of desiccation. One or two years of ample growing season moisture is also important for survival of sequoia seedlings (Demetry 1998). In some places, ancient sequoias grow in a row, suggesting that they germinated where a single log had burned and created a mineral soil seedbed (Mastroguiseppe, Crater Lake Institute, pers. comm. 2003). Sequoia cones remain closed and attached to the trees for many years, but the heat of a fire can open large quantities of cones and allow seeds to drift down into the fertile and receptive ashy seedbed (Harvey, Shellhammer, and Stecker 1980).

The 75 natural sequoia groves sprinkled through the mixed-conifer forest on the western slope of the Sierra Nevada are concentrated in SEKI and the adjacent Sequoia National Forest (Stephenson 1996). The sequoia and mixed-conifer forest in the southern Sierra occupies a narrow elevational band between about 5,500 and 7,200 feet. This highly productive and diverse fire-prone forest occurs directly upslope from the foothill forest of ponderosa pine and oaks and shares a history of frequent low- to moderate-intensity fires. Were it not for the immensity of the sequoias, the size and longevity of their companions— sugar pine, ponderosa pine, Jeffrey pine, black oak (*Quercus kelloggii*), white fir, red fir (*Abies magnifica*), and incense-cedar (*Calocedrus decurrens*)—would be widely acclaimed. Where fire and fuel treatments have been kept out of these forests, white fir and incense-cedar develop into a dense understory, and needle litter and duff accumulate up to a foot in depth. Dead wood and understory trees (ladder fuels) build to unprecedented levels, fueling explosive wildfires.

Responding to recommendations of the Leopold report, SEKI's superintendent authorized a program for restoring natural conditions to the sequoia groves (Kilgore 1970). Cooperative studies of fire ecology and fuels in sequoia forests were soon followed by experimental cutting and burning treatments designed to reduce down woody fuels, duff, and understory trees. In 1969, managers began manipulating fuels and burning at larger scales in the extensive sequoia forest on Redwood Mountain (Parsons and van Wagtendonk 1996). Researchers monitored burning conditions, fuel consumption, effects of fire on different tree species, and postfire seedling establishment in burned areas. In 1972 SEKI and Yosemite National Park established a long-term prescribed burning program based on this growing body of knowledge and experience (Parsons and van Wagtendonk 1996). During the 1970s, this program of "restoration burning" focused on removing 70–100 percent of the dead and downed fuel and killing most of the understory trees (Bancroft and others 1985). Prescribed burns were conducted in 30- to 50-acre units, using 15- to 20-person crews. At first, many of the projects (especially those in Yosemite) involved cutting understory trees and burning them in piles before conducting understory burns throughout the stand.

With more experience, SEKI relied primarily on understory burning alone, because it was more economical and less heavy-handed (Figure 10.1). The initial restoration burn often killed more than half of the trees, mainly smaller ones, and consumed most of the dead fuel and duff (Keifer, Stephenson, and Manley 2000). Many fire-killed trees topple within a decade, reestablishing down woody fuel loads of 50–90 tons per acre, similar to those in pretreatment stands (Stephenson 1996). Thus, achieving restoration for an appreciable period requires a second burn to remove woody fuel created by the first.

During the 1980s a scientific debate simmered over goals of the Park Service burning program in the sequoia and mixed-conifer forest (Parsons and van Wagtendonk 1996). Should parks try to preserve forests that looked like those of the 19th century, when Europeans first arrived? Or should they preserve ecological processes—notably fire—under which the forests evolved? Should management select which trees to remove or allow fire to make that decision? One group argued that forest structure should be restored to its presettlement state before natural processes could operate again (Bonnicksen and Stone 1982). Others responded that these forests are adapted to variations in climate and fire regimes and will recover if fire is restored to an approximation of its natural role (Parsons and others 1986).

A panel of outside experts in fire ecology, fire management, and related disciplines studied the history, status, and scientific basis for the fire management program in the Sierra Nevada national parks (Christensen and others 1987, Parsons and van Wagtendonk 1996). It rec-

Figure 10.1.
Prescribed burn in a giant sequoia grove, Sequoia and Kings Canyon National
Parks (National Park Service photo)

ommended two types of prescribed burns: "restoration fires" designed
to reduce unprecedented fuel accumulations, and "simulated natural
fires" developed to mimic the historical fire regime. The panel proposed a general goal of restoring the natural fire process but recognized
that an initial restoration burn may be necessary before simulated natural fires can be permitted. In special areas like heavily visited sequoia
groves, special measures might be needed to protect scenic values—for
example, removing understory trees or raking accumulated duff away
from the trunk to reduce extensive bark charring. The panel's concern
about inadequate knowledge to support fire restoration led SEKI to
establish a formal procedure for measuring and evaluating the effects
of fires. This monitoring program was later adopted throughout the
national park system (Caprio, pers. comm. 2003).

The panel's recommendations helped park managers clarify objectives for the overall fire program and for individual burns (Parsons and
van Wagtendonk 1996). The program's goal became to restore fire at
intervals, intensities, and seasons and with ecological effects similar to
the historical fire regime. The emphasis is on restoring the dynamic

character of historical park ecosystems rather than focusing on an individual species or a structural stage of the forest (Parsons 1990).

Today, SEKI's target for initial restoration burns is to reduce total fuel load immediately after burning by 60–80 percent and density of trees less than 32 inches in diameter to 20–100 per acre by year five after burning (Opperman, Keifer, and Trader 2001). Target conditions are based on research and experience, and once they are met, the objective shifts from forest structure to simulating the range of historical fires using lightning ignitions or management fires. SEKI sets additional targets for numbers of large trees, and on a landscape level, for forest openings and surface fuels. It periodically refines target conditions based on new knowledge (Keifer, Stephenson, and Manley 2000).

By autumn 2002 SEKI had carried out more than 200 prescribed burns covering about 45,000 acres (mostly in the sequoia and mixed-conifer forest), and Yosemite had burned 47,000 acres (Caprio, pers. comm. 2003, Parsons and van Wagtendonk 1996, van Wagtendonk, research forester, U.S. Geological Survey, pers. comm. 2003). From 1990 through 2002 SEKI burned about 27 percent of the sequoia and mixed-conifer forest, averaging about 1,700 acres per year. About half of SEKI's 10,000 acres of sequoia groves was burned between 1968 and 2002, and an additional 8 percent of the area was burned two or three times.

Despite this exemplary performance in restoring fire in the sequoia and mixed-conifer forest, approximating the historic burning cycle would require doubling the rate of burning accomplished in recent years. This dramatic increase does not account for the initial restoration burns needed in about 40 percent of the forest. Accomplishing a higher rate of annual burning is constrained by funding, smoke production, and weather and fuel moisture conditions suitable for burning. Over many years the Sierra national parks have gradually expanded their burning programs, but because the need for fire reintroduction is so great, they have to prioritize potential burning projects. Priority is based on the number of fire cycles missed (due to suppression), fuel loading, ease of control, and proximity to hazardous fuels and structures (Caprio and Graber 2000, Parsons 1990, Stephenson 1999).

Beginning in 1996 SEKI fire managers adopted computerized geographic information systems for analyzing vegetation, fuels, topography, and other landscape features (Caprio and others 1997, Lyle 2003). They use these landscape data in modeling potential fire behavior and growth. Maps made by layering different kinds of data, including the number of missed fire cycles, help in planning burns for areas most in need of fire's beneficial effects. In 1999 SEKI and cooperating agencies adopted a landscape approach for identifying and prioritizing hazardous fuels projects in the parks and surrounding lands. This interagency effort identified 91,000 acres of hazardous fuels that will be treated over several years.

Most prescribed fires in the sequoia and mixed-conifer forest are lit in late summer or fall, when the thick litter layer is relatively dry. Initial restoration fires are commonly ignited in narrow parallel strips, beginning at the control line on the leeward edge of the burn unit. This "strip head-firing" approach efficiently and uniformly reduces surface fuel accumulations, making it most appropriate for reducing the unprecedented fuel buildup linked to fire exclusion. In heavily visited groves, firing techniques are used to prevent extensive charring of trunks high above the ground or scorching sequoia canopies 100 feet or higher overhead, potentially marring the big trees' beauty (Parsons and van Wagtendonk 1996).

Once treated fuels are returned to the range of historical conditions, spot ignitions could be used to promote variable burning akin to a lightning fire (Parsons 1994). However, because the duration of smoke production must be limited, even maintenance burns are ignited so that they can be completed promptly (Caprio, pers. comm. 2003). Research ecologist Nathan Stephenson (U.S. Geological Survey, pers. comm. 2003) describes the firing technique used on a maintenance burn in 2002, where the crew lit hundreds of spots instead of continuous strips of fire, underburning 132 acres in 3 days.

At some point most of SEKI's sequoia groves may be placed in a status that customarily permits lightning fires to burn. Wherever natural fires cannot be permitted to burn, management-ignited fires will be used instead (Parsons and van Wagtendonk 1996). In 1986, a lightning ignition in the Muir Grove of giant sequoias was allowed to burn, eventually growing to 150 acres. In 1991 another of these "prescribed natural fires" burned 720 acres in the East Fork Grove (Caprio, pers. comm. 2003). Both fires exhibited behavior and effects apparently similar to historic blazes.

SEKI has established protocols to better understand and predict the effects of prescribed fires. Fire effects crews set up study plots before burning and remeasure them 1, 2, 3, and 10 years after burning to monitor fuel reduction and reaccumulation, tree mortality, regeneration, and response of herbs and shrubs (Lyle 2003). Additionally, the parks encourage studies by outside scientists concerning the effects of fires on different components of the ecosystem. Monitoring and special studies record basic information on all fires, determine whether fire management objectives are achieved, and help identify where additional fire effects research is needed (Opperman, Keifer, and Trader 2001).

Prescribed burning produces an immediate, dramatic reduction in duff, down woody fuels, and ladder fuels in the sequoia and mixed-conifer forest. It often creates small- to medium-size openings that allow giant sequoia seedlings to establish and grow rapidly (Demetry 1998, Stephenson 1996). This contrasts with the shady conditions in the unburned forest, where sequoia rarely regenerates. Shrubs such as *Ceanothus* spp. and herbs also become abundant after burning. A showy lupine (*Lupinus latifolius*) often flowers profusely after burning as a result of seeds buried in the soil (Caprio, pers. comm. 2003, Harvey, Shellhammer, and Stecker 1980, Mastrogiuseppe, pers. comm. 2003).

In 1987 a wildfire demonstrated the likely consequence of both fire exclusion and prescribed burning. Starting in a dense forest below the SEKI boundary that had not burned for nearly a century, the Pierce fire soon blew up into an inferno, lethally scorching the crowns of about two dozen "monarch" sequoias (Nichols 1989, Stephenson, pers. comm. 2003). As it roared into the upper portion of the Redwood Mountain Grove, it reached an area burned a few years earlier by park managers. Here, deprived of ladder and surface fuels, the fire dropped to the ground and was contained. In one of the burned areas on Redwood Mountain, sequoia regenerated so profusely that it is now difficult to walk through the developing thickets (Mastroguiseppe, pers. comm. 2003). Sapling thickets are thinned as additional prescribed fires are applied, and ecologists are monitoring the proportion of young trees that survive (Caprio, pers. comm. 2003). Because of sequoia's extended life span, very few individual saplings are needed to replace dying overstory trees.

SEKI informs park visitors and neighbors about the natural role of fire, prescribed burning, and other fire management activities. Prescribed fires are often conducted near park roads and trails, and visitors are informed via signs when approaching active burning projects, at park entrance stations, or through media announcements. Visitors can watch prescribed fire from a safe distance, often accompanied by a park naturalist or other interpreter to explain what is happening and answer questions. Park Service-guided nature walks lead into recently burned areas. Each spring SEKI mails a community newsletter to more than 2,000 park neighbors presenting news about the approaching fire season, scheduled prescribed burns, and where to obtain more information, including the fire information office and its Web site (www. nps.gov/seki/firesit) (Lyle 2002). SEKI also maintains an Internet Web page called the "fire information cache" (www.nps.gov/seki/fire/ indxfire.htm) that tells about the fire program and includes a large bibliography. Educational brochures describe fire ecology and fire management issues and activities. Visitors even receive complementary postcards with photographs and explanations of prescribed fires in SEKI.

In recent years SEKI has coordinated projects with the California Department of Forestry, other fire agencies, and local fire departments to reduce fuels near communities that border the parks. In some cases the parks have hired local contractors to thin, pile, and burn excess understory trees and woody debris on park land adjacent to developed areas (Lyle 2003). SEKI demonstrated removal of ladder fuel on a 2-acre plot for Wilsonia, a community surrounded by park lands, so residents could learn how to reduce fuels on their own lots. During 2002 SEKI mechanically reduced fuel on 110 acres near developments and park facilities (Caprio, pers. comm. 2003).

Despite the remarkable success of the fire restoration program in SEKI and Yosemite national parks, park managers and cooperating scientists are not complacent. Rather, they know that to mitigate the effects of a century of fire suppression, they must increase the amount of burning done each year (Parsons 1994). SEKI fire ecologist Tony Caprio (pers. comm. 2003) observed that "we may be able to reestablish pre-Euro-American burn patterns in many of our backcountry areas. . . . However, our largest contiguous area of forest is on the west slope where the constraints on burning are the most limiting." As Stephenson (pers. comm. 2003) put it, "Too many things conspire to prevent enough area from being burned to reinstate pre-Euro-American frequencies across large pieces of the landscape—most notably air quality concerns, staffing, and weather. Air quality may be the biggest limiting factor of all, and that is not likely to change any time soon."

Stephenson (pers. comm. 2003) explained that if SEKI is unable to reinstate historic fire regimes over the entire landscape, the staff may concentrate on achieving this goal in designated areas. SEKI could then use these "core areas" as benchmarks to gauge the ecological consequences of burning at longer intervals over the rest of the landscape. Caprio (pers. comm. 2003) described a core area of more than 2,000 acres that SEKI managers have established informally in the vicinity of the Atwell Grove in the East Fork Kaweah drainage. The area was originally treated with prescribed fire in 1995 and was reburned in summer 2003, with additional area added outside the 1995 burn. The unit extends from chaparral at lower elevations through the sequoia and mixed-conifer zone into the red fir forest. "Because these vegetation types had quite varying fire frequencies in the past, the second fire was applied across most of the unit but was not forced to burn throughout the whole area. This resulted in a continuous burn across most lower elevation areas but only scattered fire at higher elevations" (Caprio, pers. comm. 2003).

SEKI will need to overcome obstacles related to smoke production and burning restrictions before ratcheting up their burning program. Progress in burning also hinges on increased public understanding and acceptance of fire restoration. Finally, park managers need better knowledge of ecological effects of burning at different intensities and seasons. SEKI is developing this information by hosting one of the "Fire/Fire Surrogate Studies" sponsored by the Joint Fire Science Program of the U.S. Departments of Agriculture and Interior. Knowledge gained will help managers move from burning that removes a century of proliferating fuel to fires that re-create the variability of the historical fire regime. After all, such fires gave rise to the sequoia and mixed-conifer forests that John Muir (1894, p. 112) called "the grandest and most beautiful in the world."

Chapter 11

Western Larch/Fir

Western larch is the stately deciduous conifer that adds color and contrast to the moist inland forests of the northwestern United States and southern British Columbia. Gifford Pinchot (1947), founder of the U.S. Forest Service, singled out western larch as his favorite among all American trees. During spring and summer larch bears soft, lime-green needlelike leaves. By October the foliage turns a brilliant yellow-gold that shines in the autumn sun. Larch is the most shade-intolerant tree in the inland Northwest. To regenerate and compete successfully with its shade-tolerant associates—inland Douglas-fir, grand fir, white fir, subalpine fir, Engelmann spruce, western redcedar, and western hemlock—larch needs occasional fires or other major disturbances to prepare a suitable seedbed (Fiedler and Lloyd 1995). Larch and lodgepole pine (also shade-intolerant) regenerate readily and grow rapidly on burned sites (Fiedler 1990); thus, they often codominate new stands that spring up after mixed-severity or stand replacement fires. Larch and lodgepole pine make an odd couple. Larch is a towering, long-lived tree, while lodgepole pine is small and short-lived.

In the wettest inland areas, like parts of northern Idaho, larch remained abundant because of stand replacement fires at intervals of 100–300 years (Arno and Fischer 1995). However, much of the historic larch forest owed its existence to fires of variable intensities occurring about 30–75 years apart. Larch's exceptionally thick bark (often 6 inches through at the tree's base), nonflammable deciduous foliage, and lofty open crown help it survive all but the hottest fires. Its evergreen associates are thinned out by the mixed-severity fires, lessening competitive stress and allowing larch to attain ages of 500–1,000 years. Venerable larch trees and snags often have a rotten and partially hollow core encompassed by an outer shell of sound wood. These cavities serve as "apartment houses" for many birds and small mammals. Forests in this mixed fire regime were often dominated by widely spaced ancient larch and an occasional old Douglas-fir, along with an assortment of middle-aged and younger larch, lodgepole pine, Douglas-fir, and a smattering of other conifers and small patches of aspen. Open conditions created by periodic fires also helped produce rich undergrowth.

When fire is kept out for long periods western larch forests deteriorate. Shade-tolerant trees proliferate, causing excessive competition for moisture and nutrients that can trigger rapid decline and death of old larch trees. Sparse canopy foliage, dying tree tops, and a drastic reduction in annual-ring growth are symptoms of decline. Associated lodgepole pine trees commonly die from bark beetle attacks. Only shade-tolerant herbs and low shrubs survive beneath the dense layer of understory trees. This kind of forest structure readily supports crown fire.

Contrasting examples of restoration forestry are under way in the larch forests of western Montana that were historically molded by the mixed fire regime. Projects on the Lolo National Forest surrounding the sylvan community of Seeley Lake rely on intensive silvicultural cutting. Conversely, restoration in remote larch forests of Glacier National Park and the Bob Marshall Wilderness uses natural fires. Last, a series of different restoration treatments are being tested in a small, remnant grove of old-growth larch near the city of Missoula.

Seeley Lake Recreation Corridor

During the summer of 1988 conflagrations sweeping through Yellow-stone National Park dominated the news. Two hundred miles farther north along the Continental Divide, the gigantic Canyon Creek fire exploded eastward out of the Scapegoat Wilderness, overrunning ranches and rural homes in its wake. Meanwhile, the western flank of this 247,000-acre fire burned through remote portions of the Seeley Lake Ranger District of the Lolo National Forest in Montana. From that time forward the district's fire managers felt a sense of foreboding. Hundreds of homes and summer cabins had sprung up in ever thickening forests on private land virtually surrounded by the national forest.

Countless miles of power lines interlace dense timber to serve these dwellings, often with minimal clearance from tree crowns and only sporadic road access. These lines create a troubling new source for wild-fires. High winds topple trees onto the lines, which then arc and spew sparks. Compounding the fire protection problem, many of the residences are enveloped by hazardous forest fuels, including accumulations of pine needles and branches lying atop cedar shake roofs. Fire manager Margaret Dougherty worried about the looming threat of a summer windstorm spawning a crown fire that would sweep through the Seeley Lake community, threatening lives and destroying homes and businesses. Two small wildfires had blown up, sending flames more than 100 feet into the air. Dougherty knew that these incipient crown fires could easily have grown into a holocaust had they not been promptly doused with fire retardant from an air tanker, a resource that just happened to be available on short notice in these instances.

Dougherty sought help from scientists at the U.S. Forest Service Rocky Mountain Research Station's Fire Science Laboratory in Missoula to better understand the fire ecology of the historic larch forests and how it might inform forest management. The scientists examined a stand called Girard Grove that had never been logged and appeared to represent much of the original forest around Seeley Lake. Study of fire scars and tree ages revealed that this forest was dominated by different age groups of western larch trees ranging up to 600 years, each of which sprang up after understory fires occurring about 25 years apart on average (Arno, Smith, and Krebs 1997). Huge, rotten fire-scarred larch trees are doubtless older yet, suggesting this pattern of frequent fire extended back at least 900 years (Koch 1945). Without fires there would have been no larch. Instead, a dense tangle of shade-tolerant Douglas-fir, subalpine fir, and Engelmann spruce would have prevailed.

Most larch forests in the Northern Rockies burned less frequently than those at Seeley Lake, and in a mixed fire regime that killed many trees. As a result, the old-growth larch in these stands were found in patches consisting of one or just a few age classes. The Seeley Lake forest, in contrast, was more uniformly dominated by larch trees of many ages, including some of the oldest and largest larch in existence. Evidence from fire science, archeological studies, and historical use of the area by native peoples suggests that aboriginal burning practices were largely responsible for the pattern of frequent fires at Seeley Lake (Arno, Smith, and Krebs 1997). In the 1890s, a U.S. Geological Survey forest inspector noted: "There is no doubt that some of the fires, especially on the higher ranges, are due to lightning, but most of those in the valley seem to have been set by Indian and other hunting parties or by prospectors. The trails most frequented by Indians, as the

Figure 11.1.
Computer visualizations of the effects of the Archibald timber sale on a stand containing old-growth western larch, based on measurements of (a) pre- and (b) post-treatment stand structures as presented in Table 11.1. (S. Robertson visualizations)

Jocko and Pend Oreille, are noticeably burned, especially about the camping places" (Ayres 1901, p. 72). According to Lolo National Forest archeologist Milo McLeod, numerous artifacts suggest a sustained level of aboriginal activity (camping) in the vicinity of Girard Grove extending back 3,500 years.

Regardless of the ignition source, however, frequent fires before 1900 helped produce a magnificent, open forest of larch trees with reddish-brown trunks 3–6 feet in diameter and larch regeneration in gaps. By the 1990s fire had been kept out of the forest for nearly a century, and an understory of Douglas-fir had developed even in the unlogged Girard Grove. The 1986 Lolo National Forest Plan acknowledged the importance of using natural processes to guide forest management, and public sentiment favored treatments that would sustain a visually appealing forest of large old trees. District foresters visualized that restoring a semblance of the original conditions could reduce crown fire hazard while benefiting the many species from elk to goshawks that find forage in more open fire-maintained forests (Lyon and others 2000). Conversely, foresters recognized that withholding restoration treatments was hastening the loss of the beautiful old trees in Big Larch Campground and other recreational areas.

In 1995 the Seeley Lake Ranger District embarked on its first restoration project in the big larch forest using a conventional timber sale contract. The Archibald timber sale treated a 100-acre stand con-

Table 11.1.
Stand structures before and after treatment in the Archibald timber sale, Seeley Lake Ranger District. Data are trees per acre from an inventory conducted by S. Arno and C. Fiedler after the area was thinned and underburned. (Each letter represents an individual tree: d = Douglas-fir; w = western larch; lp = lodgepole pine; p = ponderosa pine.)

Tree dbh	Trees retained	Trees removed or killed
1–4 inches	dddddd	56 d; 3 lp
4–6	dddd	48 d; 28 lp
6–8		32 d; 4 w; 32 lp
8–10		16 d; 5 w; 12 lp
10–12	w	5 d; 16 lp
12–14	w	8 d
14–16	w	
16–18		
18–20	dd wwwwww	
20–22	w	
22–24	ww	
24–26	dww	
26–28	ww	
28–30	www	
30–32	pww	
32–40	www	
40–48	www	
Basal area/acre		
194 sq. feet pre-treatment	128 sq. ft.	66 sq. ft.

taining many old-growth larch and some large Douglas-fir trees that had survived selective logging in the early 1900s. These big trees were surrounded by thickets of small Douglas-fir, lodgepole pine, and sometimes subalpine fir and spruce. This prominent stand borders the main road encircling Seeley Lake and abuts a national forest campground and private residential properties. Large trees were retained, but treatment removed most of the small and some of the medium-size trees (less than 18 inches in diameter) to reduce crowding. Basal area of tree stems was reduced by 35 to 50 percent. Larch of all sizes, which are less numerous than under historical conditions, were retained in this "thin-from-below" treatment (Figure 11.1; Table 11.1). The goal was to reduce competition and ladder fuels, protect the larch and large trees in general, and begin returning a stand structure representative of historical conditions. Where possible, prescribed fire would be used as a follow-up to the harvesting treatment.

The sale was purchased by the Pyramid Mountain sawmill at Seeley Lake, and harvesting was carried out during winter on snowpack that averaged about 2 feet deep. Most of the trees were felled mechanically, using both small and full-size feller-bunchers. Grapple skidders hauled the bunched trees to roadside landings, where they were sorted. Despite the emphasis on removing small trees, about 1 million board feet of commercial timber was retrieved. When the intermittent market for pulpwood allowed, trees too small for sawn products were hauled to the pulp mill near Missoula. Many of the limbs and treetops were chipped and taken to the Pyramid sawmill to fuel a boiler that provides heat to dry lumber. Excess limbs and tops were burned at the landings. Logs unsuitable for lumber were set aside for public use as firewood.

Despite initial concerns that the Archibald timber sale might not be commercially viable, revenues approximately offset treatment costs. The treatments produced positive results in terms of wildfire hazard reduction, sustainability of the big larch forest, and benefits for the local economy. The sudden change of this roadside forest from a dense wall of conifers to a relatively open stand was welcomed by people who could for the first time see the magnificent larch trees. A national representative of The Wilderness Society even wrote a letter complimenting the district ranger on the project.

While the Archibald treatments were underway, the district staff began preparing a similar project on about 250 acres containing old-growth larch, Douglas-fir, and ponderosa pine as well as 140 acres of younger forest. The Morrell timber sale adjoins the northern edge of the Seeley Lake town site and extends along scenic Highway 83 for nearly a mile. A few years earlier the Montana Department of Transportation and the Forest Service had encountered stiff opposition when they proposed removing trees crowding this narrow road to improve visibility and safety.

In the old-growth areas, the Morrell sale primarily removed understory and excess mid-size trees. Both old-growth and younger forest areas were treated to retain the fire-dependent larch and ponderosa pine, reduce excessive competition, and decrease ladder fuels. In the young stands the goal was to break up continuous canopies using thin-ning from below and retention shelterwood cutting that kept the larch, ponderosa pine, and largest trees of other species. Some of the treat-ments created forested fuel breaks along existing roads and cross-country ski trails and increased the clearance along power lines running through the forest.

After harvesting, the district underburned portions of the area in the spring, shortly before the record-setting 2000 wildfire season com-menced. They resumed prescribed burning of the sale area in spring 2001. Burning was conducted soon after snowmelt in late April, dur-ing midday in sunny warm weather. The fire prescription was designed to reduce fuel concentrations and kill many of the small understory firs with minimal damage to medium- or large-size trees. Fire crews also hand piled and burned slash along the national forest boundary adja-cent to home sites. In prior years some local people complained about the danger of prescribed fire and associated, unwanted smoke; thus fire management officer Bill Oelig was pleasantly surprised by the strong public support this time around. Upon seeing the results, residents and community groups urged the district to do more burning and other fuel reduction work.

Next, the district launched the 500-acre Chain of Lakes Fuels Proj-ect to restore corridors of big larch forest extending along Highway 83 and the road encircling Seeley Lake, including popular campgrounds at Seeley Lake, Lake Inez, and Lake Alva, and national forest land con-taining leased cabins. By this time bark beetle epidemics were advanc-ing through the surrounding dense forests and also killing lodgepole pine and Douglas-fir left in recently thinned stands. District foresters contracted salvage cutting of beetle-killed trees as soon as possible to re-duce breeding habitat in dead trees and to prevent accelerating attacks.

In 2003 the district embarked on another 1,300-acre project that involves low thinning, understory fuel removal, and burning treat-ments, much of it in the big larch forest along Highway 83. They are also working with the rural fire district to assess wildfire hazard throughout the greater community—the first step of a coordinated ef-fort to reduce fuels where the threats to people and developments are greatest. The local high school removed understory thickets and thinned mid-size trees on their forest land adjacent to the athletic field. The school district hired a restoration forestry contractor and allowed the high school forestry class to participate in the work. For the first time in many years people can see the large, orange-barked ponderosa pines on the school property.

Ranger Tim Love felt that once people saw the restoration treatments in the cherished big larch forest along Highway 83, the idea of "good forestry" was no longer an abstract concept or a suspect one. Soon, many landowners carried out similar treatments around their homes and summer cabins. Love believes that growing public acceptance of restoration treatments will allow the district to develop more comprehensive projects that make openings for larch regeneration—ultimately re-creating an uneven-aged larch forest like the stands of old.

National Park and Wilderness Forests

Northward from Seeley Lake and across the crest of the Swan Range lie two broad river valleys: one is the North Fork of the Flathead in Glacier National Park, and the other is the South Fork of the Flathead in the Bob Marshall Wilderness (part of the Flathead National Forest). Both valleys are blanketed with larch–lodgepole pine forests that have never been logged. The mixed fire regime, with fire intervals averaging between 25 and 75 years, nurtured huge, ancient larch trees and younger age classes of larch and lodgepole pine arranged in intricate mosaics (Barrett, Arno, and Key 1991).

Despite ecological similarities, these two areas have different management concerns that affect the restoration of fire as an ecosystem process. In 1988 the Red Bench wildfire burned more than 26,000 acres of the North Fork valley in Glacier National Park. Sixty years of fire exclusion accompanied by massive amounts of beetle-killed lodgepole pine fueled this fire's intensity (Barrett, Arno, and Key 1991). Despite aggressive firefighting efforts, flames consumed several park buildings and killed many venerable larch trees that had previously survived up to seven fires.

After the catastrophic wildfire season of 1988, western national park and national forest fire management plans had to include parameters such as drought indicators before any lightning ignitions could be managed as prescribed natural fires—a change that greatly reduced the number and area of natural fires permitted to burn in national parks and national forest wilderness (Agee 2000). In contrast, managers in

Glacier National Park drafted a fire plan that ultimately allowed *more* natural fires to burn, especially in the North Fork drainage (Kurth 1996). Park managers also began prescribed burning to maintain the small natural grasslands in the North Fork valley that were being invaded by young conifers.

During the major wildfire season of 1994, Glacier's natural fire program made a giant step forward. Under damp June conditions, managers designated a lightning ignition near the Park's western boundary as a prescribed natural fire and named it the Howling fire for wolves howling in the area (Kurth 1996). It burned less than an acre during the first 4 weeks, but then came alive in late July. Managers agonized over the appropriateness of allowing a natural fire to burn in what had become a busy wildfire season, with potential shortages of fire personnel and equipment West-wide. The countervailing concern was whether all fires should be suppressed in a natural area that may be capable of burning only during the most active wildfire seasons. Fire growth modeling suggested that the Howling fire posed little threat to exceed acceptable boundaries; consequently, it was allowed to continue burning as a prescribed natural fire. Several experts came to Glacier to study the social and political ramifications of letting the fire burn. Rain and snow finally extinguished the fire after it had burned for 4 months, covered 2,000 acres, and required less than $200,000 to manage.

By the end of the 2000 fire season, prescribed natural fires had visited about 27,000 acres of Glacier's North Fork drainage. They burned in mixed-severity patterns, re-creating burn mosaics similar to those of historical fires (Divoky, fire ecologist, and Key, geographer, Glacier National Park, pers. comm. 2003). In 2001 the huge Moose wildfire jumped the North Fork of the Flathead River and burned 25,000 acres in the park. Park managers remembered the damage and rehabilitation expense linked to suppression efforts on the 1988 Red Bench fire, including many miles of bulldozed fire line that were ultimately little used (Benson and Kurth 1995). Confronted with the Moose fire, managers took a different tack, attempting only to slow the fire's expansion on the north and south flanks and allowing the broad eastern front to burn toward the park's alpine backcountry. Moreover, suppression was limited to aerial fire retardant and water drops and handmade fire lines applied to less than 5 percent of the fire's perimeter (Divoky and Key, pers. comm. 2003). Suppression impacts were minimal, and although the Moose fire burned under some of the driest conditions on record, it produced a mosaic of variable burning intensities and surviving trees. Stand replacement burning occurred on about 38 percent of the fire area. The 1999 Anaconda fire, a natural burn, lay in the path of the Moose fire and probably prevented it from burning many more acres (Divoky and Key, pers. comm. 2003). In 2003 Glacier National Park and the Flathead National Forest, which share boundaries along the park's west side, began developing an interagency fire management plan that will give the park additional opportunities to manage ecologically beneficial fires.

Summer 2003 produced the driest fuels and greatest area burned in northwestern Montana since record keeping began in the early 1900s. Blazes burned from mid-July through early September, their perimeters eventually encompassing 136,000 acres (13 percent) of Glacier National Park and 157,000 acres on the Flathead National Forest. The human-caused Robert fire, south of the North Fork drainage, ultimately grew to 57,000 acres, threatening hundreds of homes and other buildings within and outside the park. Many homes have wood-shingle roofs and are surrounded by dense forest intermixed with dead lodgepole pine—a highly combustible combination.

Because of extreme fire danger in 2003, all of the fires in Glacier Park were managed under the suppression alternative, but fire management officer Fred Vanhorn explained that passive suppression (a confine and contain strategy) was used extensively to minimize ecological damage, and no fire line was constructed by bulldozer. The primary tool for active suppression was to burn out fuels from roads or other anchor points that lay between developed areas and the fire front. Several burnouts covered thousands of acres and were viewed as unnecessarily large by some ecologists. Because of skilled fire management teams and relatively accurate weather forecasts, the burnouts worked well and protected developed areas. Vanhorn observed that the burnouts were of only moderate intensity and generally burned with effects similar to a natural ignition, unlike a high-intensity backfire lit in front of an advancing wall of flames.

Still, fire managers warn of inherent risks in igniting large burnouts, noting that firefighters could consider less drastic and more ecologically compatible alternatives for controlling wildfires if fuel reduction treatments were in place. For example in 2003, the 53,000-acre Wedge Canyon fire in the northern part of the North Fork Valley destroyed seven forest homes and many other structures, but spared the one home and burned lightly through the associated woodlot that had been intensively thinned and undergone fuel treatment (Jamison 2003). Before the onset of the 2003 fires, managers reduced fuels around facilities at Saint Mary and Two Medicine, on the park's east side. As a result of the fire threats experienced in 2003, Vanhorn and fire ecologist Dennis Divoky expect fuel treatments in Glacier to pick up considerably.

The small campgrounds and most buildings and facilities in Glacier Park's North Fork drainage are reached by narrow dirt roads, which provide access for prescribed burning of grasslands and for protecting people and facilities from fires. In contrast, the South Fork drainage in the Bob Marshall Wilderness has no roads, creating additional challenges for reintroducing fire. For example, it takes time to locate and evacuate the scattered parties using a large wilderness area should they become threatened by an ongoing fire. The Flathead National Forest issues fire warnings through local media, employs wilderness rangers who seek out backcountry users, and keeps in touch with the professional outfitters who host many visitors. Still, fire managers worry that some wilderness users may escape contact and become imperiled by a fire. Thick smoke and heavily forested terrain can make it difficult for uninformed users to locate an approaching fire and choose an escape route. Fire managers also want to protect some historic cabins and large bridges that span the South Fork and principal side streams.

The middle of the South Fork drainage features some dry grasslands and relict ponderosa pine groves once perpetuated by frequent fires but now invaded by Douglas-fir and other conifers (Arno, Parsons, and Keane 2000). Management restrictions in wilderness and lack of motorized access make use of management-ignited fire more difficult than in Glacier Park's North Fork drainage.

During the 2000 fire season, three blazes that started in the South Fork drainage were managed as "wildland fire use events" (formerly called "prescribed natural fires"). Another fire that started later in the season was put into suppression status but was not actually suppressed due to lack of available firefighting resources. These fires burned a total of about 8,500 acres. Crews wrapped the historic Black Bear Cabin— a two-story log building—in fire-retardant fabric and cleared ladder fuels and erected sprinklers to protect the cabin, barns, corrals, and pack bridge.

The 2000 fires burned at variable intensities, but nearly all the larch survived, including a number of 4- to 5-foot-thick patriarchs more

Figure 11.2.
Mixed-severity fire mosaic as viewed in fall 2003 in the South Fork Flathead Valley, Bob Marshall Wilderness. (photo by Steve Wirt, U.S. Forest Service)

than 500 years old. Fires killed most of the lodgepole pine, subalpine fir, and spruce, while many of the larger Douglas-fir survived. The fires created favorable conditions for regenerating larch and lodgepole pine, potentially renewing these species' historical abundance despite competition from shade-tolerant species. In a few places, stand replacement burning covered 50 acres or more, especially on steep slopes.

By the following summer, mass flowering of fireweed (*Epilobium angustifolium*), aster (*Aster conspicuous*), heart-leaf arnica, and pinegrass heralded the flush of nutrients produced by burning. Two other showy herbs—*Geranium bicknellii* and dragonhead (*Dracocephalum parviflorum*)—appeared in abundance only after fire scarified their buried seeds and opened the site. The blossoms were tended by numerous pollinating insects, while several species of woodpeckers and other birds busily harvested insects among the fire-killed trees. On moist sites that burned only at moderate intensity, the Rocky Mountain huckleberry (*Vaccinium globulare*) resprouted vigorously and will likely produce bigger berry crops in the next few years as a result of increased sunlight, soil moisture, and nutrients in the burned forest. By contrast, huckle-berry plants are often set back on severely burned sites (Fischer and Bradley 1987).

The record-breaking fire season of 2003 produced 49 fires in the Bob Marshall and Great Bear wilderness areas on the Flathead National Forest, nearly all of lightning origin. Beginning in mid-July, lightning fires in the South Fork drainage grew and merged to become the Little Salmon Complex, eventually covering 88,000 acres (Figure 11.2). At the outset, a projection of fire growth and threats beyond the wilder-ness boundary led managers to allow 12 fires in this complex to burn as wildland fire use events. Ten fires were actively suppressed and 10 received limited suppression—water or fire-retardant drops—with no direct attack by firefighters on the ground. Flathead National Forest fire specialist Steve Wirt (pers. comm. 2003) noted that in several areas fire growth was stopped or slowed when fires encountered wilderness burns that had occurred from 2 to 18 years earlier, suggesting that with-out the 20-year-old natural fire program, the 2003 fires would have grown much larger. Overall, the program to reintroduce fire in a mixed fire regime characterized by larch and lodgepole pine forest is gradu-ally restoring a more natural and manageable landscape.

Reclaiming a Remnant

In the early 1990s Vic Dupuis, a silviculturist on the Missoula Ranger District of the Lolo National Forest, ran across a small grove of old-growth larch and ponderosa pine perched high on a mountainside above the city of Missoula, Montana. Because of a complex pattern of changing land ownership in the area, this 15-acre parcel escaped early logging. Dupuis recognized that this relict forest's location near the city could be a valuable asset for educating people about forest ecology. He also recognized the old trees' vulnerability to damage as a result of fire exclusion.

Dupuis showed this "diamond in the rough" to ecologists at the Missoula Fire Sciences Laboratory. Impressed with Dupuis' find, they immediately began investigating the stand's history and how fires and fire suppression had affected its structure over the previous few centuries (Arno, Smith, and Krebs 1997). Scars on the ancient trees revealed that

16 fires had burned through this grove between the 1590s and 1889, an average of one fire every 20 years (Arno, unpublished data 1998). The longest interval between fires during that three-century period was about 34 years. Most of the fires were low-intensity underburns, but a blaze in about 1663 killed trees in parts of the stand. This historic fire regime sustained a forest dominated by old larch and ponderosa pine growing nearly 25 feet apart on average, along with a few Douglas-firs.

The last fire was an underburn in 1919, and over the following 80 years the stand missed approximately three natural fire cycles. A thick understory of Douglas-fir trees (about 700 per acre) sprang up in fire's extended absence. By the 1990s, many smaller fir were heavily infected with dwarf mistletoe, a parasitic plant that causes deformity and growth decline and creates witches brooms that promote high-intensity burning. Increment borings revealed that diameter growth of the larch and pine declined drastically after about 1950. By the 1990s, the canopy foliage was sparse and several old ponderosa pine had succumbed to bark beetle attacks.

Dupuis had hoped to simply use prescribed fire to restore this patch of old-growth forest; however, Fire Sciences Lab scientist Mick Harrington recognized that the old trees were too weak to survive any fire hot enough to kill the understory firs. Yet if the fire did not kill the firs, it would do little to rejuvenate the old trees.

Harrington, Dupuis, and their colleagues developed a demonstration study to evaluate different restoration strategies (Fiedler and Harrington 2004). The objectives of treatment were to reduce fire hazard and competition for moisture by removing the Douglas-fir thickets, create scattered openings large enough to induce regeneration of light-requiring western larch or ponderosa pine, and remove mistletoe-infected overstory trees before they could infect "clean" trees or seedlings that might become established after treatment (Fiedler and Harrington 2004). They divided the stand into five units, and each received one of the following treatments: (1) The "control" unit was protected from fire and no trees were cut, thus serving as a benchmark for comparison. (2) In the "understory cut" unit, small trees were felled, piled manually, and burned under damp, cool conditions to minimize impact on the soil or remaining trees. (3) In the "understory cut and prescribed burn" unit, the small trees were felled, creating a fuel bed that was broadcast burned under cool weather conditions to avoid damaging the old trees. Mounds of litter and duff were raked away from the old trees lest they smolder and kill the trees. (4) In the "understory/improvement cut" unit, the small trees and weaker old trees were cut. Merchantable logs were removed, some rotten logs were left in place, and understory trees and slash were burned in piles under damp, cool conditions. (5) In the "understory/improvement cut and prescribed burn" treatment, merchantable logs from weak, mistletoe-infected old trees were removed as in treatment (4). Duff mounds were raked away from the remaining old trees, and understory trees were felled, creating a fuel bed that was broadcast burned under cool weather conditions (Figure 11.3).

Harrington explained that removing the understory Douglas-firs, which postdate the last fire in 1919, along with some of the weakest old trees, returns a stand structure comparable to what would be expected if the understory fire regime had not been interrupted. Had the expected three fires burned between 1919 and the 1990s, few understory trees would have been present. Fire ecologists have found that understory fires like those historically associated with this stand will kill some large trees through damage to the tree's bole or roots. Therefore, some of the old trees alive at the beginning of this study would have been killed by 20th-century underburns were it not for fire suppression. Removing some of the weak and diseased old trees in treatments (4) and (5), as if by fire, simulates the return of a historical stand structure. Additionally, treatments (4) and (5) were designed to open the stand sufficiently—leaving about half of the tree basal area per acre—to provide opportunities for successful regeneration of larch and ponderosa pine. These treatments were prescribed because fire exclusion over an extended period prevented fire-related cycles of larch and pine regeneration. Larch saplings are present despite fire exclusion but are spindly and weak due to inadequate light and growing space. In contrast, larch saplings in nearby logged areas are sturdy and fast growing.

Harrington added that prescribed burning of the biomass generated by cutting resembles historic biomass consumption by fire. Because excessive amounts of biomass accumulated in the long fire exclusion period, prescribed burning was applied under cool, moist weather conditions. The method used in treatments (2) and (4) was "progressive pile burning," in which workers periodically fed slash into each fire—controlling the available fuel and thus heat production. This reduced the chance of injuring old trees and produced only a very small,

Figure 11.3.
(a) Pre- and (b) post-treatment views (treatment 5) from the same camera point in the remnant stand of old-growth larch, Lolo National Forest. (photos by Michael G. Harrington, U.S. Forest Service)

localized impact on soils and herbaceous and shrubby vegetation. Strip head–fires, which were used for burning in treatments (3) and (5), involve igniting a series of narrow strips along the contour, starting at the top of the unit. Strip head-fires consume excess biomass with little impact, resembling the natural fire process.

All the treatments were completed in spring 1999 (Fiedler and Harrington 2004). In the least intensive restoration treatment, (2) "understory cut," Harrington explained that 90 percent of the trees—but only the smallest ones—were removed. Basal area of living trees, a rough indicator of tree biomass, was reduced only 16 percent, from 144 to 121 square feet per acre. In the most intensive treatment, (5) "understory/ improvement cut and prescribed burn," a similar proportion (87 percent) of the trees was removed, but this reduced basal area by nearly half, from 145 to 76 square feet per acre.

In the prescribed burn treatments (3) and (5), the 19 tons per acre of slash and old woody fuel were reduced by half, mostly in the finer fuels that represent the greatest wildfire hazard. Only 35 percent of the duff was removed, indicating modest fire impacts on the soil. Harrington noted that carefully controlled ignition methods minimized crown scorch on the old trees. Despite raking duff away from tree bases, four larch trees were killed by prescribed fire igniting old fire scars. These same trees might well have been killed by natural fires had such fires not been suppressed over the last century.

Visual contrasts among treatments are already striking. Most old trees in the treatment areas have fuller crowns with healthy foliage color. The understories of treated plots are no longer choked with small trees, and the herbaceous layer is robust relative to the untreated plot (Figure 11.3).

Dr. Anna Sala and Dr. Ray Calloway of the University of Montana conducted a companion tree-level study of physiological indicators of tree vigor, and their findings corroborate the visual differences among treatments. Removing the Douglas-fir trees from the understory increased soil moisture levels compared to the control. Three years after treatment, the old-growth trees in the treated areas had higher sap flow, higher foliar nitrogen content, and higher foliage production (Sala and Calloway 2001). These indicators of improved tree vigor suggest greater resistance to insects and disease compared with trees in the untreated controls. Harrington was impressed that despite notoriously complex relationships among native trees and mountain environments, these ancient fire-dependent trees responded positively to treatments that simulated the effects of an historical fire regime.

The immediate objectives of this restoration project were to reduce extreme fire hazard, reestablish environmental conditions that promote healthy trees, and reintroduce fire as an ecological process (Fiedler and Harrington 2004). The broader objective was to provide comparative restoration treatments for managers to see and modify as needed for use in other declining larch stands.

Chapter 12

Lodgepole Pine

Lodgepole pine is the consummate fire-adapted tree of the Rockies and other high mountain ranges of the inland West. This generally small, slender conifer dominates about 60 million acres of forest between southern Colorado and the Yukon Territory. Much of the lodgepole pine forest is molded by the stand replacement fire regime, where fires kill most or all the trees in large, often irregular swaths, creating mosaics of burned and unburned patches (Arno 2000). These fires also replace a sparse undergrowth of shade-loving plants in the old forest with a luxuriant postfire community of grasses, flowering herbs, shrubs, and sometimes sprouts or seedlings of aspen—important for wildlife habitat and biological diversity.

During summer 1988 stand replacement fires engulfed a million acres of lodgepole pine forest in the greater Yellowstone National Park area. Although television network news broadcasts tended to portray these fires as an environmental disaster, over thousands of years similar fires shaped Yellowstone's forests. Historically, fires in the Yellowstone area occurred at intervals of 200–400 years and initiated long cycles of forest community development, maturation, decline, mortality, fuel accumulation, and fire (Romme and Despain 1989). In contrast, moist, warm, lower elevation areas of northern Idaho support faster growing lodgepole pine and accelerated fuel buildups, leading to stand replacement fires at intervals averaging 100 years or less (Brown 1975).

In other areas, lodgepole pine forests were molded by a mixed fire regime that included fires of low, moderate, and high intensities (Arno 2000, Zimmerman and Omi 1998). These forests have understories of grass or other fine fuels and a dry climate that allows lower intensity fires to occur at shorter intervals—sometimes averaging only 25–30 years. Some fires spread along the forest floor with flames less than a foot high, scarring but not killing the thin-barked lodgepole pines. Under drier conditions or with strong winds or abundant fuels, moderate-intensity burning kills some of the trees, thinning the forest in a patchy pattern. Occasionally, fires burn at high intensity, killing most trees—a stand replacement burn within the mixed fire regime.

In many national parks and other natural areas with lodgepole pine forests, most or all fires are suppressed to prevent them from threatening nearby commercial forests, private lands, or structures. Eventually, aided by fuel buildup, fires are likely to endanger private lands and developments. Restoration treatments could reduce wildfire hazard in these locations. Restoration forestry can also produce or simulate lower intensity fires like those of the mixed fire regime (Zimmerman and Omi 1998). In this chapter, we profile a Colorado lodgepole pine forest where prescribed burning improves habitat for a vulnerable population of bighorn sheep. In Montana, we document foresters using silvicultural cutting and prescribed burning to reduce wildfire hazard and achieve ecological and financial goals. Finally, amidst the scenic splendor of the Canadian Rockies, we see how national park managers create stand replacement prescribed fires at times and places of their choosing to mimic the effects of the historical fire regime.

Wildlife Habitat Restoration in Colorado

Jerry Chonka, a fire management officer on the Gunnison National Forest, leads one of the most unique restoration programs in fire-prone forests. Chonka and his colleagues are returning the effects of historical fires to more than 60,000 acres of rugged mountain terrain on the west slope of the Continental Divide in central Colorado. The treatment area lies northeast of the city of Gunnison in the spectacular Taylor River Canyon and extends upward to the alpine timberline on nearby Fossil Ridge. The canyon serves as a corridor for migrating bighorn sheep as they move off summer range in the alpine tundra and head down to winter range in the semiarid foothills. By 1980 the canyon's burgeoning recreational use and residential subdivisions threatened the bighorns' survival. The herd population had plunged from about 180 animals down to only 16.

Biologists recommended creating a new, safer migration corridor on the slopes of Fossil Ridge away from developed areas. The slopes had become unsuitable for bighorns because thickets of stunted lodgepole pines and other conifers had crowded out aspen, shrubs, grass, and other forage plants. Also, heavy tree cover makes sheep easy prey for coyotes and cougars. Studies showed that in the past, low- to mid-elevation slopes of Fossil Ridge were more open. They supported scattered ponderosa pine and Douglas-fir, maintained by a mixed fire regime with burn intervals averaging between 30 and 60 years. When the historic fire regime was interrupted, dense thickets of stunted lodgepole pine developed.

In the early 1980s the Gunnison Ranger District in cooperation with the Colorado Division of Wildlife began working to return a semblance of historical forest conditions, which they believed would allow bighorns to use the undeveloped slopes of Fossil Ridge as a migration route. Other benefits of restoration treatments include reducing fuel accumulations and risk of severe wildfires, controlling dwarf mistletoe infestations in lodgepole pine, rejuvenating aspen groves and ponderosa pine and Douglas-fir communities, and improving big game forage on the ridges to reduce impacts on streamside habitats.

Because the area is steep and largely inaccessible by roads, and the trees are generally too small for forest products, harvesting and other silvicultural cutting was not appropriate. Prescribed fire was selected as the principal restoration treatment. The first operational burn was conducted on 200 acres in spring 1983. By 1999, the ranger district had burned more than 28,000 acres. Then a moratorium on burning began due to severe regional drought. Over the years, burning was conducted in spring, summer, and fall, but the May through August period works best because smoke disperses well. Late summer and fall burns are often accompanied by temperature inversions that allow smoke to settle into canyons where people live and travel.

Between 1983 and the late 1990s Chonka and his colleagues wrote a dozen burn plans. The ranger district boosted efficiency by preparing three generic burn plans that fit most projects, focusing on improvement of bighorn winter range, summer range, or migration routes (Zimmerman and Omi 1998). In 2003 the ranger district was completing a comprehensive environmental analysis for a single burn plan to cover the entire 60,800-acre project area. About 37,400 acres are in lodgepole pine communities, and nearly 17,000 acres of this have been burned. One helitorch-ignited burn was conducted on 650 acres of the lodgepole pine type, but the rest of the burning has been done manually with drip torches. Approximately three-fourths of the burning killed the majority of the trees, while the remainder was low-intensity fire that caused little mortality.

Chonka likes to use places that were already burned, adjacent moist/shady slopes, or rockland with scant fuel as "natural" fire control boundaries. Sometimes the fire crew burns a certain location when control is easily accomplished—such as a south-facing slope in spring. Later, these areas serve as boundaries when burning adjacent stands under drier conditions. They conduct summer burning when spotting distances—the distance over which burning embers can be lofted and ignite new fires—are calculated to be less than 0.4 mile and when probability of ignition is less than 80 percent. Costs for hand ignition were $55–70 per acre in the late 1990s. Burning is usually accomplished using a strip head-fire technique designed to kill a large number of trees. Experience has shown that a firing crew of three can achieve good results if guided by an ignition specialist with a good vantage point for directing the burn (Zimmerman and Omi 1998).

Specific goals in the form of "desired future conditions" are developed for each type of vegetation, and burning is planned and modeled to best achieve these goals. In lodgepole pine communities containing some aspen, the goal is generally to kill as much of the pine with fire as possible and to stimulate aspen regeneration. A second burn may be planned in 20–30 years to further the same goal. Lodgepole pine stands heavily infested with dwarf mistletoe are burned in stand replacement fires so that the ensuing regeneration will develop with minimal levels of infection. Lodgepole stands without dwarf mistletoe may be left untreated or receive a low-intensity or "nonlethal" underburn.

This innovative program has evolved and improved through a lot of learning by doing. The program has generally been supported by the public, but as with any large prescribed burning venture, problems do arise. One of the early fires escaped prescription boundaries. Changing weather conditions occasionally cause smoke to settle in the populated valleys. At first some people complained about seeing dead, blackened trees, but complaints faded in a few years when lush green vegetation developed—including lodgepole pine saplings. Aerial surveys conducted by the Colorado Division of Wildlife show that bighorn use of the treatment area has increased substantially, providing evidence that the objectives of improved habitat are being met.

Reflecting on nearly 20 years of burning to restore wildlife habitat, Chonka feels that the district's efforts to define the upper limits of acceptable burning conditions have allowed its program to expand and achieve the objectives. Finding the upper limit of safe burning conditions is a balancing act, because effective fire sometimes results in erratic fires that might jump containment lines and be unsafe for ignition crews. Chonka and his colleagues have focused on developing ignition patterns, timing, and other techniques that result in ecologically effective fires that also "stay where they are supposed to."

Restoration within Commercial Forests in Montana

Farther north in the Rocky Mountains, lodgepole pine is generally short-lived and fast-growing for 60–80 years but then loses vigor and becomes vulnerable to epidemics of tree-killing mountain pine beetles. Historically, stand replacement fires at intervals between about 70 and 200 years in much of lodgepole pine's range perpetuated an ever changing landscape mosaic of young, middle-aged, and old communities that tempered the extent and severity of bark beetle epidemics.

By the 1960s fire suppression had become increasingly effective, and national forest managers began to use clear-cuts in lodgepole pine forests as a preferred alternative to fires. Clear-cuts allowed efficient mechanized harvesting of wood products, removal of fuel hazards on large patches of the landscape, and establishment of fast-growing young pines that could be harvested in short rotations before a beetle attack or wildfire was likely to intervene.

During the 1960s and 1970s, growing knowledge of forest ecology and concerns about values of wildland forests made it apparent that clear-cuts were an inadequate substitute for the ecological role of fire. Fires leave dead standing trees that become breeding grounds for insects, which in turn provide prey for an abundance of woodpeckers and other birds (Lyon and others 2000). Fires release nutrients into the soil, and the partial shade from snags aids establishment of a new forest (Miller 2000). Fires do not affect soils like the bulldozers formerly used in clear-cutting. Historical fires left irregular swathes and stringers of surviving trees that appeared more natural to the eye than the visually jolting geometric shapes of clear-cuts. The public's aversion to clear-cuts contributed strongly to the collapse of the entire national forest timber program during the 1990s.

At the same time, however, a few land managers and research foresters were devising ecologically based silvicultural treatments for lodgepole pine forests that would avoid the visual and environmental drawbacks of clear-cutting. To maintain structural features of the natural fire regime, these new treatments, termed "variable retention forestry," leave (and sometimes burn) patches of live trees and snags within a harvest unit (Franklin and others 1999). Treatment units are also more irregularly shaped than clear-cuts. Managers intend to allow the new (post-treatment) forest to grow older before the next harvest—comparable to ages under the historical fire regime. Rather than creating a large unit with only a single age class of lodgepole pine, variable retention forestry leaves some older trees to create stands with two age classes, similar to forests in a mixed fire regime. We will look at two approaches to ecologically based management of commercial lodgepole pine forests in Montana.

Bitterroot National Forest

In the late 1980s and early 1990s a deluge of environmental appeals and legal challenges to proposed timber harvesting projects prompted the U.S. Forest Service to rethink its forest management approach. Some environmentalists advocated for an end to timber harvesting on the national forests to preserve the natural environment. Many activists, however, like the public at large, accepted the policy that attempted to eliminate fire. Foresters recognized that prohibition of timber management coupled with attempts to exclude fire would produce undesirable consequences in the forest. Such a policy would also prevent the Forest Service from providing wood products to benefit society, part of its mission under the Multiple Use Act of 1960. In 1992 the chief of the Forest Service proclaimed that "ecosystem management" would become a guiding philosophy for stewardship of national forests in the western United States (Salwasser and Pfister 1994). The trouble was that foresters had not been trained in managing ecosystems.

Since the 1960s the Bitterroot National Forest had been at the center of a political maelstrom about the need to develop more environmentally compatible forest management practices (Bolle and others 1970). By the early 1990s the forest supervisor and staff were committed to demonstrating ecologically based management that still produced timber products for the local economy. This management concept was easier to visualize in the ponderosa pine forest, where some experience and research were available to help design treatments perpetuating long-lived fire-resistant trees. Foresters were skeptical about how timber management could mimic ecological processes in the higher elevation lodgepole pine forests, where fires were more severe and the trees were not fire resistant.

On the Bitterroot and many other national forests, large areas of the lodgepole pine forest type had access roads and scattered clear-cuts supporting new stands of saplings. The remaining unlogged forest was mostly over 100 years of age and heavily stocked with trees of declining vigor, vulnerable to bark beetle epidemics. Many stands were infested with dwarf mistletoe. Studies showed that prior to the early 1900s many lodgepole pine forests experienced a variety of low-, medium-, and high-intensity burns characteristic of the mixed fire regime (Arno 2000). The dry sites on the Bitterroot National Forest historically burned at average intervals of about 50 or 60 years, and this created structural diversity within stands and across the landscape (Arno and Petersen 1983, Arno, Reinhardt, and Scott 1993). By the 1990s many of these lodgepole pine forests had missed one or two natural fire cycles and had accumulated fuel that would support large stand replacement fires. Such conflagrations might trigger erosion that would produce economic and ecological damage, including loss of habitat for bull trout, a species being considered for listing under the Endangered Species Act.

For its first attempt to demonstrate ecosystem-based management in lodgepole pine forests, the Bitterroot National Forest chose Tolan Creek, a drainage abutting the Continental Divide and fraught with controversy about the effects of clear-cutting on elk habitat. A 1,700-acre clear-cut made in the 1970s—dubbed the "Oh-My-God Clearcut" in recognition of its obtrusiveness—disrupted elk travel routes during hunting season. Sula District ranger Dave Campbell and resource coordinator Stu Lovejoy shepherded the innovative Tolan Creek project that started to take shape with approval of an environmental impact statement in 1993.

The first idea was to employ a series of miniature, 1- to 3-acre clearcuts scattered across the drainage. This would remove some timber and reduce fuels with only moderate effects on elk habitat and other environmental and visual concerns. However, the forest ecologist and the silviculturist argued that this would produce a landscape pattern very different from the broader scale of the area's historical mixed fire regime. Also, burning many small clear-cuts surrounded by old lodgepole pine forest would be a logistical nightmare. Ecologist Janet Johnson (now

Janet Grove) worked with silviculturists and other resource specialists to design harvest treatments that would leave variable amounts of the mature lodgepole pines from place to place on about 500 acres (Franklin and others 1999). Then, two kinds of prescribed fire would be applied as a follow-up in different treatment units: an underburn designed to kill few trees, and a higher intensity burn intended to mimic stand replacement fire. A similar restoration project, Beaver-Woods, including 600 acres of lodgepole pine forest was soon being designed in the neighboring West Fork Ranger District.

In the Tolan and Beaver-Woods areas, interdisciplinary teams concluded that compared with historical conditions, lodgepole pine forests had become more homogeneous and dominated by old trees (Bitterroot NF 1993, 1995). They determined that fire exclusion had probably disrupted ecological processes such as nutrient cycling in the soil and re-establishment of early seral vegetation. The interdisciplinary teams recommended a desired future condition in which forest community diversity on the landscape more closely resembles historic levels, providing the mix of conditions to which the native flora and fauna are adapted (Bitterroot NF 1995). Proposed actions should fit the Forest Service's concept of ecosystem-based management for commercial forest land by approximating historic conditions and disturbance processes while meeting multiple-use objectives for a variety of resources. The interdisciplinary teams recognized that if the Forest Service hopes to practice ecosystem-based management on any significant scale, treatments must be cost-effective.

At Tolan and Beaver-Woods, harvest units were aggregated to match the natural levels of fragmentation and scale of disturbance characterizing this forest type (Bitterroot NF 1993). One of the treatments, "seed tree with reserves" removed about two-thirds of the trees and left the rest standing. Remaining trees were burned in a relatively high intensity prescribed fire designed to kill the trees and the dwarf mistletoe parasite that infects them. Burning would also provide a site suitable for vigorous natural regeneration of lodgepole pine, create snags for wildlife, and supply enough woody debris for long-term soil productivity, while still reducing wildfire hazard. At Tolan, seed trees were left in some treatment units in a uniform spacing while other units had clusters of seed trees with openings between (Figure 12.1).

Lovejoy explained that the ecological goal at Tolan and Beaver-Woods was to restore forest age- and size-class diversity at appropriate

Figure 12.1.
View of contrasting cutting treatments in a lodgepole pine forest at Tolan
Creek on the Bitterroot National Forest prior to prescribed burning and the
2000 wildfires. (U.S. Forest Service photo)

scales, create snags for wildlife, and provide woody debris for long-term
site productivity. The proposed treatments involved leaving significant
numbers of trees in a forest type that was normally clearcut. Campbell
observed that organizations formerly opposed to timber management
activities at Tolan Creek agreed with the proposed silviculture and
burning treatments that would be conducted without establishing new
roads. Trout Unlimited came out in support of the proposed treatments
saying they were preferable to the effects of a major wildfire or a more
extensive timber sale. Cutting treatments, leaving between 25 and 75
percent of the overstory trees in different units, were conducted between 1994 and 1996. Prescribed burning was done in 1997, 1998, and
1999. Then, in August 2000 the whole area was swept by huge regional
wildfires, giving foresters a chance to assess effectiveness of treatments
in reducing fire damage.

Patience was required at Tolan Creek while waiting for the right
burning conditions to meet the objectives of killing most residual trees
while minimizing risk of losing control at unit boundaries. When the

conditions were right, burning crews weren't always available. A 100–acre unit was successfully burned at Tolan Creek in late June 1999. Dry (red) slash in the unit produced enough intensity to kill the seed trees, while the lack of slash in adjacent areas made it fairly easy to confine the fire. The fire consumed roughly 70 percent of the down woody fuel. When wildfire swept through the entire area in August 2000, this prescribed burn unit did not reburn, and the abundant, newly germinated pine seedlings survived. This and other treated units surrounded an uncut patch of old lodgepole pine forest that underburned lightly in the 2000 wildfire, killing few live trees. Some other untreated patches around the outer edge of the Tolan treatments also experienced low-intensity underburning in the 2000 wildfire, whereas most of the surrounding untreated forest was swept by stand replacement fire. Stand replacement burning in the 2000 wildfire led to an erosion blow-out and debris flow in a small, intermittent stream course next to the Tolan units in an area that was unlogged and unroaded.

Despite killing the remaining trees in the harvest unit, the 1999 prescribed burn produced only moderate soil heating as indicated by the surviving dominant undergrowth plants—beargrass (*Xerophyllum tenax*) and whortleberry (*Vaccinium scoparium;* Arno, Simmerman, and Keane 1985). In adjacent stands, the 2000 wildfire consumed most of the down woody fuel and killed most of the beargrass and whortleberry. Post-burn vegetation was mainly fireweed, lupine, and pinegrass, much of which was flowering in 2002.

Evaluating the treatments at Tolan and Beaver-Woods in 2003, Lovejoy and Campbell feel they implement ecosystem-based management principles and that similar treatments hold promise for use in other lodgepole pine forests. At Beaver-Woods, a 117-acre lodgepole pine harvest unit, retaining about one third of the trees, was successfully burned in September, 2002. Both the Tolan and Beaver-Woods projects proved cost-effective for commercial harvesting, producing a combined total of more than 5 million board feet of timber from the lodgepole pine units. Logs were sold to sawmills and plywood plants, and the highest quality lodgepole pine was sold to log home manufacturers.

Despite the success of the Tolan and Beaver-Woods projects application of similar treatments has been postponed because the 2000 wildfires burned more than 300,000 acres of the Bitterroot National Forest and attention shifted to management of burned areas. This includes installing large capacity culverts to prevent erosion and accommodate increased flows from the heavily burned forest, and salvaging some fire-killed trees to reduce landscape-scale fuel accumulations when dead trees fall. If more projects like Tolan and Beaver-Woods had been conducted in the commercial forest area, perhaps less wildfire rehabilitation work would be needed.

Tenderfoot Creek Experimental Forest

Forest scientist Ward McCaughey and fire scientist Colin Hardy from the Forest Service's Rocky Mountain Research Station are conducting an ambitious study of ecologically based treatments in high-elevation lodgepole pine forests on the Tenderfoot Creek Experimental Forest in central Montana. This study tests the feasibility of different treatments for maintaining ecological values while the forest provides products and services for society. Cutting treatments (with and without burning treatments) were designed to emulate effects of the historical fire regime by maintaining moderate fuel hazards. In 1992, McCaughey began monitoring quality and quantity of stream flow in the study area. Planning the study and designing treatments began in 1997, harvesting treatments were conducted in 2000, and the first burning treatments occurred in 2002.

The study area is located at 7,000 feet in the Little Belt Mountains, about 20 miles north of White Sulphur Springs on the Lewis and Clark National Forest. It lies at the headwaters of Tenderfoot Creek, a critical cold-water tributary of the Smith River—a blue-ribbon trout stream and primary irrigation source for many ranches. Water shortages plague both anglers and irrigators during late summer in dry years. Lodgepole pine dominates the continuous forest that covers the area's gentle to moderately steep slopes.

Ecological consultant Steve Barrett (Kalispell, Montana) described the area's fire history based on dates of fire scars and fire-initiated age classes of trees. He produced a map that characterizes the extent of fires back to 1580 (Flora and McCaughey 1998). Stand replacement fires burned through the forest at intervals of 100–300 years or longer, and lower intensity fires occurred between the big burns. About half of the experimental forest is covered by even-aged lodgepole pine stands that arose after a stand replacement fire. The remaining half consists of two-aged stands arising after low- to moderate-intensity fires thinned the forest and made room for a new age class of saplings. The two-aged stands range in size from a few acres to about 1,000 acres.

McCaughey and Hardy designed experimental cutting and prescribed burning treatments to mimic these historical disturbance patterns and maintain spatial and biological diversity. They are measuring treatment effects on erosion, water quality, and water quantity throughout the year and comparing them with untreated forest using paired subwatersheds equipped with monitoring flumes. Water-flow monitoring will detect whether these treatments provide increased water production and a change in timing of peak flows by allowing more snow to accumulate and by providing more effective shade to slow the rate of snowmelt. They are also evaluating undergrowth vegetation and noxious weed response to treatment, creation of snags and their use by wildlife, forest fuels before and after treatment, soil nutrients, tree regeneration, tree growth and mortality, and windthrow.

McCaughey and Hardy are testing two different forms of "retention shelterwood" cutting systems designed to remove enough of the overstory to make room for a new age class of young trees while retaining some overstory trees for an indefinite period to benefit structural diversity. The uniform shelterwood cut leaves evenly spaced shelter trees, while the group cutting leaves small patches of trees (1/4–2 acres in size) surrounded by heavily cut openings and corridors. The forests are mostly 100–200 years old, and dominated by trees averaging about 10 inches in diameter. Before treatment the forest averaged 600 trees per acre, and after cutting, about 250. Basal area averaged about 180 square feet per acre before cutting and 60–90 square feet afterwards.

The Tenderfoot study has eight units of uniform shelterwood harvest and eight units of grouped shelterwood cuttings. Four units of each set were underburned after harvest, and four were left unburned. A feller-buncher harvested and transported the trees to a roadside landing with tops and branches still attached; thus, there was relatively little slash (limbs and tops) to support prescribed burning. However, there were sizeable quantities of dead and down trees, and considering that lodgepole pine has little fire resistance, the duff, broken-off branches, and down trees provided adequate fuel for low-intensity burning that still allowed many remaining overstory trees to survive.

The treatments moderately reduced litter and duff, and slightly increased large fuel loadings (Table 12.1). Large fuels are likely to increase during the next 20 years as fire-killed trees continue to fall. The harvest

Table 12.1.
Average quantities of fuel (tons per acre) before and after treatment in a lodgepole pine forest at Tenderfoot Creek Experimental Forest, Montana.

	Preharvest	Postharvest	Postburn
Duff and litter	20	20	13
Small woody fuels (0–3 in. diam.)	3.6	6.7	3.4
Large woody fuels (3+ in. diam.)	11	16	14

and burn treatments may approximate the effect of repeated fires that gave rise to young lodgepole pine communities. These treatments contain lower fuel levels than result from a single stand replacement fire.

In addition to the four different harvest and burn treatments carried out in the 16 research units, two uncut units were burned in a moderate-intensity fire designed to emulate historical thinning fires. Six of the ten burn units were prescribe-burned in 2002 at an average cost of $189 per acre. The 16 treatment units cover a total of 778 acres, and together with the two untreated control units used for comparisons, occupy four small watersheds that are monitored by flumes.

Hardy, reflecting on what he has learned from the Tenderfoot Project, noted that prescribed fire can indeed be used in partially cut lodgepole pine stands, but that tree mortality after prescribed burning may be higher than planned. McCaughey found it interesting and a bit surprising that water quantity and quality were not significantly affected by the treatments, which occurred during years of below-average snow accumulation.

Demand for the small timber removed in the shelterwood cutting treatments was good. The timber sale was purchased and harvested by a sawmill located more than 200 miles away across a high mountain pass. Total purchase price was $858,457, and after subtracting the national forest's costs for developing and administering the sale, the net return was about $353,000. The volume of timber sold was 5.25 million board feet, enough to build about 400 modern-day homes. Following completion of the sale, the Forest Service allowed the public to retrieve firewood from slash piles that would have otherwise been burned.

The treatments incorporated timber harvest, maintained some forest cover, and stimulated the development of a new forest. They provided more of the structural diversity important for wildlife habitat than a single-aged forest arising from a clear-cut or stand replacement fire. The biggest logistical problem in conducting the study was getting enough days within prescription to complete burning within a single burning season.

Returning Fire to Banff National Park

In 1979 the Canadian Parks Service adopted a policy permitting active management of national park ecosystems under certain conditions (Woodley 1995), a revolutionary change from the traditional practice of trying to eliminate fire from the parks. The agency, now called Parks Canada, developed a comprehensive policy recognizing fire as an important ecological process that should be returned to its historical role. Parks Canada considered simply letting some lightning fires burn, as is done in some large wilderness areas and Yellowstone National Park, but deemed this too risky to people and facilities in the parks and to neighboring lands. Instead, it chose active management with prescribed fire as the restoration method. A restoration program based on management fires requires intensive study of historical fire regimes followed by planning and monitoring to ensure that management fires approximate historical fire effects. The program must make scientifically based decisions regarding where, when, and how to conduct burning.

Under the guidance of conservation biologist Cliff White and fire management specialist Ian Pengelly, Banff National Park has built one of the leading fire restoration programs in western North America. Banff, jewel of the Canadian Rockies, covers 1.6 million acres (660,000 ha), including the rugged alpine backbone of the Continental Divide and a series of deep glacial valleys and towering ridges that rise up to the east. The park attracts 4 million visitors a year and hosts thousands of residents in its town-sites and resorts. Banff and three adjacent national parks—Jasper, Yoho, and Kootenay—together encompass 5 million acres (2 million ha). Still other large provincial and national parks are situated not far from Banff and its neighbors along the crest of the Rockies.

Fire managers used prescribed fire on more than 13,000 acres (5,300 ha) in Banff National Park between 1983 and 1994 (White and others 2004). Fire-dependent lodgepole pine communities comprise the principal forest type in the region around Banff, and the burning pro-

Figure 12.2.
A stand-replacement prescribed burn in Banff National Park, June 2003.
(Randy Komar photo)

gram attempts to regenerate them using stand replacement fire (Figure 12.2). Moderate-intensity fires are applied to dry-site Douglas-fir stands, aspen groves, and mountain grasslands. Vocal opposition halted prescribed burning in Banff and the neighboring national parks in the early 1990s awaiting two independent reviews of the ecological health of the parks. The reviews recommended that prescribed burning continue, and in 1997 Banff's new management plan specified the goal of maintaining native vegetation communities to reflect historical forest conditions and disturbance patterns.

Specific objectives for accomplishing this broad goal include (1) restoring fire's role in modifying vegetation communities except where limited by public safety and health, major facilities, or neighboring lands; (2) restoring key fire-dependent vegetation such as aspen, willows, and grasslands; (3) determining vegetation patterns and age-class distributions that will ensure natural biodiversity; and (4) improving public awareness of natural disturbances such as fire and the management implications of these disturbances. The plan sets an annual burning target of at least 50 percent of the long-term historical average using prescribed fires and lightning fires. To be successful, park staff recognize that they must cooperatively develop the burning program and related aspects of park management with neighboring landowners and management agencies.

The 1997 management plan ushered in a new burning program that more than tripled previous activity. Burning averaged 5,000 acres (2,000 ha) annually from 1998 through 2003, exceeding the 50 percent target. Area burned per year is one of the few ecological goals that is quantified in park management plans (Pengelly, unpublished presentation 2003). Changes to the National Parks Act in 2000 brought new emphasis and legislative support for ecosystem-based management. Now many more parks have fire management objectives similar to Banff for maintaining an historic rate of burning. Spurred by this goal, Jasper and Kootenay National Parks used prescribed fire and wildfire confinement strategies to burn in large areas in 2003–2004.

The restoration burning program at Banff National Park inspires others, demonstrates a working strategy, and indicates how to gain support from the public, biologists, and other land owners and agencies. Most prescribed burning in Banff has been in lodgepole pine forests that historically burned at intervals averaging between 50 and 300 years (White and others 2004). Fire history studies indicate that the scarcity of large wildfires around Banff and neighboring parks over the last 70 years is unprecedented in the previous 500 years and probably results from fire suppression rather than climate change (Pengelly, unpublished presentation 2003).

Studies show that lightning-ignited fires occur much more frequently west of the Continental Divide and in the western part of Banff National Park (Wierzchowski, Heathcott, and Flannigan 2002). Eastern portions of the park, despite fewer lightning ignitions, had markedly shorter intervals between fires, according to fire history studies. These findings confirm anthropological evidence indicating that human-caused fires have been important for hundreds of years or longer in the eastern areas, which are within traditional hunting grounds of the Blackfeet and other native tribes (Kay and others 1999, Nisbet 1994, Stewart 2002). Indians may have burned to maintain open corridors and meadows to attract plains bison, which were a prime food source (White and others 2001). Thus, it appears that historic fire regimes in Banff National Park can be maintained only by restoring human-ignited fires. Currently, fire managers are allowing for 5–10

percent of Banff's fire regime to be maintained by unsuppressed lightning fires, but they suspect that such fires will be too uncommon to
contribute even this small fraction to the fire restoration program (Pengelly, unpublished presentation 2003).

Park managers use a comprehensive ecological survey and maps of
site types, fuel types, and stand origination dates to determine desired
future conditions for the forest landscape, including locations and sizes
of areas to be treated (White and others 2004). Changes in forest development (succession) through time are modeled across the landscape.
Age classes of stands in a given area are compared with historic fire intervals to see how much of the forest is overdue for burning. This helps
determine burning priorities and points to practical considerations like
smoke impacts and potential difficulties in controlling a burn.

Pengelly (unpublished presentation 2003) observed that planned
burns would ideally match all of the characteristics of historical fire
regimes, including fire intervals, fire sizes, effects on tree canopies, effects on the soil, and season of burning. However, it is clearly not feasible to re-create historic stand replacement fires that today would pose
great hazard and loss to society. The Banff program uses a compromise
approach by setting good-sized prescribed stand replacement fires—
often about 2,500 acres (1,000 ha)—using natural boundaries and minimal fire line control. Crews sometimes end up containing or herding
the edges of a fire for 2 weeks or longer. Managers have burned often
along the park's eastern boundary to help contain future fires that will
be ignited farther west within the park (White and others 2004). These
boundary fires may allow park managers the latitude to burn in mid-
summer, as they did with more than 2,500 acres (1,000 ha) of the
Fairholme burn in 2003.

Banff's fire managers use several techniques to achieve stand replacement burning with good control at moderate expense. Pengelly
estimated that the average burning cost is about US$35 per acre ($105
Canadian per ha). In mountainous terrain, major differences in fuel
moisture often coincide with changes in aspect; thus, part of the fire
perimeter could adjoin a less flammable slope (Pengelly, unpublished
presentation 2003). Fire managers often try to burn coniferous forests
on west- or south-facing slopes in late May, when the ground has recently become snow free and adjacent cooler aspects are still snow covered. At this time new herbaceous growth has not yet developed, surface
fuels are cured, and conifer foliage is relatively dry and flammable. These

conditions allow a crown fire to develop, which produces less smoke and little smoldering due to high moisture levels in the surface fuels. A tactic fire managers use in early fall is to burn a lodgepole pine forest when adjacent grasslands and deciduous fuel types are still green. Sometimes burns are scheduled just ahead of forecasted season-ending rain and snow. Near developments, fire managers create forested fuel breaks as insurance against wildfire or possible problems with prescribed fire (White and others 2004).

The fire restoration program has benefited by informing the public about the role of fire and cooperating with other landowners to address their concerns. For instance, Parks Canada has been working with other agencies and communities to develop a cooperative approach for reducing threats of severe bark beetle epidemics (Banff National Park 2002). By the year 2000, beetle epidemics were building to the highest levels ever observed, with British Columbia recording 14 million acres (5.7 million ha) of outbreaks. Because of fire suppression, most lodgepole pine stands in Banff and adjacent parks are more than 100 years old and highly susceptible to beetle attacks. Parks Canada reasons that approximating the historical fire regime will reduce the spread of catastrophic bark beetle epidemics through the parks and into adjacent provincial and privately owned forests. Banff's land managers are designing the prescribed burning program to break up the continuity of old, beetle-susceptible forests. Restoring a forest age distribution more consistent with historic conditions should also reduce susceptibility to beetles on a landscape scale.

Similarly, biologists worry that postfire communities rich in wildlife forage are gradually vanishing as a result of fire suppression. The legume sweetvetch (*Hedysarum* spp.), the shrub buffaloberry, and the sprouting (suckering) hardwood quaking aspen all depend on periodic fires to maintain any abundance in the lodgepole pine zone. These and other fire-dependent forage plants are critical for supporting populations of elk and grizzly bear and indirectly for meeting the needs of wolves. Important ecological functions and associated human benefits provide justification and guidance for the fire restoration program in Banff and other nearby parks.

Chapter **13**

Whitebark Pine

Until the late 1970s, most foresters and ecologists knew little about a slow-growing high-mountain conifer called whitebark pine. During the next 20 years scientists learned that this obscure tree is actually a critical component or "keystone species" in high mountain ecosystems (Tomback, Arno, and Keane 2001). Healthy whitebark pine populations are the centerpiece of an interconnected, high-elevation world of plants and animals. Whitebark pines also shelter the snowpack and stabilize thin, rocky soils, helping protect the quality of water flowing from alpine sources.

Whitebark pine cone crops are an important and sometimes crucial food source for squirrels, certain birds, black bears, and especially grizzly bears, which are listed as an endangered species in the United States outside of Alaska. Wildlife biologists in the Rocky Mountains learned that when whitebark pine produces a bountiful cone crop, the high fat content in the nutlike seeds ensures ample nutrition for grizzly bears entering hibernation and throughout the following year (Mattson, Kendall, and Reinhart 2001). Good cone crops contribute to reproductive success by allowing well-nourished females to produce larger litters of cubs. When whitebark pine seeds are available, grizzlies in the greater Yellowstone National Park area seldom prowl around ranches or campsites in search of food, thereby avoiding conflicts with humans that lead to bears getting killed.

The revelation of whitebark pine's significance for grizzly bears was just one small part of a fascinating ecological story that was beginning to unfold. Although whitebark pine is the key species in its high-mountain ecosystem, fire was soon identified as the primary disturbance that perpetuates this tree in the Rocky Mountains and the other inland mountain ranges where it flourishes (Arno 1986). Paradoxically, the emerging story of whitebark pine shows that despite occupying remote, high-elevation country, largely in national parks and wilderness areas, this remarkable tree is declining due to unintended consequences of human activities. Humans accidentally introduced a Eurasian fungal disease—white pine blister rust (*Cronartium ribicola*)—that has weakened and killed much of the whitebark pine. Also, the long-established policy of trying to eliminate fire in forests has especially affected whitebark pine. Reinstating fire is the first step in restoring whitebark pine and its habitat in regions where it is fire-dependent, and several restoration projects that include fire are now underway in Idaho and Montana.

However, before delving into specific restoration activities, we first need to understand the components of whitebark pine's fire-dependent ecosystem. Whitebark pine stands produce abundant cone crops at intervals of about 2–5 years. The cones, which take 2 years to mature, contain nutritious seeds about the size of a pea that are locked inside tightly closed cones. Unlike those of most other conifers, whitebark pine's cone scales do not spread open when the seeds ripen. Furthermore, whitebark seeds lack the papery wings found on most conifer seeds. Without a means of dispersal, whitebark pine seeds cannot fall to the ground or be carried by the wind to places where they might germinate. Instead, they have to be physically extracted from the cone by animals, and few are up to the task. One that is, the pine squirrel, "harvests" the closed cones in late summer by deftly nipping them from the branches, then collects and stores the cones in hollow logs, stump holes, and heaps on the ground known as middens. Black bears and grizzlies eagerly hunt for squirrel caches, crush the cones under their paws, and separate the seeds as best they can, then spit out the woody cone scales somewhat like a human eating sunflower seeds. Chipmunks, ground squirrels, deer mice, other rodents, and several species of birds also dine on any loose seeds generated by cone caching. Pine squirrels and bears continue to feed on seeds for as long as 12 months after they are cached (Mattson, Kendall, and Reinhart 2001). When first emerging from their dens in the spring, bears often paw through several feet of remaining snowpack to raid a cone cache.

Despite the millions of seeds harvested by squirrels, very few ever produce whitebark pine seedlings. Another major seed predator, Clark's nutcracker, is directly responsible for establishing virtually all whitebark pine trees (Tomback 2001). This jaylike bird competes with squirrels to harvest whitebark pine seeds. While squirrels chatter away and nip cones down, nutcrackers communicate to each other with a "kra-a-a" and other calls as they work their way through the tree tops, alighting on cones and hammering into them with their long, sharp beaks. They quickly pull out the contents, seed by seed, diverting them into the nutcracker's version of a food bag—a special throat pouch that can hold 100 or more seeds.

What nutcrackers do next is crucial for maintaining whitebark pine populations. The birds fly off with a pouch full of seeds and land nearby or as far as several miles away (Tomback 2001), caching their bounty by burying 1–15 seeds at a time about an inch deep. Biologist Diana Tomback of the University of Colorado at Denver has studied this mutually beneficial relationship between nutcrackers and whitebark pine since the 1970s. She and other biologists have observed the nutcracker's pinpoint accuracy in relocating thousands of seed caches that were deposited as many as 9 months earlier (Tomback 2001). Fortuitously, nutcrackers also leave many seed caches unharvested, especially following large cone crops, and the unclaimed seeds become future whitebark pine forests. Nutcrackers prefer to cache seeds in open areas created by recent burns or other disturbances, or on severely windswept sites. These are good places for the slow-growing whitebark saplings to get established in the absence of faster growing or more shade-tolerant conifers that out-compete them for growing space. Nearly all whitebark pine trees originate from these nutcracker-sown seed caches.

In places where fire is rare and competition from shade-tolerant conifers is intense, such as the crest of the Cascade Range, whitebark pine is confined to a narrow strip at the uppermost limit of trees. By contrast, in high mountains farther inland where fire is common, whitebark pine occupies a broad zone of subalpine forest because it is well suited to colonizing disturbed sites exposed to harsh growing conditions. Fire exclusion has now greatly reduced the amount of burning in whitebark pine habitats, in part because extensive burning in this high country historically occurred only when fires covered vast areas at all elevations, a situation that is not permissible today. Due to reduced burning in subalpine forests, whitebark pine is out-competed by other conifers, making it easy prey for bark beetle attacks.

Whitebark pine's primary nemesis, blister rust, has killed or fatally weakened most of the whitebark trees in many northwestern mountain ranges, and this disease is increasing in the greater Yellowstone region

(Kendall and Keane 2001). A few whitebark pine trees are resistant to blister rust, and abundant regeneration from resistant trees could potentially counteract the rust's onslaught (Hoff and others 2001). However, burned areas are needed for successful regeneration of new seedlings, and breeding programs are necessary to ensure that enough seeds from rust-resistant trees are available to produce seedlings in suitable sites. Thus, prescribed burning and propagation of rust-resistant seedlings are key components of whitebark pine restoration projects.

Ecologist Bob Keane at the U.S. Forest Service's Fire Sciences Laboratory in Missoula, Montana, has studied whitebark pine communities since the 1980s. He has developed models that simulate growth, mortality, and successional change in whitebark pine stands through time. Keane's models simulate whitebark's response to disturbances such as blister rust epidemics, bark beetle outbreaks, fires, and prolonged absence of fire (Keane 2001). The models reveal factors driving whitebark's widespread and sometimes catastrophic decline. Expanding blister rust and bark beetle epidemics, and a dearth of open, burned sites are allowing other conifers to replace whitebark (Kendall and Keane 2001). Tomback is concerned that seed-producing whitebark pine are becoming so scarce in some areas that cone cutting by squirrels and seed harvesting by nutcrackers will prevent regeneration, rather than help it. Also, without fire to create openings and kill competing fir and spruce, nutcrackers will find few open areas to cache seeds where they can develop into whitebark pine trees. The few rust resistant pines might not pass this trait along to new generations because there are seldom openings for seedling establishment.

Tomback studied large, quarter-century-old burns in whitebark pine habitats of the Northern Rockies. She found that burned areas that had seed sources nearby regenerated well to whitebark pine, presumably because birds transported the seeds (Tomback 1994). Fir and spruce regeneration depend on wind transport, and their seeds tend to travel shorter distances into big burns. Therefore, a potentially effective treatment for restoring whitebark pine is to allow lightning fires to burn high-elevation habitats wherever possible. This approach is being followed in a few large national parks and wilderness areas; however, even in these reserves lightning fires often must be snuffed out near area boundaries. The majority of natural areas are considered too small to permit significant return of natural fires (Agee 2000).

Allowing lightning fires to burn whenever possible is important, but studies in a large wilderness area show that this practice alone is not sufficient for returning fire to whitebark pine habitats (Brown and others 1994). Creating numerous suitable sites for whitebark pine regeneration could help counteract the effects of fire exclusion, beetle epidemics, and blister rust. This is where prescribed fires and perhaps cutting treatments can serve as substitutes for the decades of suppressed natural fires.

Prescribed burning in whitebark pine habitats presents a challenge because they become dry enough to burn only in late summer. At that time, nearby lower elevation forests are tinderboxes in danger of severe wildfire. At lower elevations, early-season spring burning can be effective if it is conducted soon after the snowpack melts and before new grass, herb, and shrub leaves develop. In high-elevation whitebark pine stands, however, by the time the snowpack has finally melted in July, green-up is already well underway. Here, prescribed burning is generally limited to early autumn, after a hard frost has caused leaf-fall from huckleberry and other deciduous plants, creating fine fuels that help carry a fire. Frost also induces dormancy in beargrass and other evergreen plants, reducing plant moisture contents to 40–50 percent, which is low enough to sustain fire (Keane 2002).

Keane has found that a few days of sunny weather after a cold front that brings light snow and sharp frost is often sufficient to dry surface fuels—a situation commonly occurring in late September or early October (Figure 13.1). He prefers burning at midday during sunny weather when relative humidity is near or below 30 percent. Moderate winds can disperse the smoke column and allow fire to expand through the fuel bed. Fire coverage is generally patchy with scattered torching of subalpine fir clumps and thickets. Surface burning is often incomplete at first, but fire can smolder for days in rotten logs and duff and then creep into unburned patches on warm dry afternoons.

Since 1994 Keane has worked with fire managers to apply prescribed burning in restoration projects on the Bitterroot, Lolo, and Flathead national forests (Montana) and the Clearwater, Targhee, and Salmon-Challis national forests (Idaho). Where feasible, they first fell some of the fir and spruce trees to create cured slash, allowing an autumn fire to burn hot enough to cover a greater proportion of the area and torch dense patches of trees. Burning is focused in areas of suitable

Figure 13.1.
Prescribed burn in whitebark pine habitat in early autumn. (U.S. Forest Service photo)

habitat where few cone-bearing whitebarks remain. Some small white-bark pines are killed by fire, but in these crowded stands they proba-bly would not have matured enough to bear cones. The more intense the prescribed fire, the greater the number of competing conifers that will be killed. The charred ground attracts nutcrackers to cache seeds in places suitable for new whitebarks to develop.

In areas where blister rust has killed or badly damaged most of the mature whitebark pines, Keane suggests planting treated sites with rust-resistant seedlings. In areas heavily affected by rust, a small percentage of mature whitebark pines remain undamaged and periodically bear cone crops. The proportion of rust-resistant individuals among seedlings produced from these cones is expected to be higher than in the general population. The Forest Service tree nursery at Coeur d'Alene, Idaho, nurtures crops of these potentially more resistant seedlings for planting on restoration sites. The hardest part is finding and protecting enough of the developing cones by early July to keep them from being consumed by squirrels or nutcrackers. Horticulturist Karen Burr safeguards the maturing cones in the tree crowns using cages made from hardware cloth. In areas where only a few cone-bearing whitebark pine trees survive, animals normally harvest all unprotected seeds (Burr, Eramian, and Eggleston 2001).

Keane's largest restoration study site sits atop Beaver Ridge on the Clearwater National Forest in Idaho, near Lolo Pass. During dry warm weather in late September 2002, forest managers burned a 200-acre area, part of which contained felled fir trees (Keane 2002). Under these ideal conditions fire burned in a highly variable pattern, in some places torching out patches of tall fir and spruce trees, in others killing trees by surface burning or thinning them out by low-intensity burning. Vir-tually any fire favors whitebark pine over fire-sensitive subalpine fir, but fires that create relatively large openings are most beneficial be-cause they can give whitebark pine saplings a head start over compet-ing conifers.

The best prospect for restoring whitebark pine on a landscape scale is convincing forest and park managers to allow more lightning fires to burn in its high-elevation habitat (Campbell 2001). Effective restora-tion also depends on continuing progress in propagating rust-resistant seedlings (Hoff and others 2001). The small restoration treatments that Keane and his colleagues are conducting hold promise, but only if they can be refined and greatly expanded. To this end, the Whitebark Pine Ecosystem Foundation is leading a rangewide assessment of this species as a basis for prioritizing restoration projects. Further information on whitebark pine ecology and restoration activities is available on the foundation's Web site (www.whitebarkfound.org).

Chapter 14

Restoring Aspen and Conifers across a Ranger District

Taking advantage of a strong market for forest residues and a congressional mandate to reduce hazardous fuels, the Eagle Lake Ranger District of the Lassen National Forest has developed a broad program of forest restoration. The district's restoration initiative follows the concept of ecosystem-based management by attempting to restore a semblance of historical vegetative conditions and the processes that produced them. The key ingredient is the staff's dedication to developing, testing, and improving restoration strategies. They begin designing restoration by gathering information about past and current ecological conditions. Then they analyze information, consult with experts, plan the project, test treatments, and monitor results. Finally, they evaluate to see if the approach is meeting restoration goals, or if revised methods are needed.

The Eagle Lake Ranger District is located in a mountainous, sparsely populated region of northeastern California. The district extends about 30 miles west and north from the small city of Susanville and adjoins the eastern boundary of Lassen Volcanic National Park. It covers about 300,000 acres of the volcanic upland that connects the southern end of the Cascade Range to the northern end of the Sierra Nevada. Most of the land lies between elevations of 4,500 and 6,500 feet, with scattered peaks rising 1,000 feet higher. The district supports relatively dry forest habitats that typify the eastern slope of the southern Cascades and northern Sierra Nevada. During the 1990s, studies of ecological evidence revealed that the principal vegetation types were commonly outside the range of their historical conditions (McKelvey and others 1996, Taylor 1999). This includes sagebrush/grassland, now colonized by young conifers; open-grown ponderosa pine/bunchgrass communities, now supporting dense stands of trees; mixed conifer/ shrub communities, now experiencing senescence and heavy mortality; and aspen/riparian-broadleaved communities, now replaced by conifers. Gruell (2001) compared dozens of historical landscape photographs with recent retakes and documented similar changes in vegetation since the 19th century. The district has restoration projects underway in all of these vegetation types.

History of Forest Management on the Eagle Lake Ranger District

Asked why his district pioneered such an expansive restoration program, ranger Bob Andrews sketched events starting in the 1970s. At that time Forest Service recognized that thickening forests and accumulating fuels were promoting increasingly dangerous wildfires (Pyne 1982). To combat this problem, federal wildland fire policy shifted from its narrow focus on suppression to a broader program of managing fire and fuels (Nelson 1979). The federal government also began cooperatively planning biomass energy plants with the state of California. As a response to the 1970s oil shortage and a federal initiative to develop domestic energy sources, these plants would supply electricity to the power grid. By the mid-1980s, five energy plants in northern California were using hog-fuel chips from small trees and logging slash to produce about 150 megawatts of power. Within several years, the Eagle Lake Ranger District was providing 5,000 semitrailer vans full of chips annually to help keep the biomass plants running. The low thinning treatments that produce the hog fuel also provide an average of 10 million board feet of small sawlogs annually. The power plants pay enough for chips to partially offset the cost of removing, chipping, and hauling nonmerchantable trees thinned from dense forests. Sending forest fuels to a biomass plant is often the least expensive way of disposing of them. By 2003, the district had removed the excess small trees on about 40,000 acres of forest in conjunction with the biomass energy program.

The biomass energy and fuel reduction program enabled the district to explore concepts of forest restoration, but first the staff had to adopt an ecological perspective. This viewpoint emerged in the mid-1980s with an interdisciplinary planning project aimed at restoring stream habitat for the Eagle Lake trout (*Oncorhynchus mykiss aquilarum*), an isolated subspecies whose populations were declining.

In the early 1990s, another interdisciplinary team convened to deal with fuel buildups resulting from mass mortality of white fir (*Abies concolor* var. *lowiana*). The team discovered that the catastrophic die-off was linked to drought and overcrowded forests resulting from fire exclusion. They concluded that resolving the underlying problem called for a long-term management strategy.

At this time, the Forest Service's Washington, D.C., office was promoting "ecosystem management"—an approach to maintaining forests that attempts to restore the effects of historical processes such as fire and natural succession (Salwasser and Pfister 1994). District wildlife biologist Tom Rickman was interested in how past successional changes had affected wildlife habitat. He compared historic vegetation identified from 19th-century land survey records and early 1940s aerial photographs with modern vegetation on the same sites. District personnel helped persuade ecologists from universities and research stations to study successional changes and fire history in different vegetation types on the district. One alarming revelation was that conifer encroachment and excessive use by deer and cattle were displacing aspen groves, a critical habitat for wildlife. Ecological studies also showed that in past centuries frequent fires maintained the dry pine forests as scattered trees growing amid productive semiarid grassland (Taylor 1999). Historical records and accounts revealed that by the late 1800s unregulated livestock grazing had devastated much of the bunchgrass. By the mid-20th century, suppression of fires and selective harvesting of large trees allowed small trees to proliferate.

Andrews recalls a pivotal incident occurred while the district's interdisciplinary team was inspecting a beetle-killed stand that had been salvage-logged and planted to ponderosa pine. Silviculturist Al Vazquez pulled up some seedlings of *Ceanothus* shrubs to keep them from competing with tree regeneration. In response, biologist Rickman plucked out a pine seedling to emphasize that trees suppress *Ceanothus* and other forage plants important for wildlife. This helped district personnel expand their consciousness from concern primarily about trees to considering all vegetation. As time went on, the district staff learned more about past and present conditions and the ecological implications of the changes. They agreed to devise management plans aimed at restoring habitats based on the range of historical conditions. Benefits of restoration include wildfire hazard reduction, diverse wildlife populations, and sustainable harvest of forest products.

In 1998 Congress passed the Herger-Feinstein Quincy Library Group Forest Recovery Act, which required implementing a system of forested fuel breaks, group-selection and individual tree-selection units, and riparian area management on seven ranger districts, including the Eagle Lake District. The fuel breaks, termed defensible fuel profile zones (DFPZs), are designed and strategically situated—usually along roads—to reduce the size of stand replacement fires. The DFPZs are about one-quarter mile wide, fairly open strips dominated by fire-tolerant trees, with most surface and ladder fuels removed. The act specifies that DFPZs are the initial step in a long-term fuel reduction program aimed at area-wide fuel treatment. A long-term program might employ the selection system to perpetuate relatively open uneven-aged stands that include old growth. In addition to wildfire protection, the act promotes treatments intended to ensure a flow of timber to help maintain jobs and infrastructure in timber-dependent communities. The government covered the costs of implementing the DFPZs, allowing the district to expand its restoration activities.

Continuing wildfire threats to forest communities created public support for the district's fuel treatments. In May 2001 a human-caused forest fire forced evacuation of Susanville's hospital. In September 2002 the Cone fire burned 2,000 acres on the district, largely within Blacks Mountain Experimental Forest. A towering wall of flames roared through the untreated forest. However, when this crown fire reached stands that had previously been thinned and underburned, it cooled and became a controllable surface fire that killed few trees. The district quantified the effectiveness of these treatments in reducing wildfire damage (Vazquez and Hood 2003). They also produced educational posters demonstrating the differential behavior of the Cone fire in treated and untreated stands. Wildfire suppression costs exceeded $1,700 per acre, whereas the thinning and underburning treatments that saved trees and permitted control of the fire had a net cost of only about $200 per acre.

During the 1990s much of the emphasis in wildlife management focused on preserving dense forests for sensitive species such as the spotted owl, pine marten, and fisher. However, Rickman and his colleagues on the Eagle Lake District recognized that dense forests represented a highly unstable condition caused by ecological imbalances. Livestock overgrazing a century ago initiated changes by removing the grassy fine fuels that allowed fires to spread. Historically, strong competition from grasses also limited the establishment of conifer seedlings. Then, beginning in the early 1900s, exclusion of fire allowed copious tree regeneration, further compounding the downward spiral of a fire-dependent ecosystem.

The resulting, disrupted forest communities were highly susceptible to destructive wildfire, insects, and disease, contrasting sharply with the open-grown fire-adapted forests of the past. Rickman became convinced that instead of trying to protect unnaturally dense stands, the district should restore functioning old-growth ecosystems. These would have structures like historical stands, including fire-dependent herbs, shrubs, and trees. The restored landscape would have appropriate proportions of early successional vegetation such as meadows, aspen groves, shrubfields, and pine savannas.

In 1993 Congress ordered a comprehensive study of the status of forests in the Sierra Nevada and southern Cascades to assist the government in making policy to guide management. The final report on the Sierra Nevada Ecosystem Project, published in 1996, emphasized the ecological importance of fire in these forests and the problems caused by continuing attempts to exclude it. Nevertheless, the Sierra Nevada Forest Plan Amendment (also called the "Sierra Nevada Framework") that appeared in January 2001 disrupted restoration activities by placing heavy constraints on thinning in overcrowded forests. Instead, the amendment relied primarily on prescribed fire for restoration, not recognizing the extreme difficulty of using fire alone to remove large numbers of excess trees without damaging the remaining trees. In 2003 the Forest Service regional office was rethinking this amendment and considering revisions that would allow Eagle Lake and other districts to resume and improve upon their restoration activities.

Despite such discouraging constraints, the Eagle Lake Ranger District's vegetation management objective is to restore structure and species composition similar to that of the original fire-maintained landscapes. This management direction is based on the premise that maintaining an ecosystem within its range of natural variability is the most scientifically credible way of sustaining habitat for viable populations of native species. The district's restoration program is informed by knowledge from published research, scientific studies, historical inventories, and measurements of current conditions. When current vegetation is far outside the range of conditions that occurred historically, restoration may require a series of corrective treatments conducted over

Figure 14.1.
Aspen regeneration following a restoration treatment, Eagle Lake Ranger District, Lassen National Forest. (S. Arno photo)

a considerable period. In the short term, silvicultural cutting, prescribed burning, and other practices are designed to incrementally move vegetative communities toward desired conditions.

Restoration of Aspen Groves

The district's most intensive restoration efforts are to save the disappearing aspen groves—a process that silviculturist Vazquez compares to administering life-saving CPR. Aspen provides critical nesting habitat for several species of songbirds and is heavily used as forage by big game and livestock. Historically, frequent fires reduced competition from conifers and stimulated aspen to sucker (resprout) from their extensive root system. Photographs and range appraisals of the district from as early as the 1920s indicate a lack of aspen reproduction that was linked to grazing. During recent decades aspen throughout much of the West has been giving way to conifers or has been overused and damaged by big game and livestock (Bartos 2001). Nevertheless, only

a few ranger districts or other land managers have made large-scale efforts to restore aspen.

The Eagle Lake District inventoried and mapped aspen groves, including the tiny remnants nearly shaded out by conifers, using criteria
that assess conifer competition and the success of aspen regeneration.
Based on the latest scientific knowledge, the district made management
recommendations for each grove (Shepperd 2001). As of 2002, about
75 percent of the district had been surveyed, including 430 aspen
groves that cover 2,500 acres. More than 80 percent of these are considered at high risk of being lost. Environmental analyses have called
for conifer removal or fencing to protect most aspen groves. By summer 2003 more than 100 groves had been treated. Groves treated in
1999 responded with a three-fold increase in the number of aspen
stems per acre (Figure 14.1). Long-term monitoring plots and photo
points are established in representative stands to determine the response
to treatments. Depending on monitoring results, additional treatments
such as prescribed burning or ground ripping may be implemented
to stimulate root suckers.

Restoration of Ponderosa Pine Stands

Ponderosa pine now dominates lower elevations and dry forest sites on
the Eagle Lake District. The district staff was astonished when they
compared historic and current vegetation on these sites. Large areas that
showed in 1941 aerial photos as meadow or dry grassland sprinkled
with saplings appear as thick forest in recent photos. The tree invasion
actually started much earlier. A range report from 1910 stated that
conifer reproduction was so abundant on heavily grazed sites that
stockmen predicted trees would replace grass if fire was not returned
to the range.

General Land Office surveys from the 1870s, forest reconnaissance
reports from the 1910s, 1946 inventory data from virgin stands, and recent ecological studies show that most 19th-century ponderosa pine
stands on the district had an average of only 20–30 medium and large
trees (greater than 12 inches in diameter) per acre and few small trees
(Taylor 1999). These stands were open-grown—less than 30 percent
canopy coverage and sometimes even a savanna—which fostered a
lush grass undergrowth. The open structure developed in response to

low-intensity burning that occurred about every 5–10 years, a pattern that continued until the late 1800s (Taylor 1999). When the Forest Service officially recognized that fire exclusion helped produce dense pine forests prone to crown fires, it proposed remedies in the form of thinning, fuel removal, and prescribed burning.

The Eagle Lake District staff takes a broader view of the consequences of fire exclusion. They conclude that the replacement of meadow, mountain grassland, and open grassy forest by conifer thickets has degraded plant diversity and habitat values for many wildlife species. They reason that excessive fuels are just a symptom of a damaged ecosystem requiring restoration. Rickman agrees with Covington and Moore (1994b), who compared the population explosion of trees that followed disruption of the natural fire cycle to the overpopulation, forage depletion, and mass die-offs that plagued western deer herds when predators were removed in the early 1900s.

Even today it is easy to tell which pine stands represent invaded grasslands and which ones were historically open forests. Relict old-growth ponderosa pine trees or old stumps are present among the younger trees on sites that were originally forested. However, remnants of old growth are absent from the young stands that occupy former grasslands. Most of the ponderosa pine encroachment occurred in the first half of the 1900s, but other encroachment, including lodgepole pine saplings colonizing meadows in frost-prone basins, didn't occur until the 1960s or later.

As of 2003, the district had removed young trees from small areas of former meadows and grasslands, but on many thousands of acres it had begun the process of re-creating open, old-growth pine forests. The relict ponderosa pine trees are often 3–4 feet thick and 400 years old or older, with eye-catching platy orange bark. Old pines are physiologically weaker than the young trees that now surround them (Biondi 1996), and vulnerable to bark beetle attacks. Removing young trees from around these ancient pines is a top priority for the district.

The district's long-term objective, or "Desired Future Conditions," for the ponderosa pine communities includes mixtures of open- and medium-canopied stands with basal areas ranging from 25 to 100 square feet per acre. The stands will be dominated by large trees, commonly with 10 or more trees per acre greater than 24 inches in diameter. The understory will be open and grassy with only small, scattered patches of tree regeneration. Because of frequent burning there will be little fuel accumulation, and no more than two standing snags and fallen trees per acre.

The district often uses DFPZ funding to initiate restoration. One of these projects is the Bidwell DFPZ timber sale, which was nearing completion in 2003. It included restoring 20 acres of aspen, 18 acres of tree-invaded meadow, and more than 300 acres of ponderosa pine forest on a relatively productive site. The initial treatment was a low thinning that reduced stand density from 800 trees per acre to 107. Thinning lowered the average basal area from 327 square feet per acre to 139, while average tree diameter nearly doubled to 15 inches. Tree canopy cover was reduced by about half, to 34 percent. The treatment area occupies gentle terrain, and existing roads provide access. Whole-tree harvesting was done using a feller-buncher, and trees were processed at landings into sawlogs and hog-fuel chips. Harvesting removed about 45 tons of biomass chips and more than 3,000 board feet of small sawlogs per acre. The sale generated more than $200 per acre in revenue, while the cost of preparing, marking, and administering the sale was about $145 per acre.

Harvesting equipment that travels repeatedly over the same area can severely compact soils. The Eagle Lake District hosted a study of the effects of subsoil "ripping" to rehabilitate compacted areas. A crawler tractor pulling knifelike blades slanted upward "rips" or lifts the subsoil several inches, yet the ground surface remains substantially in place. Preliminary results suggest that ripping reduces harvest-related compaction, so it is being applied to major skid trails and landings on many sites. Increasingly, harvesting is done on snowpack or frozen ground to reduce or eliminate soil compaction and to avoid disturbing nesting goshawks and other sensitive species.

The district's fire staff typically underburns restoration units 1 or 2 years after thinning. This allows time for the remaining trees to gain vigor in response to the increased growing room, moisture, and nutrients. With whole-tree removal and chipping of slash, only modest amounts of woody fuel remain after thinning. The accumulated duff and pine needle litter is a more consistent fuel, and duff mounds several inches thick are common at the base of old-growth trees. Still, the underburns usually cause little mortality in overstory trees. The goal of burning is commonly to reduce surface and ladder fuels by 50–70 percent and to stimulate production and diversity of grasses, other herbs, and shrubs, which are important features of wildlife habitat. Prescribed fire is used as a surrogate for the frequent fires of the pre-1900 period—recycling soil nutrients and restoring an approximation of natural ecological processes and their myriad unknown effects. Burning is conducted either in spring or fall during a window of opportunity when fuel moisture, weather, and smoke dispersal are favorable. Some of the large ponderosa pine restoration units being burned contain stringers of riparian habitat. Prescribed fire is often allowed to spread into these areas to help rejuvenate early successional shrubs and broadleaved trees.

The district burns about 4,000 acres annually, although windows of opportunity and the actual extent of burning vary considerably among years. In fall 2001, favorable conditions allowed crews of 10–15 people to underburn 2,300 acres of thinned forest in a 5-day period for about $50 per acre—one-third less than the average cost of underburning. The large units in this project were surrounded by roads, making fire-line construction unnecessary. Monitoring showed a significant increase in grass cover during the first year after burning. The district staff is also tracking response of bitterbrush and other shrubs and comparing effects of spring versus fall burning.

District personnel are particularly interested in the effects of fire on old-growth trees so they can identify situations in which special protection may be needed, such as previously scarred trees or trees with fine roots growing in accumulated duff. Although the original ponderosa pine forest was largely dominated by old growth, only a small fraction of these trees remains. The district's long-term goal is to return forests that again feature large old pines. The initial low thinning and fuel reduction treatments will be followed by some form of selection cutting—now being studied—to regenerate new age classes of pine and ultimately develop fire-resistant, uneven-aged stands.

Restoration of Mixed-Conifer/Shrub Communities

The western slope of the Sierra Nevada and southern Cascades harbors a rich mixed-conifer forest highlighted by massive sugar pines with spreading upper limbs bearing foot-long cones. Although this diverse forest assemblage occurs locally in small areas of the Eagle Lake Ranger District, a dry inland climate generally restricts the mixed conifer zone to domination by just white fir and ponderosa and Jeffrey pines. The ecologically comparable Jeffrey pine replaces ponderosa at about 6,000 feet in elevation. Prior to 1900, frequent mixed-severity fires created a shifting mosaic of forest patches with different structure and composition (Taylor 1999). These included postfire shrubfields, young pine/shrub communities, patches of open-grown mature pine, and old pine with a fir understory.

Fire exclusion and selective logging of the large pines accelerated succession to crowded stands of the shade-tolerant white fir (Taylor 1999). *Ceanothus,* bittercherry, willow, elderberry, and other fire-dependent shrubs important for wildlife died out. In the 1980s and early 1990s prolonged drought triggered insect epidemics that killed vast numbers of firs. Dead firs in turn created fuel accumulations that could rapidly kindle a wildfire.

After conducting several sanitation/salvage harvests in heavily damaged mixed-conifer forests during the 1990s, Vazquez concluded that he was only applying a bandage to a broken ecosystem. Instead, he wanted to enhance and protect the remaining old-growth pines and allow them to regenerate. The techniques chosen would need to replace a fir-dominated landscape with a patchwork of different forest communities, many of which featured pine and early successional shrubs. Meanwhile, very restrictive prescription guidelines were being developed for the greater Sierra Nevada region to preserve "old forest" areas for the spotted owl and some other sensitive species. To test the conflicting concepts about how to maintain mixed-conifer forests, the district decided to apply and evaluate two contrasting treatments on Harvey Mountain in a dense fir forest containing old-growth pine.

In the "nonmerchantable thinning" treatment, small trees up to 10 inches in diameter were removed from within 30 feet of dominant old pines. This approach was consistent with the recommendations for preserving "old forest" in the 2001 Sierra Nevada Forest Plan Amendment. After thinning, the stand averaged about 65 percent fir and 35 percent pine. The small trees removed produced very little revenue to offset treatment cost, which averaged about $1,000 per acre. This expense precludes application on any significant scale. The non-merchantable thinning removed enough of the ladder fuels to reduce the hazard of crown fire for perhaps 20 years until a fir understory redevelops. Treatment improved growing conditions for the old pines but did not open the stand enough to encourage natural regeneration of pine or a major increase in seral shrubs.

The other technique, a "comprehensive thinning," removed almost all of the fir up to 24 inches in diameter, leaving an open stand of nearly pure pine. The value of harvested fir nearly paid for treatment, leaving a cost to the district of only $11 per acre. The harvest removed virtually all ladder fuels. Comprehensive thinning increased available soil moisture as determined by district monitoring, which enhanced conditions for survival of the old-growth pine. The stand is also sufficiently open to encourage regeneration of pine and shrubs. Fir will regenerate from seed blown in from adjacent stands, but it will probably be several decades before it can develop into extensive thickets. The thinned stand can be treated with prescribed fire, which would further stimulate regeneration and forage and return an important ecological process.

Selection Systems for Maintaining Forests

Much of the district's mixed-conifer forest needs thinning and lacks young pines. The Herger-Feinstein Quincy Library Group Act required that group-selection cutting be implemented on about 700 acres per year in numerous small openings of 2 acres or less, but with all trees greater than 30 inches in diameter retained. The district received approval for 400 acres of group-selection cuttings scattered across several sections of land west of Pegleg Mountain. The small cutting units are laid out sparsely—only 6–12 per square mile. As of 2003, the district had more than 700 acres of group-selection units in various stages of implementation. About 300 acres of these are located in previously thinned stands, where they add structural diversity. Some were positioned to remove pockets of encroaching fir or clumps of dwarf mistletoe-infected trees. Selection-cutting units were spatially arranged so they could be reentered every 20 years to create a new age class. The 2001 forest plan amendment set restrictions that disrupted this process; but in 2003 revisions were proposed that would restore the district's ability to keep up its selection-cutting program. Still, Vazquez is concerned about the feasibility of maintaining a large-scale group-selection system, which schedules treatments over long time frames, if it is highly vulnerable to shifts in regional forest policy.

Canopy-closure requirements for sensitive wildlife species heavily restrict the application of regeneration cutting, including selection cutting. Still, the district's group-selection program is a tool for returning elements of the historic fuel conditions, stand structure, and undergrowth composition. Continuing similar group-selection treatments over the decades in other patches within the overall area will help produce a multi-aged, mixed pine-fir forest patterned after forests of the past. Prescribed burning is planned after harvesting is complete.

The district staff is up to its eyebrows evaluating and adapting management to better achieve restoration. They haven't figured out how to address all restoration needs, given the heavy restrictions placed on forest treatments. For example, how can they restore a large-patch mosaic that historically characterized some high-elevation true fir stands? They question guidelines that simply try to preserve forest cover while ignoring how much today's forest deviates from the range of historical conditions and the implications of such distortions. Wildlife biologist Rickman states these concerns succinctly: "Preserving the unnatural is folly."

Chapter 15

Restoring Fire on a Wilderness Landscape

Viewed from a small plane or a mountaintop, Idaho's Clearwater River and Salmon River backcountry spreads to hazy horizons as an endless succession of rugged ridges and dark canyons. Despite its rocky composition, this landscape is mostly covered with trees. South-facing slopes in the driest canyons are clothed with patches of ponderosa pine, grassland, and sagebrush. At the other extreme, north-facing slopes in humid areas harbor nearly impenetrable jungles of spruce, hemlock, fir, and 25-foot-tall shrubs, including mountain maple, serviceberry, Scouler willow, elderberry, and mountain-ash. Ecosystems in the Clearwater and Salmon river mountains were molded over thousands of years by recurrent fires. Stand replacement fires predominated in the north. Farther south, dry canyons hosted frequent understory fires while other sites were subject to the mixed fire regime. This rough, inaccessible country has a long history of hard-fought battles to suppress fires, but it now boasts the most extensive program to restore natural fires in the United States (Figure 15.1).

As of 2003, more than 4 million acres of designated wilderness and nonwilderness backcountry in northern and central Idaho and the adjacent edge of Montana—an area nearly as large as New Jersey—were being managed to restore the natural role of fire. The Hells Canyon Wilderness along the Snake River in Idaho and Oregon, which lies just beyond a narrow, inhabited stretch of the Salmon River canyon, is also part of the natural fire restoration program. Still other lands in the Clearwater-Salmon region are being considered for inclusion by 10 national forests—the Clearwater, Nez Perce, Idaho Panhandle, Lolo, Bitterroot, Payette, Salmon-Challis, Boise, Sawtooth, and Wallowa-Whitman. The remote territory under this program extends about 200

Figure 15.1.
Postfire mosaic (foreground) and snow–avalanche community patterns, Selway–Bitterroot Wilderness. (S. Arno photo)

miles northward from the Sawtooth Wilderness near Stanley, Idaho,
to the Mallard-Larkins Pioneer Area southeast of St. Maries. Along the
Salmon River canyon, the restoration area stretches 100 miles west to
east, from the vicinity of Riggins to the headwaters of the Bitterroot
River in Montana.

Impetus for Restoring Fire

The Great Idaho fire of 1910 engulfed more than 3 million acres, including a huge swath of the Clearwater drainage (Pyne 2001). This
holocaust damaged or destroyed several backwoods communities and
served as the impetus for the U.S. Forest Service's campaign to eliminate forest fire. However, in spite of mobilized manpower and equipment, major fires again swept much of this region in 1919, 1926, 1929,
and 1934. Fire suppression relied on punching roads into steep country, carving out a network of trails suitable for pack trains, and establishing dozens of fire lookouts atop ridges and peaks. In 1935, Elers

Koch, a widely respected forester with 30 years experience in fire suppression, expressed second thoughts. Koch (1935) argued that road building and development in the name of fire protection was detrimental to the erosion-prone canyons, harmed the character of this wild country, and would ultimately fail to minimize fire. Since the area had little potential for supplying timber, Koch questioned why it was important to rid it of fire, which he viewed as an intrinsic part of the natural environment. Koch (1935, 1998) concluded his commentary with the prescient recommendation that the Forest Service abandon its effort to remove fire from this remote region.

Koch's eloquent logic failed to influence the fire exclusion advocates who held sway in the Forest Service administration. However, 30 years later, increasing evidence of the seminal role of fire in maintaining western forest ecosystems spawned proposals to restore fire in national parks and wilderness areas (Leopold and others 1963, Kilgore and Briggs 1972). Then in 1971, Bud Moore, a Forest Service fire administrator who had spent much of his life in the Clearwater backcountry, initiated a pilot program to restore natural fires (Moore 1996). This was a revolutionary event in the agency that had initiated the national campaign to eliminate fire. In 1972, with the help of Bitterroot National Forest supervisor Orville Daniels, fire scientist Bob Mutch, and others, the natural fire program was launched in one small part of the Selway-Bitterroot Wilderness (SBW) in Idaho's Clearwater drainage. In 1979 the program was expanded to cover the entire SBW, and beginning in 1985 it encompassed 3 million acres of the SBW and the neighboring Frank Church/River of No Return Wilderness (FC/RNRW). By the dawn of the 21st century the fire restoration program also included nearby smaller wilderness areas as well as several remote areas outside wilderness.

The Wilderness Act of 1964 specified that wilderness areas are protected to allow natural forces to operate without human interference; therefore, neither natural fire nor prescribed fire can be used in wilderness to improve wildlife habitat or for any other specific benefit. However, the new restoration programs include use of prescribed (management-ignited) fires outside and even inside wilderness, where careful study indicates a need to reduce unprecedented and potentially damaging fuel accumulations before permitting lightning fires to burn. In other words, human-ignited prescribed fire could be justified in wilderness if it were a necessary step before allowing natural fires to resume.

Before land managers can permit natural fire to burn in a wilderness or other area they must develop a "wildland fire use guidebook" that specifies appropriate management response to all fires in the area. Ironically, a fire management program complying with the National Environmental Protection Act must be completed before installing a natural fire program.

Evolution of the New Fire Policy

Traditionally, federal fire policy called for aggressive suppression of all fires, with a goal of achieving control by 10 A.M. the day after the fire was first reported. In 1978 a newly enacted fire policy allowed a more flexible suppression response based upon risk to natural resources and property, firefighter safety, and economic efficiency (Benedict, Swan, and Belnap 1991). Options included everything from full-blown suppression to surveillance and limited suppression. This gave fire managers much more flexibility in matching suppression response to the values at risk. The new policy also opened doors for increased use of "prescribed natural fires" (PNFs), which are lightning fires burning under previously defined conditions in designated areas.

During the 1980s, fire management plans enacted in the SBW and FC/RNRW allowed large areas to be burned under PNFs and a "wildfire confinement" strategy. This approach employs monitoring and uses only limited suppression tactics to keep fires from escaping designated boundaries or threatening property. Monitoring a wildfire that is being managed under a confinement strategy requires both ground and aerial reconnaissance to record fire behavior and weather conditions, map the fire's perimeter, and report changes. Between 1979 and 1990, the total area of fire receiving limited or no suppression was 150,000 acres, about 12 percent of the SBW (Brown and others 1994). The PNF and wildfire confinement strategies returned more fire to the SBW and FC/RNRW than had been experienced in previous decades, providing benefits to the ecosystem, lessening firefighter exposure to safety hazards, lowering suppression costs by several million dollars, and reducing impacts of suppression activities on the land (Benedict, Swan, and Belnap 1991).

Despite the program's success, still more fire is needed to approximate the historical fire-generated landscape mosaic (Oppenheimer and Dickinson 2003). Analysis of the extent of wildfires and PNFs from

1979 through 1990 in the SBW indicates that the annual area burned averaged only about 60 percent of the historical fire regime (Brown and others 1994). The largest departures occurred in the low-elevation ponderosa pine and the high-elevation whitebark pine ecosystems, where the restoration program was burning only about 40 percent of historical levels. Yet the ponderosa pine type was experiencing a higher proportion of stand replacement burning than was characteristic of the historical fire regime.

During the 1988 season, fires that burned through the greater Yellowstone National Park region were portrayed as a disaster on national news broadcasts and sometimes attributed to a "let it burn" policy. The natural fire programs were relatively new and had not been tested in a dramatic wildfire season like 1988, when withering drought and a series of massive cold fronts bombarded much of the West with dry lightning and unrelenting gale-force winds. After the 1988 blowup, all PNF programs were suspended and an interagency review established new criteria and procedures that had to be met by each area before natural fires would be allowed (USDA-USDI 1989). Another severe wildfire season in 1994 produced 34 firefighter fatalities, leading to even greater outcry. Another formal review of federal fire policy was commissioned after the 1994 season, further strengthening accountability of the federal fire program (Zimmerman and Bunnell 2000).

For a decade following the 1988 fire season, waning political support eroded the wilderness fire programs (Agee 2000). In 1989 fire managers had to incorporate new, more restrictive management criteria for wilderness fire that were based on thoroughly assessing the risk of managing a long-duration fire and on external issues such as smoke. Not a single criterion was based on meeting objectives for returning fire to wilderness ecosystems. Explosive wildfire seasons in 2000, 2002, and 2003 helped neutralize earlier setbacks to natural burning programs by delivering fire on such an enormous scale throughout the West that many wilderness blazes had to be left without active suppression.

Federal fire management policy is continually being reviewed and adjusted (Zimmerman and Bunnell 2000). It directs federal agencies to achieve a balance between suppression to protect life, property, and resources, and use of fire to regulate fuels and maintain healthy fire-dependent ecosystems. The policy enacted in 1995 eliminates many of the previous limitations to expanding the use of fire, and it improved the decision process for allowing natural fire to play its ecological role

(USDI/USDA 1995). Previously, all fires were classified as "wildfires" or "prescribed fires," and the designation chosen for each new fire limited the range of management options available. Under the 1995 policy, all fires not ignited by managers are considered "wildland fires" and they receive "appropriate management responses," which include a broad range of tactical options. This policy advocates greater use of fire for accomplishing resource benefits, such as restoring ecosystem processes, while implementing an effective suppression program. The 1995 policy states that fire management should have a foundation based on safety of firefighters and the public, sound risk management, the ecological role of fire, and application of the best available science.

Data for the 1994–1998 fire seasons suggest that the 1995 policy was having a favorable effect in returning fire to the Clearwater–Salmon region. The number of wildland fires managed for resource benefits— "wildland fire use" (WFU), formerly called PNF—showed an increasing trend (Zimmerman and Bunnell 2000). Byron Bonney, (Florence, MT, pers. comm. 2003) retired fire staff officer for the Clearwater/Nez Perce Zone, cites evidence that the WFU status is gaining acceptance. The area burned in prescribed natural fires (PNF and WFU) on the Clearwater and Nez Perce national forests averaged less than 3,000 acres per year between 1979 and 1994 but increased to nearly 8,000 acres per year between 1995 and 1999. While PNFs accounted for only 16 percent of the total area burned between 1979 and 1994, they comprised 69 percent of the area burned between 1995 and 1999.

Restoring Fire on the Land

The 1978 fire policy allowed national forest managers to develop a fire management plan for restoring fire through the use of PNFs. The plan used a flowchart process to guide decisions about each new fire based on weather, fuel moisture, firefighting resources, hazards, and social concerns such as smoke (Benedict, Swan, and Belnap 1991). This determined whether the fire would be managed as a PNF or wildfire. The 1985 Savage Creek fire on the Payette National Forest illustrates such a flexible response to wildfire. The fire burned 12,000 acres of generally remote land that was interspersed with private ranches and valuable timber, and was suppressed wherever it threatened these assets. However, the head of the fire was spreading into remote high-country adjacent to wilderness. This section of the fire was managed under a confinement strategy using natural terrain barriers as designated boundaries. These different strategies lowered suppression costs by an estimated $2 million and reduced possible negative effects from fire line construction on erosive terrain.

Under the 1978 policy, little money was available to support monitoring and management of PNFs, while funding for suppression was ample (Daniels 1991). Also, administrative problems often discouraged reclassification of PNFs as wildfires when conditions changed. Bonney (pers. comm. 2003) explained that changing the status of a fire from PNF to wildfire meant that the fire could no longer be called beneficial. A stigma of failure accompanied this change even though it was within Forest Service policy guidelines. Funding of the fire would also have to change from appropriated funding for managing PNFs to emergency Fire Fighting Funds that could not be used to provide resource benefits. The 1995 policy revision mitigated these problems by lumping all fires not ignited by managers into one funding category, "wildland fires," thus giving managers more flexibility to design "appropriate management responses" that can change as conditions change.

During the late 1990s, national forests in the Clearwater and Salmon river drainages developed management plans that allow use of lightning fires in several areas outside of designated wilderness. The Clearwater Fire Management Unit, located north of the SBW, encompasses 515,000 acres where lightning fires can be used for resource benefit— designated as "wildland fire use" (WFU) (Clearwater National Forest 1999). Within this remote nonwilderness landscape managers use lightning ignitions to restore fire for the maintenance of historical ecosystem processes except in the limited areas where the Forest Plan emphasizes recreation or timber production.

Under the 1995 policy revision, the decision to allow a lightning fire to burn (WFU) or to initiate an appropriate suppression response considers many factors and involves several fire/resource specialists (Clearwater National Forest 1999). Within 2 hours after a fire is discovered, a team of experts either classifies it as WFU or designates it for suppression. The following elements are considered before designating WFU: threats to the area boundary and to life and property can be alleviated; effects on cultural and natural resources are acceptable; forecast weather and risk indicators are acceptable; and the regional and national fire situation is acceptable.

A risk assessment for a given wildland fire and the probability of the fire exceeding the area designated for WFU are part of the analysis process. The decision for WFU considers potential effects of smoke on populated areas (not often a problem in this remote region), proportion of a watershed to be burned in any 10-year period, habitat for endangered species, and protection of structures. Each day the fire is subject to evaluation regarding whether to keep it under WFU status or to assign suppression. Under WFU, managers may need to prevent fire spreading along one flank to keep it within the designated area, or they may need to protect a historic structure or administrative facility.

Between 1993 and 2002, PNFs and WFUs covered 122,000 acres in the entire Clearwater and Salmon river backcountry on the Clearwater, Nez Perce, Payette, Salmon-Challis, Sawtooth, and Bitterroot national forests (Oppenheimer and Dickinson 2003, Bitterroot National Forest 2003). From 1990 through 1998 the natural fire program (PNF and WFU) in the 1.2-million-acre SBW allowed 100 fires to burn 8,300 acres, while the remaining 516 blazes that were classified as wildfires burned 27,000 acres (Clearwater National Forest 1999). This illustrates that while PNF and WFU status is a principal feature of the fire restoration program, the "confinement" response to wildfires actually returns more fire to the landscape. In severe wildfire seasons with high levels of firefighting activity west-wide, such as 2000 and 2002, most new fires in the Clearwater and Salmon river backcountry were placed in a suppression status. However, many of these were allowed to burn under a confinement strategy except where they posed an immediate threat to structures or private property. The combined effects of PNF/WFU and confinement-strategy wildfires have returned natural fires to the landscape on an impressive scale. As an example, 46 percent of the 2.3-million-acre FC/RNRW was visited by fire between 1985 and 2000. About half of this burned area resulted from confinement wildfires in 2000 alone.

The multiple benefits of allowing suppression fires to burn under "confinement" are illustrated by comparing strategies used on two huge fires in the Salmon River country during 2000. Both burned in a mosaic of varying severities commonly associated with a mixed fire regime. The Clear Creek fire, closer to but not directly threatening communities, was subjected to a $71 million suppression effort, and 200 miles of fire lines were bulldozed that ultimately were not needed (Barker 2000). It burned 217,000 acres, including portions of the

FC/RNRW. Meanwhile, the more remote 182,000-acre Wilderness Complex fire was monitored and allowed to burn with very little suppression effort and little environmental damage.

Despite the impressive extent of burning since about 1980, the fire restoration program in the Clearwater and Salmon river mountains has not adequately treated ponderosa pine habitats in the semiarid canyons. These sites historically burned in understory fires at intervals of about 10–25 years (Barrett 1988). As a result of effective suppression, many pine stands have missed several natural fire cycles. Competition from thickets of young trees causes physiological stress in the old trees, hampering production of pitch needed to combat bark beetle attacks. The buildup of surface and ladder fuels puts canyon watersheds at risk of uncharacteristic stand replacement fires (Nez Perce National Forest 1999). Such fires are costly and often impossible to suppress, pose safety risks to firefighters, and accelerate soil loss, which degrades water quality and aquatic habitat for threatened populations of salmon, steelhead, and bull trout. In July 2003, two firefighters were overrun and killed by a canyon wildfire that was being fought to mitigate its potential threat to 35 residences (Barker 2003).

National forests are proposing to conduct spring and fall prescribed fires to reduce fuel accumulations and return to a semblance of historical conditions in about 200,000 acres of the Salmon River canyon, much of it in the FC/RNRW (Brown 1992–93, Nez Perce National Forest 1999). Pre- and postburn monitoring will evaluate the effectiveness of prescribed fire. After reducing fuels with prescribed fire, managers hope to allow lightning fires to resume their natural role in this spectacular but fragile canyon habitat.

Sustaining Success: The Challenge

Armed with officially sanctioned plans and procedures, one might suppose that national forest managers would be able to fulfill a mission of returning fire to an undeveloped region. In reality, the fire restoration program in the Clearwater and Salmon river backcountry still encounters opposition within the 90-year-old federal fire suppression bureaucracy, whose traditional mandate was eliminating fire. Most fire restoration occurs during years of extreme wildfire activity when attention is focused on potential damage to communities and dwellings dispersed within or adjacent to this backcountry.

Byron Bonney (pers. comm. 2003) notes that during years of high fire activity prior to 1999, regional- or national-level administrators suspended the option of declaring new ignitions as WFU. National forest managers still had the capability to declare any fire a wildfire and take whatever suppression response best met objectives. A national forest might receive 50 or more new lightning starts from one storm, so new fires in remote areas were often assigned low priority for suppression. Because action was delayed, the fires grew larger and more difficult to suppress later. Managers would probably have put such fires under confinement strategy and managed them similar to a WFU, but they could not claim any benefits to the ecosystem. Large fires managed under WFU require funding, aerial reconnaissance, and a team of specialists for monitoring and planning limited suppression. Bonney observed that beginning in about 1999, fires designated WFU have been put on equal footing with suppression fires in vying for fire management resources because of greater emphasis on restoring fire to ecosystems. He sees this as a welcome shift from the traditional mentality that presumes every fire should be attacked with all-out suppression.

The success of this broad-scale restoration program depends on extraordinary commitment by local fire management personnel, district rangers, and forest supervisors. The natural fire program has perhaps the highest risks and consequences of any operation within the federal land management agencies. Fire is by nature unpredictable, and losing control of a designated natural fire (WFU) can have devastating professional consequences. If the responsible officials are risk-averse, they will be reluctant to designate WFU no matter how great the potential benefits. During past periods of high wildfire activity, regional officials pressured local managers to suppress new lightning fires and fight ongoing fires in the backcountry. Local managers often resisted and instead allowed fire restoration to continue. Such commitment is crucial to long-term success of the natural fire program. Local managers have a strong sense of mission and shared satisfaction in returning fire despite the difficulties and constraints. Bonney believes that these personal commitments have turned the tide in recent years toward restoring fire and thus more natural forest landscapes—even during years with high fire-suppression activity.

The Wildland-Urban Interface Is Crucial

Pressure from residents of the wildland–urban interface (WUI) is a growing obstacle to landscape-scale restoration of fire. The sheer size of the Clearwater and Salmon backcountry reduces but does not eliminate concerns about fire from nearby suburban areas or people who have cabins on old mining claims in the mountains. Paradoxically, rapid population growth at the edge of national forests, national parks, and wilderness could argue for expanded use of managed fire rather than clinging to the myth of fire exclusion. Veteran fire behavior specialist Bob Mutch (2001) concluded that a successful fire restoration program becomes a self-regulating process. During the 2000 fire season he observed that burns from previous years were limiting the spread and intensity of new wilderness fires.

The largest suburban area affected by the Clearwater and Salmon region's fire program is Montana's Bitterroot Valley, located along the eastern boundary of the SBW. In 1988 three major wildfires spread eastward from the SBW and threatened valley residences, although damage to private land was averted. After the 1988 fires in Yellowstone and elsewhere raised national concerns, SBW managers eliminated PNFs on the east slope of the Bitterroot Range for the next 10 years. They also reduced the number of fires allowed immediately west of the Bitterroot crest in Idaho. Later, managers agreed to permit small, innocuous fires largely confined to subalpine rocklands in this eastern portion of the SBW.

The Bitterroot national forest proposed creating forested fuel breaks by thinning some of its land between the SBW and the forested home sites in the Bitterroot Valley, but local opposition prevented many of these projects. Forest managers conducted several prescribed burns to reduce fuel buildup above the west side of the Bitterroot Valley, but these operations are continually hampered by smoke regulations and complaints about smoke from residents. Ironically, the wildfires of 2000 and 2003 produced smoke levels that were orders of magnitude more severe and prolonged than any smoke from prescribed fire (Devlin 2001, 2003).

In some regions, teams of fire specialists and air quality regulators have developed plans that allow prescribed fire to serve as a prevention or mitigation measure for wildfire (Arno and Allison-Bunnell 2002,

Core and Peterson 2001, Sandberg and others 2002). Fire managers need to convince residents and air-quality regulators that smoke is inevitable, but it can be mitigated by actively managing fire and fuels. Mutch (2001) is one of many fire experts advocating that people who live in the forest need to adapt to an environment where fire and smoke are inseparable.

In order to maintain support for a natural fire program, managers must continually remind WUI residents and the public at large of the ecological and practical necessity of proactive fire management. Education about the natural role of fire can influence people to accept management of fire and forest fuels (McCool and Stankey 1986, Shindler and Toman 2003). Programs such as *Firewise* (www.firewise. org) and *FireWorks* (Smith and McMurray 2000) can be effective. So can simple tools such as tree cross-sections featuring multiple fire scars and historic photo comparisons showing undesirable changes in modern forests linked to fire exclusion.

Bonney (pers. comm. 2003) points out that the Clearwater and Nez Perce National Forests together average nearly 400 lightning fires per year, and that for more than 50 years the majority of these blazes were suppressed. Had these thousands of fires burned naturally, they undoubtedly would have produced forests and wildlife habitats much different than today's. Although fire exclusion has disrupted this wilderness ecosystem, managers of the Clearwater and Salmon River country are now demonstrating how to return the primeval fire process.

Part III

Conclusions

Part III concludes the book by placing restoration forestry in a broad perspective and specifying factors critical for its success. We summarize how restoration forestry uses knowledge of historical natural processes as the basis for managing for different landowner goals. Restoration forestry provides for ecological sustainability of the forest and the resources and amenity values important to humans. It also allows highly developed countries to sustainably manage natural forests rather than exploiting them or those of less developed countries.

Chapter 16

The Restoration Imperative

The compelling case for forest restoration today parallels legendary ecologist Aldo Leopold's call for watershed restoration early in the 20th century. In a 1920 memo to the supervisor of Arizona's Prescott National Forest, Leopold wrote that the time for "investigative work" had passed. "What is needed is a series of actual demonstrations, to test and improve techniques and to serve as examples to private interests" (Meine 1988, p. 186). But the stakes associated with restoring the West's forests are higher than those of restoring the Prescott's watersheds in Leopold's time—these have regional and even global implications.

Naturally functioning forest ecosystems are gemstones of the western landscape and the biosphere, providing important wildlife habitat, sustaining flows of fresh water, and moderating climate. The native forests that blanket the West's mountain ranges and spill out into the valleys and high plains are truly marvels of nature. The largest trees in the world, the tallest, and the oldest all occur here, as do the most productive and densest stands. Although plantations of introduced species or genetically "improved" native species are common in much of the world and elsewhere in the United States, western forests are dominated by native vegetation and molded by natural processes such as fire—or were until recently.

Although natural fires can be returned to their historical role in some secluded backcountry areas with mixed or stand replacement fire regimes, we must rely on judicious tree cutting (at least initially) and prescribed burning to restore most other fire-prone forests in the West. Removing trees in restoration treatments can offer multiple rewards; it can help fulfill a range of ecological goals and, where appropriate, provide for human resource needs. Today, relatively few residents in the

U.S. and other developed countries have any direct connection with the resources that provide their food and shelter, yet they depend more than ever on paper products and buildings in their daily lives, and wood is the most environmentally sustainable building material (Dekker-Robertson and Libby 1998, Koch 1992). Use of wood also contributes less to global warming than does use of steel, aluminum, concrete, brick, or plastics (Kershaw, Oliver, and Hinckley 1993).

Numerous regulatory constraints reduced timber harvests from the national forests by the year 2000 to about 15 percent of pre-1990 levels (Culbert 2004), with unintended environmental consequences. When Americans forego using wood from domestic forests, they do not go without. Consumer demand is met by importing wood and by substituting other materials that have greater impact on the global environment (Berlik, Kittredge, and Foster 2002, Koch 1992, Uusivuori and Kuuluvainen 2001). Fortunately, forest restoration strategies could provide a substantial flow of wood products from western forests while returning an approximation of historical conditions and natural processes (Fiedler 2003, Fiedler and others 2001). A recent analysis in Montana showed that if just 1 percent of the forests in the historical understory fire regime were treated annually, the volume of wood produced as a *byproduct* of restoration treatments would boost current timber production in the state by nearly half (Keegan, Fiedler, and Morgan, 2004).

A growing threat to western forests is conversion to suburban and commercial development. This irreversible process diminished forestland by 2.2 million acres in Washington State alone between 1970 and 1992 (Washington State Department of Natural Resources 1998) and is expanding through many popular areas of the West. Still, the most widespread disruption to western forests comes from attempts to exclude fire. Past logging that removed large, fire-resistant trees and encouraged a dense growth of small trees compounded this problem. Decline also occurs in natural areas that are protected from logging but denied any kind of natural or prescribed fire. The good news is that restoration forestry can begin reversing the decline of western forests linked to fire exclusion and high-grade logging.

The preceding 10 chapters document how some exemplary land managers are going about restoring both public and private forestlands across the West. These chapters highlight distinctive projects conducted on different ownerships under diverse goals. A common thread running through these projects is the aim to create forest structures where fire can once again serve as a beneficial process, rather than as a destructive aberration. But these examples are few and far between, together accounting for only a tiny proportion of the acres that could potentially benefit from restoration forestry. Most of the projects we present focus on stand-level restoration, which seems necessarily the first step in application. Longer term success requires that restoration be accomplished over much larger landscapes across the West. Only then can the natural disturbance processes such as fire, insects, and disease operate in ways that are healthy and sustainable. However, expanded application of restoration forestry depends on a diverse infrastructure and a realistic regulatory environment.

Infrastructure Is Paramount

Restoration forestry cannot be conducted at any significant scale without a supporting infrastructure. Sawmills, pulp mills, wafer-board and plywood plants, post-and-pole plants, latilla and viga makers (latillas are ceiling materials and vigas are beams used in southwestern buildings), and log home manufacturers are all key components of infrastructure. Small to moderate volumes of timber suitable for one or more of these facilities are commonly produced in restoration projects, helping offset treatment costs. Some restoration projects can pay for themselves, or even turn a profit, but only if markets are readily available (Fiedler and others 2004). Absence of markets within a reasonable transporting distance can easily kill an otherwise economically feasible project.

Availability of markets for waste material and mill residues is another critical and often overlooked component of needed infrastructure. A considerable volume of the material to be removed in restoration projects consists of trees too small for conventional solid wood products. Even for commercial-size trees, only about 40 percent of the merchantable log becomes lumber. The remainder must be dealt with as a residue. Pulp mills, particle-board and wafer-board plants, and biomass generation facilities provide outlets in some areas for the large volume of low-value wood recovered in restoration projects. They also serve as an important revenue source for residues created by sawmills and other wood-processing facilities.

Colorado, Arizona, and New Mexico have lost most of their timber-processing industry in recent years, and with it the potential to utilize the mountains of wood that must be removed if we hope to restore forests. Most of the facilities closed because they could not obtain a dependable supply of wood or because they could not process small-diameter trees. Forest inventories reveal that the volume of timber needing removal to restore forests already accessible by road exceeds the amount required for new mills, but there is no long-term assurance that this material will be made available.

New markets, products, and uses for low-value wood may help expand restoration efforts. In recent years, small plants have been established to utilize waste wood to fuel industrial boilers, generate electric power, or heat schools or other buildings, often partially funded with grants from the Forest Service or other agencies. Congressional representatives and community development organizations promote facilities that use waste wood or produce new products from small trees because of the local jobs they create. Maintaining and improving local and regional markets for wood is essential to restoration and cannot be taken for granted in today's highly competitive global economy.

People skilled in designing and implementing restoration treatments are another key component of infrastructure. Traditional forestry focused on deciding which trees to cut and on efficiently removing value from the forest. Restoration forestry is most concerned with deciding which trees to leave, and treatment prescriptions are designed to create sustainable conditions adapted to natural disturbances. Then these treatments are implemented as efficiently as possible.

Although a conceptual basis for restoration forestry can be acquired in college and professional education, success requires people who are familiar with all facets of a project. This includes the species, sites, and ecological disturbances characteristic of an area, silvicultural techniques appropriate for restoration objectives, suitable equipment and skillful operators to do the work, and available markets. Such comprehensive knowledge can come only from careful observations over a number of years in one area. A continuing obstacle to greater restoration activity on the national forests—the ownership with the greatest need and potential for restoration—is the agency's policy of moving professionals from job to job and place to place every few years. Many Forest Service employees move on to a new assignment before understanding the issues, infrastructure, and ecological context of their previous station. They are not at a location long enough to develop a sense of place and the human relationships and trust needed to successfully carry out quality restoration projects. Nor can they see the effects of treatments they prescribed in the past, and learn from them.

The Environmental Regulation Paradox

Another critical requirement for broad-scale restoration of federal lands is a flexible regulatory environment that "fits" the dynamic nature of natural systems. Jack Ward Thomas, well-known wildlife biologist and retired chief of the U.S. Forest Service, points out the need to update, revise, and coordinate environmental laws and regulations, many enacted in the 1970s (Thomas 2002). Although individual pieces of legislation (or guidelines for their implementation) may have been appropriate for their intended purpose, the combined effect of many such laws and regulations is to hamper active management of any kind. Quoting Thomas (p. 1), "The combined effect of these laws resulted in the predominant use of preservation strategies (static management) to protect the habitat of species considered rare, threatened, or endangered (T&E species) due to habitat dwindling in either amount or effectiveness. None of these laws prescribed actions required to achieve management objectives." Thomas, who is equally respected for his environmental ethic and straight talk, gives this disturbing assessment of today's regulatory environment: "The system that governs the planning and management of the public lands is, or should be, recognized as a 'snafu' decades in the making" (Thomas 2002, p. 7).

Unlike today's overlapping and sometimes conflicting regulatory morass, an integrated and realistic environmental regulation framework should address both short- and long-term risks to forests—including risks of passive management. In an article titled "The Fallacy of Passive Management," University of Washington fire ecologist Jim Agee warns of the unintended consequences of "passive" management in western forests (Agee 2002). He notes that after considerable forest exploitation in the last century and a move toward restoration in this century, there is a temptation to "let nature take its course" and allow forests to recover naturally. He cautions, "such a passive approach to management is not a sustainable forest strategy in ecosystems that have a substantial history of natural disturbance, including forests on almost every continent." He recalls pointing to an area on a map during a recent summer and remarking about its vulnerability to severe wildfire. "Three

Figure 16.1.
Heavy mortality in ponderosa pine, central Arizona, resulting from bark beetle attack. Trees without foliage and trees with pale foliage are dead. (C. Fiedler photo)

weeks later the 200,000-acre Wenatchee Fire destroyed most old-growth and late-successional structures in the area. Passive management was a dismal failure" (Agee 2002). Agee concurs that late-successional reserves are an important feature of the landscape; he takes issue with a policy of delineating them and expecting them to remain intact in the West's fire-prone environment.

For decades, United States and Canadian land management organizations fought to keep fire out of forests. Over a period of 70 years these organizations learned a hard lesson and now champion integration of natural and prescribed fire into forest management. But it will not be easy to get from where forest conditions are today to where fire can again play a more natural role. Since 2000, western wildfires have raged through fuel-clogged forests from British Columbia south to California, Arizona, and New Mexico, burning more than 1,000 homes in 2003 alone. Wildfires such as the Cerro Grande, Bitterroot Complex, Biscuit, and Rodeo-Chediski became household words. The U.S. government alone has spent more than $1 billion annually in recent years trying to suppress wildfires. A similar amount is expended

Figure 16.2.
Forest homes destroyed in central Arizona by the 2002 Rodeo-Chediski wild-fire. (Photo by Humphrey's Type 1 USDA/USDI Southwest Region Incident Management Team)

in often futile attempts to avert erosion and reforest heavily burned watersheds. This massive spending purchases a very large Band-Aid—it does nothing to correct the underlying problems that afflict fire-prone forests. Similar funding used for restoration forestry in strategic locations could reduce fire threats to humans and property and lessen irreversible damage to forest environments (Fiedler and others 2001, Finney 2001, Stephens 1998).

But this is not just about fire. It is about the overall resilience of western forests to natural disturbances, including insects, disease, and climate change. The effects of dramatic departures from historically sustainable forest conditions are beginning to erupt on the landscape. One needs only to visit northern New Mexico and central Arizona to witness the ecological tragedy that can befall dense forests in drier environments. Massive killing of large pines by bark beetles across central Arizona (Figure 16.1) and intense crown fires, such as the Rodeo-Chediski (Figure 16.2), in ponderosa pine forests not adapted to them are grim testimony that the ecological "laws of gravity" cannot be suspended indefinitely (Trachtman 2003). On a recent trip to the Southwest, a colleague in New Mexico remarked that the only consolation one derives out of this calamity is to say, "I told you so." Small consolation, indeed.

In the aftermath of 4 severely destructive wildfire years within the last 10, and several decades of conflict over environmental laws, westerners are struggling to define their relationship with forests. Congress recently passed "forest restoration" legislation (HR 1904) promoting fuel reduction, thinning, and prescribed burning treatments. Whether this legislation translates into actual restoration forestry projects or something quite different in the name of "restoration" and "fire hazard reduction" remains unclear. Will the primary influence come from those who oppose human intervention in forests and litigate to prevent all but a few minimalist activities such as thinning the smallest trees? Or will the initiative be seized by those who wish to return to a 1960s brand of logging on public lands—an approach that will ultimately fail because of overwhelming public disapproval?

There is, however, one dramatically different alternative. If the restoration approach described in this book were implemented in an open and credible way, building on demonstrated successes, it could lead to a new kind of forestry in the West. Restoration forestry could provide a new future for altered, vulnerable, and damaged forests. It could foster a new appreciation of the dynamic nature of western forests and the integral role of fire. Perhaps most importantly, it could define a *positive* role for people in their relationship with forests.

References

Agee, J. K. 1993. *Fire ecology of Pacific Northwest forests*. Island Press, Washington, D.C.

———. 1998. The landscape ecology of western forest fire regimes. *Northwest Science* 72, Special Issue, 24–34.

———. 2000. Wilderness fire science: a state-of-knowledge review. pp. 5–22 *in USDA Forest Service, Rocky Mountain Research Station, Proceedings 15*, vol. 5, Ogden, Utah.

———. 2002. The fallacy of passive management of western forest reserves. *Conservation Biology in Practice* 3(1):18–25.

Allen, C. D. 2001. Runoff, erosion, and restoration studies in pinyon-juniper woodlands of the Pajarito Plateau. pp. 24–26 *in* P. S. Johnson, ed. *Water, watersheds, and land use in New Mexico. New Mexico Decision-Makers Field Guide 1*. New Mexico Bureau of Mines and Mineral Resources, Socorro, New Mexico.

———. 2002. Lots of lightning and plenty of people: an ecological history of fire in the upland Southwest. pp. 143–193 *in* T. R. Vale, ed. *Fire, native peoples, and the natural landscape*. Island Press, Washington, D.C.

Allen, C. D., and D. Breshears. 1998. Drought-induced shift of a forest-woodland ecotone: rapid landscape response to climate variation. *Proceedings of National Academy of Sciences USA* 95:14839–14842.

Allen, C. D., M. Savage, D. Falk, K. Suckling, T. Swetnam, T. Schulke, P. Stacey, P. Morgan, M. Hoffman, and J. Klingel. 2002. Ecological restoration of southwestern ponderosa pine ecosystems: a broad perspective. *Ecological Applications* 12(5): 1418–1433.

Anderson, M. K., and M. J. Moratto. 1996. Native American land-use practices and ecological impacts. pp. 187–206 *in Sierra Nevada Ecosystem Project: Final report to Congress, volume II*. University of California, Centers for Water and Wildland Resources, Davis, California.

Arno, S. F. 1976. *The historical role of fire on the Bitterroot National Forest*. USDA Forest Service, Intermountain Forest and Range Experiment Station, Research Paper 187, Ogden, Utah.

———. 1980. Forest fire history in the northern Rockies. *Journal of Forestry* 78(8): 460–465.

————. 1986. Whitebark pine cone crops: A diminishing source of wildlife food. *Western Journal of Applied Forestry* 1:92–94.

————. 1999. Undergrowth response, Shelterwood Cutting Unit. pp. 36–37 *in USDA Forest Service, Rocky Mountain Research Station, General Technical Report 23*, Ogden, Utah.

————. 2000. Fire regimes in western forest ecosystems. pp. 97–120 *in USDA Forest Service, Rocky Mountain Research Station, General Technical Report 42*, vol. 2, Fort Collins, Colorado.

Arno, S. F., and S. Allison-Bunnell. 2002. *Flames in our forest: Disaster or renewal?* Island Press, Washington, D.C.

Arno, S. F., and W. Fischer. 1995. *Larix occidentalis*—fire ecology and fire management. pp. 130–135 *in USDA Forest Service, Intermountain Research Station, General Technical Report 319*, Ogden, Utah.

Arno, S. F., and G. Gruell. 1983. Fire history at the forest–grassland ecotone in southwestern Montana. *Journal of Range Management* 36:332–336.

————. 1986. Douglas-fir encroachment into mountain grasslands in southwestern Montana. *Journal of Range Management* 39:272–275.

Arno, S. F., and T. Petersen. 1983. *Variation in estimates of fire intervals: a closer look at fire history on the Bitterroot National Forest.* USDA Forest Service Intermountain Forest and Range Experiment Station, Research Paper 301, Ogden, Utah.

Arno, S. F., D. Parsons, and R. Keane. 2000. Mixed-severity fire regimes in the Northern Rocky Mountains: Consequences of fire exclusion and options for the future. pp. 225–232 *in USDA Forest Service, Rocky Mountain Research Station, Proceedings 15*, vol. 5, Ogden, Utah.

Arno, S. F., E. Reinhardt, and J. Scott. 1993. *Forest structure and landscape patterns in the subalpine lodgepole pine type: A procedure for quantifying past and present conditions.* USDA Forest Service Intermountain Research Station, General Technical Report 294, Ogden, Utah.

Arno, S. F., J. Scott, and M. Hartwell. 1995. *Age-class structure of old growth ponderosa pine/Douglas-fir stands and its relationship to fire history.* USDA Forest Service Intermountain Research Station, Research Paper 481, Ogden, Utah.

Arno, S. F., D. Simmerman, and R. Keane. 1985. *Forest succession on four habitat types in western Montana.* USDA Forest Service Intermountain Forest and Range Experiment Station, General Technical Report 177, Ogden, Utah.

Arno, S. F., H. Smith, and M. Krebs. 1997. *Old growth ponderosa pine and western larch stand structures: Influences of pre-1900 fires and fire exclusion.* USDA Forest Service Intermountain Research Station, Research Paper 495, Ogden, Utah.

Ayres, H. B. 1901. Lewis and Clark Forest Reserve, Montana. pp. 27–80 in *21st Annual Report, Part V. U.S. Department of Interior, Geological Survey.*

Baker, W.L., and D. Shinneman. 2004. Fire and restoration of piñon-juniper woodlands in the western United States: a review. *Forest Ecology and Management* 189:1–21.

Bancroft, L., T. Nichols, D. Parsons, D. Graber, B. Evison, and J. van Wagtendonk. 1985. Evolution of the natural fire management program at Sequoia and Kings Canyon National Parks. pp. 174–180 *in USDA Forest Service, Intermountain Forest and Range Experiment Station, General Technical Report 182*, Ogden, Utah.

Banff National Park. 2002. *Regional forest management strategy: Environmental screening report.* Parks Canada, Banff, Alberta.

Barbouletos, C. S., L. Morelan, and F. Carroll. 1998. We will not wait: Why prescribed fire must be implemented on the Boise National Forest. pp. 27–30 *in Proceedings—Tall Timbers Fire Ecology Conference 20.* Tall Timbers Research Station, Tallahassee, Florida.

Barker, R. 2000. Fire officials weigh damage in wake of Clear Creek fire. *Idaho Statesman*, 22 September, Boise, Idaho.

———. 2003. Firefighters didn't know they were in danger. *Idaho Statesman*, 10 August, 1A, 6A. Boise, Idaho.

Barnard, J. 2003. Reality review faults Northwest Forest Plan. *Missoulian*, 29 June, B1, 2. Missoula, Montana.

Barrett, S. W. 1988. Fire suppression's effects on forest succession within a central Idaho Wilderness. *Western Journal of Applied Forestry* 3(3):76–80.

Barrett, S. W., and S. Arno. 1982. Indian fires as an ecological influence in the Northern Rockies. *Journal of Forestry* 80(10):647–651.

Barrett, S. W., S. Arno, and C. Key. 1991. Fire regimes of western larch-lodgepole pine forests in Glacier National Park, Montana. *Canadian Journal of Forest Research* 21:1711–1720.

Barrett, S. W., S. Arno, and J. Menakis. 1997. *Fire episodes in the inland Northwest (1540–1940) based on fire history data.* USDA Forest Service Intermountain Research Station, General Technical Report 370, Ogden, Utah.

Bartos, D. L. 2001. Landscape dynamics of aspen and conifer forests. pp. 5–14 *in USDA Forest Service, Rocky Mountain Research Station, Proceedings 18.* Fort Collins, Colorado.

Beattie, M., C. Thompson, and L. Levine. 1983. *Working with your woodland: a landowner's guide.* University Press of New England. Hanover, New Hampshire.

Becker, R. 1995. Operational considerations of implementing uneven-aged management. pp. 67–81 *in University of Montana, Montana Forest and Conservation Experiment Station, Miscellaneous Publication 56,* Missoula, Montana.

Benedict, G. W., L. Swan, and R. Belnap. 1991. Evolution and implementation of a fire management program which deals with high-intensity fires on the Payette National Forest in central Idaho. pp. 339–351 in *Proceedings—Tall Timbers Fire Ecology Conference 17.* Tall Timbers Research Station, Tallahassee, Florida.

Benson, N. C., and L. Kurth. 1995. Vegetation establishment on rehabilitated bulldozer lines after the 1988 Red Bench Fire in Glacier National Park. pp. 164–167 *in USDA Forest Service Intermountain Research Station, General Technical Report 320,* Ogden, Utah.

Berlik, M. M., D. Kittredge, and D. Foster. 2002. *The illusion of preservation: a global environmental argument for the local production of natural resources.* Harvard Forest Paper No. 26., Harvard University, Petersham, Massachusetts.

Beukema, S., E. Reinhardt, J. Greenough, W. Kurz, N. Crookston, and D. Robinson. 2000. *Fire and fuels extension; model description.* Working draft prepared by ESSA Tech. Ltd., Vancouver, British Columbia, for USDA Forest Service, Rocky Mountain Research Station, Moscow, Idaho.

Biondi, F. 1996. Decadal-scale dynamics at the Gus Pearson Natural Area: evidence for inverse (a)symmetric competition? *Canadian Journal of Forest Research* 26: 1397–1406.

Biswell, H. H. 1968. Forest fire in perspective. pp. 43–63 in *Proceedings—Tall Timbers Fire Ecology Conference* 7. Tall Timbers Research Station, Tallahassee, Florida.

————. 1989. *Prescribed burning in California wildlands vegetation management.* University of California Press. Berkeley, California.

Biswell, H. H., H. Kallander, R. Komarek, R. Vogl, and H. Weaver. 1973. Ponderosa fire management: a task force evaluation of controlled burning in ponderosa pine forests of central Arizona. *Tall Timbers Research Station, Miscellaneous Publication* 2, Tallahassee, Florida,

Bitterroot National Forest. 1993. *Final environmental impact statement and record of decision, Tolan Creek timber sale.* USDA Forest Service. Hamilton, Montana.

Bitterroot National Forest. 1995. *Final environmental impact statement and record of decision, Beaver-Woods vegetation management project.* USDA Forest Service. Hamilton, Montana.

Bitterroot National Forest. 2003. *Fire records.* USDA Forest Service. Hamilton, Montana.

Bolle, A. W., R. Behan, W. Pengelly, R. Wambach, G. Browder, T. Payne, and R. Shannon. 1970. *Report on the Bitterroot National Forest.* Select Committee of the University of Montana, Missoula. For U.S. Senator Lee Metcalf, Washington, D.C.

Bonnicksen, T. M. 2000. *America's ancient forests: From the ice age to the age of discovery.* John Wiley and Sons, New York.

Bonnicksen, T. M., and E. Stone. 1982. Managing vegetation within U.S. national parks: a policy analysis. *Environmental Management* 6:101–102, 109–122.

Botkin, D. B. 1990. *Discordant harmonies: a new ecology for the twenty-first century.* Oxford University Press, New York.

Boyd, R., ed. 1999. *Indians, fire and the land in the Pacific Northwest.* Oregon State University Press, Corvallis, Oregon.

Brown, J. K. 1975. Fire cycles and community dynamics in lodgepole pine forests. pp. 429–456 in D. M. Baumgartner, ed. *Proceedings—Management of lodgepole pine ecosystems symposium.* Cooperative Extension, Washington State University, Pullman, Washington.

————. 1992–93. A case for management ignitions in wilderness. *Fire Management Notes* 53–54 (4):3–8.

————. 2000. Introduction and fire regimes. pp. 1–8 *in USDA Forest Service, Rocky Mountain Research Station, General Technical Report 42*, vol. 2, Fort Collins, Colorado.

Brown, J. K., S. Arno, S. Barrett, and J. Menakis. 1994. Comparing the prescribed natural fire program with presettlement fires in the Selway-Bitterroot Wilderness. *International Journal of Wildland Fire* 4:157–168.

Brown, R. 2001. *Thinning, fire, and forest restoration*. Defenders of Wildlife, Washington, D.C. (Available at www.biodiversitypartners.org).

Burr, K. E., A. Eramian, and K. Eggleston. 2001. Growing whitebark pine seedlings for restoration. pp. 325–345 *in* D. F. Tomback, S. Arno, and R. Keane, ed. *Whitebark pine communities: ecology and restoration*. Island Press, Washington, D.C.

Byler, J. W., M. Marsden, and S. Hagle. 1990. The probability of root disease on the Lolo National Forest, Montana. *Canadian Journal of Forest Research* 20:987–994.

Campbell, D. 2001. Whitebark pine and fire management: Avoiding danger in the long run. *Nutcracker Notes* 1:13. Whitebark Pine Ecosystem Foundation, Missoula, Montana.

Caprio, A. C., and D. Graber. 2000. Returning fire to the mountains: Can we successfully restore the ecological role of pre–Euroamerican fire regimes to the Sierra Nevada? pp. 233–241 *in USDA Forest Service, Rocky Mountain Research Station, Proceedings 15*, vol. 5, Ogden, Utah.

Caprio, A. C., C. Conover, M. Keifer, and P. Lineback. 1997. Fire management and GIS: a framework for identifying and prioritizing fire planning deeds. *in Proceedings—1997 ESRI GIS Conference*, San Diego, California.

Caprio, A. C., L. Mutch, T. Swetnam, and C. Baisan. 1994. *Temporal and spatial patterns of giant sequoia radial growth response to a high severity fire in A.D. 1297*. Contract report to the California Department of Forestry and Fire Protection, Mountain Home State Forest. (Abstract in "bibliography" at www.nps.gov/seki/fire/fire_bib.htm

Carle, D. 2002. *Burning questions: America's fight with nature's fire*. Praeger Publishers, Westport, Connecticut.

Chapman, H. H. 1926. *Factors determining natural reproduction of longleaf pine on cut-over lands in LaSalle Parish, Louisiana*. Yale University, School of Forestry, Bulletin No. 16, New Haven, Connecticut.

Christensen, N. L., L. Cotton, T. Harvey, R. Martin, J. McBride, P. Rundel, and R. Wakimoto. 1987. *Review of fire management program for sequoia-mixed conifer forests of Yosemite, Sequoia, and Kings Canyon National Parks*. Final report to the National Park Service, Washington, D.C.

Clary, D. A. 1986. *Timber and the Forest Service*. University of Kansas Press, Lawrence, Kansas.

Clearwater National Forest. 1999. *Clearwater fire management unit: Wildland fire use guidebook*. Orofino, Idaho.

Clements, F. E. 1910. *The life history of lodgepole burn forests*. USDA Forest Service, Bulletin 79, Washington, D.C.

Cooper, C. F. 1960. Changes in vegetation, structure, and growth of southwestern pine forests since white settlement. *Ecological Monographs* 30(2):129–164.

Core, J. E., and J. Peterson 2001. State smoke management programs. *In* C. C. Hardy, R. D. Ottmar, J. L. Peterson, and others, comp. *Smoke management guide for prescribed and wildland fire: 2001 edition.* National Interagency Fire Center, National Wildfire Coordinating Group, NWCG-PMS-420-2, Boise, Idaho.

Cottrell, W. H., Jr. 2004. *The book of fire,* 2nd ed. Mountain Press, Missoula, Montana.

Covington, W. W. 1995. Implementing adaptive ecosystem restoration in western long-needled pine forests. pp. 44–48 *in USDA Forest Service, Rocky Mountain Forest and Range Experiment Station, General Technical Report 278,* Ogden, Utah.

Covington, W. W., and M. Moore. 1994a. Postsettlement changes in natural fire regimes and forest structure: Ecological restoration of old-growth ponderosa pine forests. *Journal of Sustainable Forestry* 2(1/2):153–182.

———. 1994b. Southwestern ponderosa pine forest structure: changes since Euro-American settlement. *Journal of Forestry* 92(1):39–47.

Cronon, W. 1996. The trouble with wilderness; or, getting back to the wrong nature. pp. 69–90 *in* W. Cronon, ed., *Uncommon ground: rethinking the human place in nature.* W. W. Norton and Company, New York.

Culbert, J. 2004. Unpublished data on annual harvests, 1905–2003. USDA Forest Service, Washington, D.C.

Daniel, T. W., J. Helms, and F. Baker. 1979. *Principles of silviculture.* McGraw-Hill, New York.

Daniels, O. L. 1991. A forest supervisor's perspective on the prescribed natural fire. pp. 361–366 in *Proceedings—Tall Timbers Fire Ecology Conference 17.* Tall Timbers Research Station, Tallahassee, Florida.

Davenport, D. W., D. Breshears, B. Wilcox, and C. Allen. 1998. Viewpoint: Sustainability of piñon-juniper ecosystems—a unifying perspective of soil erosion thresholds. *Journal of Range Management* 51:231–240.

Dekker-Robertson, D. L., and W. Libby. 1998. American forest policy—global ethical tradeoffs. *BioScience* 48(6):471–477.

Demetry, A. 1998. A natural disturbance model for restoration of Giant Forest Village, Sequoia National Park. pp. 142–159 *in* W. R. Keammerer and E. Redente, ed. *Proceedings of High Altitude Revegetation Workshop No. 13,* Fort Collins, Colorado. Water Resources Research Institute, Information Series No. 89.

Despain, D. G. 1990. *Yellowstone vegetation.* Roberts Rinehart Publishing, Boulder, Colorado.

Devlin, S. 2001. Clear picture of filthy air: study provides comprehensive analysis of pollution caused by wildfires of 2000. *Missoulian,* 4 February, A1, A12. Missoula, Montana.

Devlin, S. 2003. Gritty blanket clings to city. *Missoulian,* 23 August, 1A. Missoula, Montana.

Dieterich, J. H. 1980. *Chimney Spring forest fire history.* USDA Forest Service, Rocky Mountain Forest and Range Experiment Station, Research Paper 220, Fort Collins, Colorado.

Egan, D., and M. Anderson. Ecological Restoration. 2003. Introduction to theme issue: Native American land management practices in national parks. *Ecological Restoration* Vol. 21(4):237–310.

Evans, J. W. 1990. *Powerful Rockey: the Blue Mountains and the Oregon Trail, 1811–1883.* Eastern Oregon State College. Pika Press, Enterprise, Oregon.

Everett, R., D. Schellhaas, D. Spurbeck, P. Ohlson, D. Keenum, and T. Anderson. 1997. Structure of northern spotted owl nest stands and their historical conditions on the eastern slope of the Pacific Northwest Cascades, USA. *Forest Ecology and Management* 94:1–14.

Fazio, J. R. 1987. *The woodland steward.* The Woodland Press, Moscow, Idaho.

Fiedler, C. E. 1990. *Natural regeneration following clearcutting in the spruce-fir zone of western Montana.* Ph.D. dissertation. University of Minnesota, Twin Cities.

———. 1995. The basal area-maximum diameter-q (BDq) approach to regulating uneven-aged stands. pp. 94–109 *in University of Montana, Montana Forest and Conservation Experiment Station, Miscellaneous Publication 56.* Missoula, Montana.

———. 1999. Stand structure in response to selection cutting and burning. pp. 31–34 *in USDA Forest Service, Rocky Mountain Research Station, General Technical Report 23,* Ogden, Utah.

———. 2000a. Silvicultural treatments. pp. 19–20 *in* H. Y. Smith, ed. *The Bitterroot Ecosystem Management Research Project: What we have learned.* USDA Forest Service, Rocky Mountain Research Station, Proceedings 17.

———. 2000b. Restoration treatments promote growth and reduce mortality of old-growth ponderosa pine (Montana). *Ecological Restoration* 18:117–119.

———. 2002. Natural process-based management of fire-adapted western forests. pp. 147–151 *in* D. M. Baumgartner, L. Johnson, and E. DePuit, ed. *Small diameter timber: resource management, manufacturing, and markets conference.* Proceedings—Washington State University Cooperative Extension, MISC0509, Pullman, Washington.

———. 2003. The future of Montana's forests: Forest management. pp. 27–30 *in* P. F. Kolb, ed. *The governor's conference on the future of montana's forests: crafting a vision for landowners and managers.* Montana Forest and Conservation Experiment Station, The University of Montana, Missoula, Montana.

Fiedler, C. E., and J. Cully. 1995. A silvicultural approach to develop Mexican spotted owl habitat in Southwest forests. *Western Journal of Applied Forestry* 10:144–148.

Fiedler, C. E., and M. Harrington. 2004. Restoring vigor and reducing hazard in an old-growth western larch stand (Montana). *Ecological Restoration* 22:133–134.

Fiedler, C. E., and C. Keegan. 2003. Reducing crown fire hazard in fire-adapted forests in New Mexico. pp. 39–48 *in USDA Forest Service, Rocky Mountain Research Station, Proceedings 29,* Fort Collins, Colorado.

Fiedler, C. E., and D. A. Lloyd. 1995. Autecology and synecology of western larch. pp. 118–122 *in USDA Forest Service, Intermountain Research Station, General Technical Report GTR-INT-319,* Ogden, Utah.

Fiedler, C. E., S. Arno, C. Keegan, and K. Blatner. 2001. Overcoming America's wood deficit: an overlooked option. *BioScience* 51(1):53–58.

Fiedler, C. E., R. Becker, and S. Haglund. 1988. Preliminary guidelines for uneven-aged silvicultural prescriptions in ponderosa pine. pp. 235–241 in D. M. Baumgartner and J. E. Lotan, comp. and ed. *Ponderosa pine: The species and its management*. Washington State University Cooperative Extension, Pullman, Washington.

Fiedler, C. E., C. Keegan, S. Arno, and D. Wichman. 1999. Product and economic implications of ecosystem restoration. *Forest Products Journal* 49:19–23.

Fiedler, C. E., C. Keegan, T. Morgan, and C. Woodall. 2003. Fire hazard and potential treatment effectiveness: A statewide assessment in Montana. *Journal of Forestry* 101(2):7.

Fiedler, C. E., C. Keegan, C. Woodall, and T. Morgan. 2004. *A strategic assessment of crown fire hazard in Montana: Potential effectiveness and costs of hazard reduction treatments*. USDA Forest Service, Pacific Northwest Research Station, General Technical Report 622, Portland, Oregon.

Filip, G. M. 1994. Forest health decline in central Oregon: A 13-year case study. *Northwest Science* 68(4):233–240.

Finney, M. A. 2001. Design of regular landscape fuel treatment patterns for modifying fire growth and behavior. *Forest Science* 47(2):219–228.

Fischer, W. C., and A. Bradley. 1987. *Fire ecology of western Montana forest habitat types*. USDA Forest Service, Intermountain Research Station, General Technical Report 223, Ogden, Utah.

Fitzgerald, S. A., ed. 2002. *Fire in Oregon's forests: risks, effects, and treatment options*. Oregon Forest Resources Institute, Portland, Oregon.

Flora, G. E., and W. McCaughey. 1998. *Environmental assessment: Tenderfoot Creek Experimental Forest, Vegetative Treatment Research Project*. On file at USDA Forest Service, Rocky Mountain Research Station, Missoula, Montana.

Foster, D. R., D. Knight, and J. Franklin. 1998. Landscape patterns and legacies resulting from large, infrequent forest disturbances. *Ecosystems* 1:497–510.

Franklin, J. F., D. Berg, D. Thornburgh, and J. Tappeiner. 1999. Alternative silvicultural approaches to timber harvesting: Variable retention harvest systems. pp. 111–139 in K. A. Kohm and J. F. Franklin, ed. *Creating a forestry for the 21st century*. Island Press, Washington, D.C.

Friederici, P. 2003a. ed. *Ecological restoration of southwestern ponderosa pine forests*. Island Press, Washington, D.C.

Friederici, P. 2003b. The "Flagstaff Model." pp. 7–25 in *Ecological restoration of southwestern ponderosa pine forests*. Island Press, Washington, D.C.

Fulé, P. Z., C. McHugh, T. Heinlein, and W. Covington. 2001a. Potential fire behavior is reduced following forest restoration treatments. pp. 28–35 in *USDA Forest Service, Rocky Mountain Research Station, Proceedings 22*, Ogden, Utah.

Fulé, P. Z., A. Waltz, W. Covington, and T. Heinlein. 2001b. Measuring forest restoration effectiveness in hazardous fuels reduction. *Journal of Forestry* 99(11):24–29.

General Accounting Office. 1999. *Western national forests: A cohesive strategy is needed to address catastrophic wildfire threats*. U.S. General Accounting Office, House of Representatives, Committee on Resources, Report to the Subcommittee on Forests and Forest Health RCED-99-65, Washington, D.C.

Gottfried, G., T. Swetnam, C. Allen, J. Betancourt, and A. Chung-MagCoubrey. 1995. Pinyon-juniper woodlands. pp. 95–132 *in* D. M. Finch and J. Tainter, tech. eds. *Ecology, diversity, and sustainability of the middle Rio Grande basin*. USDA Forest Service General Technical Report, RM-GTR-268, Fort Collins, Colorado.

Gray, A. N., and J. Franklin. 1997. Effects of multiple fires on the structure of southwestern Washington forests. *Northwest Science* 71:174–185.

Gray, R. W. 2001. Historic vs. contemporary interior Douglas-fir structure and process: managing risks in overly-allocated ecosystems. pp. 40–46 *in Proceedings of the Fire Maintained Ecosystems Workshop*, May 2000, Whistler, B.C. British Columbia Ministry of Forests, Squamish Forest District, and Forestry Continuing Studies Network, Vancouver, British Columbia.

Gray, R. W., and B. Blackwell. In press, a. The maintenance of key biodiversity attributes through ecosystem restoration operations. *in Proceedings from the 2002 Fire Conference: Managing fire and fuels in the remaining wildlands and open spaces of the southwestern United States*. USDA Forest Service, Pacific Southwest Research Station, Proceedings, Berkeley, California.

Gray, R. W., and B. Blackwell. In press, b. Fuel management strategies in 60 year old Douglas-fir/ponderosa pine stands in the Squamish Forest District, British Columbia. *in Proceedings from the 2002 Fire Conference: Managing fire and fuels in the remaining wildlands and open spaces of the southwestern United States*. USDA Forest Service, Pacific Southwest Research Station, Proceedings, Berkeley, California.

Greenlee, J. M., and J. Langenheim. 1990. Historic fire regimes and their relation to vegetation patterns in the Monterey Bay area of California. *American Midland Naturalist* 124:239–253.

Gruell, G. E. 1983. *Fire and vegetative trends in the Northern Rockies: Interpretations from 1871–1982 photographs*. Intermountain Forest and Range Experiment Station, General Technical Report 158, Ogden, Utah.

———. 1985a. Fire on the early western landscape: an annotated record of wildland fires 1776–1900. *Northwest Science* 59(2):97–107.

———. 1985b. Indian fires in the Interior West: a widespread influence. pp. 68–74 *in USDA Forest Service, Intermountain Forest and Range Experiment Station, General Technical Report 182*, Ogden, Utah.

———. 2001. *Fire in Sierra Nevada forests: A photographic interpretation of ecological change since 1849*. Mountain Press, Missoula, Montana.

Gruell, G. E., J. Brown, and C. Bushey. 1986. *Prescribed fire opportunities in grasslands invaded by Douglas-fir: State-of-the-art guidelines*. USDA Forest Service, Intermountain Research Station, General Technical Report 198, Ogden, Utah.

Gruell, G. E., W. Schmidt, S. Arno, and W. Reich. 1982. *Seventy years of vegetal change in a managed ponderosa pine forest in western Montana—implications for resource management.* USDA Forest Service, Intermountain Research Station, General Technical Report 130, Ogden, Utah.

Habeck, J. R. 1961. The original vegetation of the mid-Willamette Valley, Oregon. *Northwest Science* 35:65–77.

Hall, F. C. 1976. Fire and vegetation in the Blue Mountains: Implications for land managers. pp. 155–170 in *Proceedings—Tall Timbers Fire Ecology Conference 15.* Tall Timbers Research Station, Tallahassee, Florida.

Hansen, A. J., T. Spies, F. Swanson, and J. Ohmann. 1991. Conserving biodiversity in managed forests: Lessons from natural forests. *BioScience* 41(6):382–392.

Harrington, M. G. 1999. Stand structure response to harvesting and prescribed burning on shelterwood cutting and commercial thinning units. pp. 28–31 *in USDA Forest Service, Rocky Mountain Research Station, General Technical Report 23,* Ogden, Utah.

————. 2000. Fire applications in ecosystem management. pp. 21–22 *in USDA Forest Service, Rocky Mountain Research Station, Proceedings 17,* Ogden, Utah.

Hartesveldt, R. J., and H. Harvey. 1968. The fire ecology of sequoia regeneration. pp. 65–77 in *Proceedings—Tall Timbers Fire Ecology Conference 7.* Tall Timbers Research Station, Tallahassee, Florida.

Harvey, H. T., H. Shellhammer, and R. Stecker. 1980. *Giant sequoia ecology.* U.S. Department of Interior, National Park Service, Science Monograph 12, Washington, D.C.

Hastings, B. K., F. Smith, and B. Jacobs. 2003. Rapidly eroding pinyon-juniper woodlands in New Mexico: Response to slash treatment. *Journal of Environmental Quality* 32:1290–1298.

Hoff, R. J., D. Ferguson, G. McDonald, and R. Keane. 2001. Strategies for managing whitebark pine in the presence of white pine blister rust. pp. 346–366 *in* D. F. Tomback, S. Arno, and R. Keane, ed. *Whitebark pine communities: ecology and restoration.* Island Press, Washington, D.C.

Hoxie, G. L. 1910. How fire helps forestry. *Sunset* 34:145–151.

Hunt, C. B. 1967. *Physiography of the United States.* W. H. Freeman and Company, San Francisco.

Jacobs, B.F., R. Gatewood, and C. Allen. 2002. *Watershed restoration in degraded piñon-juniper woodlands: A paired watershed study.* Final report to USGS-BRD Research/NPS Natural Resource Preservation Program. December 31, 2002.

Jamison, M. 2003. 'A lot of luck' preserves one North Fork man's oasis. *Missoulian,* 31 July A1–2. Missoula, Montana.

Johannessen, C. L. 1971. The vegetation of the Willamette Valley. *Annals of the Association of American Geographers* 61(2):286–302.

Johnson, C. G., Jr., R. Clausnitzer, P. Mehringer, and C. Oliver. 1994. *Biotic and abiotic processes of eastside ecosystems.* USDA Forest Service, Pacific Northwest Research Station, General Technical Report 322, Portland, Oregon.

Kalabokidis, K. D., and R. Wakimoto. 1992. Prescribed burning in uneven-aged stand management of ponderosa pine/Douglas-fir forests. *Journal of Environmental Management* 34:221–235.

Kappel, T. 2002. Sustainable forestry at the E Bar L. *Big Sky Landmarks*, summer 2002, pp. 21–22. The Nature Conservancy, Helena, Montana.

Kay, C. E., C. White, I. Pengelly, and B. Patton. 1999. *Long-term ecosystem states and processes in Banff National Park and the central Canadian Rockies.* Occasional Report No. 9. National Parks Branch, Parks Canada. Ottawa.

Keane, R. E. 2001. Successional dynamics: modeling an anthropogenic threat. pp. 159–192 *in* D. F. Tomback, S. Arno, and R. Keane, ed. *Whitebark pine communities: ecology and restoration.* Island Press, Washington, D.C.

———. 2002. Burning for whitebark pine. *Nutcracker Notes* 3:14–15. Whitebark Pine Ecosystem Foundation, Missoula, Montana.

Keane, R. E., K. Ryan, T. Veblen, C. Allen, J. Logan, and B. Hawkes. 2002. *Cascading effects of fire exclusion in Rocky Mountain ecosystems: A literature review.* USDA Forest Service, Rocky Mountain Research Station, General Technical Report 91, Ogden, Utah.

Keegan, C. E., C. Fiedler, and T. Morgan. 2004. Wildfire in Montana: Potential hazard reduction and economic impacts of a strategic treatment program. *Forest Products Journal* 54(7/8):21–25.

Keifer, M., N. Stephenson, and J. Manley. 2000. Prescribed fire as the minimum tool for wilderness forest and fire regime restoration: A case study from the Sierra Nevada, California. pp. 266–269 *in USDA Forest Service, Rocky Mountain Research Station, Proceedings 15,* vol. 5, Ogden, Utah.

Kendall, K. C., and R. Keane. 2001. Whitebark pine decline: infection, mortality, and population trends. pp. 221–242 *in* D. F. Tomback, S. Arno, and R. Keane, ed. *Whitebark pine communities: ecology and restoration.* Island Press, Washington, D.C.

Kershaw, J. A., Jr., C. Oliver, and T. Hinckley. 1993. Effect of harvest of old growth Douglas-fir stands and subsequent management on carbon dioxide levels in the atmosphere. *Journal of Sustainable Forestry* 1(1):61–77.

Kilgore, B. M. 1970. Restoring fire to the sequoias. *National Parks and Conservation* 44(277)(October):16–22.

Kilgore, B. M., and G. Briggs. 1972. Restoring fire to high elevation forests in California. *Journal of Forestry* 70(5):266–271.

Kilgore, B. M., and G. Curtis. 1987. *Guide to understory burning in ponderosa pine-larch-fir forests in the Intermountain West.* USDA Forest Service, Intermountain Research Station, General Technical Report 233, Ogden, Utah.

Kitts, J. A. 1919. Forest destruction prevented by control of surface fires. *American Forestry* 25:1264, 1306.

Knight, D. H. 1996. The ecological implications of fire in Greater Yellowstone: A summary. pp. 233–235 *in* J. M. Greenlee, ed. *The ecological implications of fire in Greater*

Yellowstone. Proceedings—Second Biennial Conference on the Greater Yellowstone Ecosystem. International Association of Wildland Fire, Fairfield, Washington.

Koch, E. 1935. The passing of the Lolo Trail. *Journal of Forestry* 33(2):98–104.

———. 1945. The Seeley Lake tamaracks. *American Forests* 51(1):21, 48.

———. 1998. *Forty years a forester: 1903–1943.* Mountain Press, Missoula, Montana.

Koch, P. 1992. Wood versus nonwood materials in U.S. residential construction: some energy-related global implications. *Forest Products Journal* 42(5):31–42.

Kurth, L. L. 1996. Examples of fire restoration in Glacier National Park. pp. 54–55 *in USDA Forest Service, Intermountain Research Station, General Technical Report 341,* Ogden, Utah.

Langston, N. 1996. The uses of history in restoration. pp. 36–40 *in* D. L. Peterson and C. Klimas, ed. *The role of restoration in ecosystem management.* Society for Ecological Restoration, Madison, Wisconsin.

Leiberg, J. B. 1899. Bitterroot Forest Reserve. pp. 253–282 in *U.S. Geological Survey, 19th Annual Report, Part V.*

Leopold, A. 1924. Grass, brush, timber, and fire in southern Arizona. *Journal of Forestry* 22(6):1–10.

———. 1949. *A Sand County almanac and sketches here and there.* Oxford University Press, New York.

Leopold, A. S., S. Cain, C. Cottam, I. Gabrielson, and T. Kimball. 1963. Wildlife management in the national parks. *Transactions of the North American Wildlife and Natural Resources Conference* 28:28–45.

Lewis, H. T. 1973. *Patterns of Indian burning in California: ecology and ethnohistory.* Anthropology Paper No.1. Ballena Press, Ramona, California.

———. 1985. Why Indians burned: Specific versus general reasons. pp. 75–80 *in USDA Forest Service, Intermountain Forest and Range Experiment Station, General Technical Report 182,* Ogden, Utah.

Lyle, J. 2002. *Fire and fuels information—2002.* Sequoia and Kings Canyon National Parks, Three Rivers, California.

———. 2003. *Fire and fuels management.* Sequoia and Kings Canyon National Parks, Three Rivers, California.

Lynch, D. L., W. Romme, and M. Floyd. 2000. Forest restoration in southwestern ponderosa pine. *Journal of Forestry* 98(8):17–24.

Lyon, L. J., M. Huff, R. Hooper, E. Telfer, D. Schreiner, and J. Smith. 2000. *Wildland fire in ecosystems: effects of fire on fauna.* USDA Forest Service, Rocky Mountain Research Station, General Technical Report 42, vol.1, Ogden, Utah.

Maffei, H., and B. Tandy. 2002. Methodology for modeling the spatial and temporal effects of vegetation management alternatives on late successional habitat in the Pacific Northwest. pp. 69–77 *in USDA Forest Service, Rocky Mountain Research Station, Proceedings 25.* Ogden, Utah.

Martin, R. E. 1990. Goals, methods, and elements of prescribed burning. pp. 55–66 *in* J. D. Walstad, S. Radosevich, and D. Sandberg, ed. *Natural and prescribed fire in Pacific Northwest forests.* Oregon State University Press, Corvallis, Oregon.

Mattson, D. J., K. Kendall, and D. Reinhart. 2001. Whitebark pine, grizzly bears, and red squirrels. pp. 121–136 *in* D. F. Tomback, S. F. Arno, and R. E. Keane, ed. *Whitebark pine communities: ecology and restoration.* Island Press, Washington, D.C.

McCool, S. F., and G. Stankey. 1986. *Visitor attitudes toward wilderness fire management policy 1971–84.* USDA Forest Service, Intermountain Research Station, Research Paper 357, Ogden, Utah.

McEvoy, T. J. 1998. *Legal aspects of owning and managing woodlands.* Island Press, Washington, D.C.

———. 2004. *Positive impact forestry.* Island Press, Washington, D.C.

McGinnis, N. 2002. Fighting fire with fire. *Squamish Chief,* 17 August, p. 8. Squamish, British Columbia.

McKelvey, K. S., C. Skinner, C. Chang, D. Erman, S. Husari, D. Parsons, J. van Wagtendonk, and C. Weatherspoon. 1996. An overview of fire in the Sierra Nevada. pp. 1033–1040 *in Sierra Nevada Ecosystem Project: Final report to Congress, volume II.* Centers for Water and Wildland Resources, University of California. Davis, California.

McLean, H. 1993. The Boise Quickstep. *American Forests* 99(1–2):11–14.

Meine, C. 1988. *Aldo Leopold: his life and work.* University of Wisconsin Press, Madison.

Miller, M. 2000. Fire autecology. pp. 9–34 *in USDA Forest Service, Rocky Mountain Research Station, General Technical Report 42,* vol. 2, Fort Collins, Colorado.

Milstein, M. 2000. Spotted owl complicates solutions to fires in forests. *Oregonian,* 26 November, A-29, 34. Portland, Oregon.

Monnig, E., and J. Byler. 1992. *Forest health and ecological integrity in the Northern Rockies.* USDA Forest Service, Northern Region, FPM Report 92-7, Missoula, Montana.

Moore, B. 1996. *The Lochsa story: land ethics in the Bitterroot Mountains.* Mountain Press, Missoula, Montana.

Morgan, P., G. Aplet, J. Haufler, H. Humphries, C. Hope, M. Moore, and D. Wilson. 1994. Historical range of variability: a useful tool for evaluating ecosystem change. *Journal of Sustainable Forestry* 2:87–111.

Morris, W. G. 1934. Forest fires in Oregon and Washington. *Oregon Historical Quarterly* 35:313–339.

Muir, J. 1894. *The mountains of California.* [republished 1961. Doubleday and Company, New York.]

Muri, G. 1955. *The effect of simulated slash burning on germination, primary survival and taproot ratios of Engelmann spruce and alpine fir.* Research Note No. 14, University of British Columbia, Forestry Club, Vancouver, B.C.

Mutch, R. W. 2001. Practice, poetry, and policy: Will we be better prepared for the fires of 2006? *Bugle* 18(2):61–64.

Mutch, R. W., S. Arno, J. Brown, C. Carlson, R. Ottmar, and J. Peterson. 1993. *Forest health in the Blue Mountains: A management strategy for fire-adapted ecosystems.* USDA Forest Service, Pacific Northwest Research Station, General Technical Report 310, Portland, Oregon.

Nash, R. 1973. *Wilderness and the American mind.* Yale University Press, New Haven, Connecticut.

Nelson, T. C. 1979. Fire management policy in the national forests: a new era. *Journal of Forestry* 77:723–725.

Nez Perce National Forest. 1999. *Salmon River Canyon Project: Draft environmental impact statement.* Grangeville, Idaho.

Nichols, H. T. 1989. Managing fire in Sequoia and Kings Canyon national parks. *Fremontia* 16(4):11–14.

Nisbet, J. 1994. *Sources of the river.* Sasquatch Books, Seattle.

Northey, J. K. 2002. Making the most out of your slash. *Montana Tree Farm News* 22:10. (Available at www.mttreefarm.org).

Oppenheimer, J., and I. Dickinson. 2003. *Fire in Idaho: An analysis of fire policy in Idaho.* Idaho Conservation League, Boise, Idaho (Available at www.wildidaho.org).

Opperman, T., M. Keifer, and L. Trader. 2001. Meeting resource management objectives with prescribed fire. pp. 135–142 *in Proceedings of the 11th Conference on Research and Resource Management in Parks and Public Lands.* The George Wright Society, Hancock, Michigan.

Oregonian. 2003. Case study for the fire bill. (editorial) p. F-4. Portland, Oregon.

Parsons, D. J. 1990. Restoring fire to the Sierra Nevada mixed conifer forest: Reconciling science, policy and practicality. pp. 271–279 *in* H. G. Hughes and T. Bonnicksen, ed. *Proceedings—First Annual Meeting, Society for Ecological Restoration.* University of Wisconsin, Madison.

———. 1994. *Objects or ecosystems? Giant sequoia management in national parks.* USDA Forest Service, Pacific Southwest Research Station, General Technical Report 151, Berkeley, California.

———. 2000. The challenge of restoring natural fire to wilderness. pp. 276–282 *in USDA Forest Service, Rocky Mountain Research Station, Proceedings 15,* vol. 5, Ogden, Utah.

Parsons, D. J., and J. van Wagtendonk. 1996. Fire research and management in the Sierra Nevada national parks. pp. 25–48 *in* W. Halvorson and G. Davis, ed. *Science and ecosystem management in the national parks.* University of Arizona Press, Tucson.

Parsons, D. J., D. Graber, J. Agee, and J. van Wagtendonk. 1986. Natural fire management in national parks. *Environmental Management* 10:21–24.

Paysen, T. E., R. Ansley, J. Brown, G. Gottfried, S. Haase, M. Harrington, M. Narog, S. Sackett, and R. Wilson. 2000. pp. 121–159 *in USDA Forest Service, Rocky Mountain Research Station, General Technical Report 42,* vol. 2, Ogden, Utah.

Pearson, G. A. 1923. *Natural reproduction of western yellow pine in the Southwest.* USDA Forest Service, Bulletin 1105, Washington, D.C.

———. 1933. A twenty-year record of changes in an Arizona pine forest. *Ecology* 14:272–285.

Pfister, R. D., B. Kovalchik, S. Arno, and R. Presby. 1977. *Forest habitat types of Montana.* USDA Forest Service, Intermountain Forest and Range Experiment Station, General Technical Report 34, Ogden, Utah.

Pinchot, G. 1899. The relation of forests and forest fires. *National Geographic* 10:393–403.

————. 1947. *Breaking new ground*. Harcourt Brace Jovanovich, Inc. Reprinted, 1972, University of Washington Press, Seattle.

Polley, H.W., H. Mayeux, H. Johnson, and C. Tischler. 1997. Viewpoint: Atmospheric CO_2, soil water, and shrub/grass ratios on rangelands. *Journal of Range Management* 50:278–284.

Powell, J.W. 1891. *Testimony to Congress. Eleventh annual report of the U.S. Geological Survey, 1889–1890, part II irrigation*, 207–208. Washington, D.C.

Pyne, S.J. 1982. *Fire in America: A cultural history of wildland and rural fire*. Princeton University Press, Princeton, New Jersey.

————. 1984. *Introduction to wildland fire*. John Wiley and Sons, New York.

————. 1997. *World fire: The culture of fire on Earth*. University of Washington Press, Seattle.

————. 2001. *Year of the fires: The story of the great fires of 1910*. Viking Penguin, New York.

Quigley, T. M., R. Haynes, and R. Graham, technical ed. 1996. *Integrated scientific assessment for ecosystem management in the interior Columbia Basin*. USDA Forest Service, Pacific Northwest Research Station, General Technical Report 382, Portland, Oregon.

Reid, B. 1998. A clearing in the forest: New approaches to managing America's woodlands. *Nature Conservancy* 48(6):18–24.

Romme, W. H., and D. Despain. 1989. Historical perspective on the Yellowstone fires of 1988. *BioScience* 39:695–699.

Romme, W.H., L. Floyd-Hanna, and D. Hanna. 2003. Ancient piñon-juniper forests of Mesa Verde and the West: a cautionary note for forest restoration programs. pp. 335–350 *in USDA Forest Service, Rocky Mountain Research Station, Proceedings RMRS-O-29*, Fort Collins, Colorado.

Rothermel, R. C., R. Hartford, and C. Chase. 1994. *Fire growth maps for the 1988 Greater Yellowstone area fires*. USDA Forest Service, Intermountain Research Station, General Technical Report 304, Ogden, Utah.

Sala, A., and R. Callaway. 2001. *Physiological responses of old-growth ponderosa pine and western larch to restoration cutting and burning treatments*. USDA Forest Service, Rocky Mountain Research Station, Progress report RMRS-99563-RJVA. Missoula, Montana.

Salwasser, H., and R. Pfister. 1994. Ecosystem management: from theory to practice. pp. 150–161 *in USDA Forest Service, Rocky Mountain Forest and Range Experiment Station, General Technical Report 247*, Fort Collins, Colorado.

Sandberg, D., R. Ottmar, J. Peterson, and J. Core. 2002. *Wildland fire in ecosystems: effects of fire on air*. USDA Forest Service, Rocky Mountain Research Station, General Technical Report 42, vol. 5, Ogden, Utah.

Savory, A., and J. Butterfield. 1999. *Holistic resource management*, 2nd ed. Island Press, Washington, D.C.

Scott, J. H. 1998. *Fuel reduction in residential and scenic forests: a comparison of three treatments in a western Montana ponderosa pine stand*. USDA Forest Service, Rocky Mountain Research Station, Research Paper 5, Ogden, Utah.

Shepperd, W. D. 2001. Manipulations to regenerate aspen ecosystems. pp. 355–366 *in USDA Forest Service, Rocky Mountain Research Station, Proceedings 18*. Fort Collins, Colorado.

Shindler, B., and E. Toman. 2003. Fuel reduction strategies in forest communities: a longitudinal analysis of public support. *Journal of Forestry* 101(6):8–15.

Shinn, D. A. 1980. Historical perspectives on range burning in the Inland Pacific Northwest. *Journal of Range Management* 33:415–422.

Sisters Ranger District. 2001. *McCache Vegetation Management Environmental Assessment*. USDA Forest Service, Deschutes National Forest, Sisters, Oregon.

Smith, D. M. 1997. *The practice of silviculture: Applied forest ecology*. John Wiley and Sons, New York.

Smith, D. O. in review. Closing canopies and changing trophic energy pathways in western conifer forests: where do we go from here? Manuscript submitted for publication to *Transactions of the Wildlife Society, Western Section*. Sacramento, California.

Smith, H.Y., and S. Arno, ed. 1999. *Eighty-eight years of change in a managed ponderosa pine forest*. USDA Forest Service, Rocky Mountain Research Station, General Technical Report 23, Ogden, Utah.

Smith, J.K., and N. McMurray. 2000. *FireWorks curriculum featuring ponderosa, lodgepole, and whitebark pine forests*. USDA Forest Service, Rocky Mountain Research Station, General Technical Report 65, Fort Collins, Colorado.

Stalling, D. 2003. The Burnt Fork Ranch: on the cutting edge of stewardship. *Bugle* 20(3):32–39.

Stephens, S. L. 1998. Evaluation of the effects of silviculture and fuels treatments on potential fire behavior in Sierra Nevada mixed-conifer forests. *Forest Ecology and Management* 105:21–35.

Stephenson, N. L. 1996. Ecology and management of giant sequoia groves. pp. 1431–1467 *in Sierra Nevada Ecosystem Project: Final report to Congress, vol. II*. University of California, Centers for Water and Wildland Resources, Davis, California.

————. 1999. Reference conditions for giant sequoia forest restoration: structure, process, and precision. *Ecological Applications* 9(4):1253–1265.

Stewart, O. C. 2002. *Forgotten fires: Native Americans and the transient wilderness*. University of Oklahoma Press, Norman.

Stickney, P. F. 1990. Early development of vegetation following holocaustic fire in Northern Rocky Mountain forests. *Northwest Science* 64(5):243–246.

Swetnam, T. W. 1990. Fire history and climate in the southwestern United States. pp. 6–17 *in USDA Forest Service, Rocky Mountain Research Station, General Technical Report 191*, Fort Collins, Colorado.

————. 1993. Fire history and climate change in giant sequoia groves. *Science* 262:885–889.

Sydoriak, C. A., C. Allen, and B. Jacobs. 2000. Would ecological landscape restoration make the Bandelier Wilderness more or less of a wilderness? pp. 209–215 *in* D. N. Cole, S. McCool, W. Borrie, and F. O'Loughlin (comps.). *Proceedings:*

Wilderness Science in a Time of Change Conference—Volume 5: Wilderness ecosystems, threats, and management. USDA Forest Service, Rocky Mountain Research Station, Proceedings RMRS-P-15-VOL-5. Ogden, Utah.

Sydoriak, C. A., C. Allen, and B. Jacobs. 2001. Would ecological landscape restoration make the Bandelier Wilderness more or less of a wilderness? *Wild Earth* 10(4):83–90.

Taylor, A. H. 1999. *Changes in fire regimes, land use, and forest structure since European settlement in the Lassen National Forest, California.* Final report for cost share agreement between Lassen National Forest and The Pennsylvania State University, University Park, Pennsylvania.

Thomas, J. W. 2002. *Dynamic vs. static management in a fire-influenced landscape—the Northwest Forest Plan.* Text of presentation at the conference "Fire in Oregon Forests," Oregon Forest Resources Institute, Portland, Oregon.

Tomback, D. F. 1994. Effects of seed dispersal by Clark's nutcracker on early postfire regeneration of whitebark pine. pp. 193–198 *in USDA Forest Service, Intermountain Research Station, General Technical Report 309,* Ogden, Utah.

———. 2001. Clarks nutcracker: Agent of regeneration. pp. 89–104 *in* D. F. Tomback, S. Arno, and R. Keane, eds. *Whitebark pine communities: ecology and restoration.* Island Press, Washington, D.C.

Tomback, D. F., S. Arno, and R. Keane. 2001. The compelling case for management intervention. pp. 3–25 *in* D. F. Tomback, S. Arno, and R. Keane, eds. *Whitebark pine communities: Ecology and restoration.* Island Press, Washington, D.C.

Touchan, R., C. Allen, and T. Swetnam. 1996. Fire history and climatic patterns in ponderosa pine and mixed-conifer forests of the Jemez Mountains, northern New Mexico. pp. 33–46 *in* C. D. Allen, tech. ed., *Fire effects in southwestern forests: Proceedings of the Second La Mesa Fire Symposium.* USDA Forest Service, Rocky Mountain Research Station, General Technical Report RM-GTR-286, Fort Collins, Colorado.

Trachtman, P. 2003. Fire fight. *Smithsonian* (August) pp. 43–52.

Turner, N. J. 1999. Time to burn: Traditional use of fire to enhance resource production by Aboriginal peoples in British Columbia. pp. 185–218 *in* R. Boyd, ed. *Indians, fire and the land in the Pacific Northwest.* Oregon State University Press, Corvallis, Oregon.

Turner, N. J., L. Thompson, M. Thompson, and A. York. 1990. *Knowledge and usage of plants by the Thompson Indians of British Columbia.* Royal British Columbia Museum, Memoir No. 3. Victoria, British Columbia.

USDA Forest Service and USDI Bureau of Land Management. 1994. *Record of decision for the amendments to Forest Service and Bureau of Land Management planning documents within the range of the northern spotted owl/Standards and guidelines for management of habitat for late-successional and old-growth forest related species.* Final environmental impact statement.

USDA-USDI. 1989. Final report and recommendations of the Fire Management

Policy Review Team and summary of public comments; notice. *Federal Register* 54(115):25660–25678, 16 June.

USDI/USDA. 1995. *Federal wildland fire management policy and program review.* Final report. National Interagency Fire Center, Boise, Idaho.

Uusivuori, J., and J. Kuuluvainen. 2001. Substitution in global wood imports in the 1990s. *Canadian Journal of Forest Research* 31(7):1148–1155.

Vancouver Sun. 2002. The risk of doing nothing about forest fires. (editorial) 7 October, A-10. Vancouver, British Columbia.

Vazquez, A., and L. Hood. 2003. *Evaluation of thinned and unthinned stands within the Cone Fire, Blacks Mountain Experimental Forest.* Draft report. Eagle Lake Ranger District, Lassen National Forest, Susanville, California.

Wallowa Valley Ranger District. 2000. *Environmental assessment for the Buck Vegetation Management Project.* Wallowa-Whitman National Forest, Enterprise, Oregon.

Waring, R. H., and G. Pitman. 1985. Modifying lodgepole pine stands to change susceptibility to mountain pine beetle attack. *Ecology* 66:889–897.

Washington State Department of Natural Resources. 1998. *Our changing nature: natural resource trends in Washington State.* Olympia, Washington.

Weaver, H. 1943. Fire as an ecological and silvicultural factor in the ponderosa pine region of the Pacific Slope. *Journal of Forestry* 41(1):7–14.

———. 1968. Fire and its relationship to ponderosa pine. pp. 127–149 in *Proceedings— Tall Timbers Fire Ecology Conference 7.* USDA Forest Service, Tall Timbers Research Station, Tallahassee, Florida.

White, A. S. 1985. Presettlement regeneration patterns in a southwestern ponderosa pine stand. *Ecology* 66:589–594.

White, C. A., E. Langemann, C. Gates, C. Kay, T. Shury, and T. Hurd. 2001. Plains bison restoration in the Canadian Rocky Mountains? Ecological and management considerations. pp. 152–160 in D. Harmon, ed. *Crossing boundaries in park management: Proceedings of the 11th Conference on Research and Resource Management in Parks and Public Lands.* The George Wright Society, Hancock, Michigan.

White, C. A., I. Pengelly, M. Rogeau, and D. Zell. 2004. *Landscape fire regimes and vegetation restoration in Banff National Park, Alberta.* Occasional Paper BNP-2003-01. Parks Canada, Banff National Park, Alberta.

Wickman, B. E. 1992. *Forest health in the Blue Mountains: The influence of insects and diseases.* USDA Forest Service, Pacific Northwest Research Station, General Technical Report 295, Portland, Oregon.

Wierzchowski, J., M. Heathcott, and M. Flannigan. 2002. Lightning and lightning fire, central cordillera, Canada. *International Journal of Wildland Fire* 11:41–51.

Wilcox, B. P., D. Breshears, and C. Allen. 2003. Ecohydrology of a resource-conserving semiarid woodland: Temporal and spatial scaling and disturbance. *Ecological Monographs* 73(2):223–239.

Wilcox, B. P., J. Pitlick, C. Allen, and D. Davenport. 1996. Runoff and erosion from a rapidly eroding pinyon–juniper hillslope. pp. 60–77 in M. G. Anderson and S. Brooks, ed. *Advances in Hillslope Processes*, Vol. 1. John Wiley and Sons, New York.

Wilkinson, T. 2001. Prometheus unbound. *Nature Conservancy* 51(3):12–20.

Woodley, S. 1995. Playing with fire: vegetation management in the Canadian Parks Service. pp. 30–33 *in USDA Forest Service, Intermountain Research Station, General Technical Report 320*. Ogden, Utah.

Wooton, E. O. 1908. *The range problem in New Mexico.* New Mexico College of Agriculture and Mechanic Arts, Agriculture Experiment Station Bulletin No. 66. Las Cruces, New Mexico.

Zimmerman, G. T., and D. Bunnell. 2000. The federal wildland fire policy: Opportunities for wilderness fire management. pp. 288–297 *in USDA Forest Service, Rocky Mountain Research Station, Proceedings 15*, vol. 5, Ogden, Utah.

Zimmerman, G. T., and P. Omi. 1998. Fire restoration options in lodgepole pine ecosystems. pp. 285–297 in *Proceedings—Tall Timbers Fire Ecology Conference 20.* Tall Timbers Research Station. Tallahassee, Florida.

About the Authors

Stephen F. Arno, now retired, was research forester with the USDA Forest Service Rocky Mountain Research Station. He is coauthor of *Flames in our Forest: Disaster or Renewal?* (Island Press), and has been restoring his family's uneven-aged ponderosa pine forest for 30 years.

Carl E. Fiedler is research professor at the University of Montana. He teaches silviculture, conducts research on uneven-aged management, and presents short courses on silviculture, fire, and restoration forestry throughout the West.

Index

Aesthetic appeal, importance of, 80
Agee, Jim, 207
Agriculture Department, U.S. (USDA), 130
Alders, 24–25
Allen, Craig, 59, 61
American Forests, 101
Anasazi people, 60
Anders, Warren, 118, 119
Andrews, Bob, 176, 177
Animal protection and Northwest Forest
    Plan, 92–93
Archibald timber sale in Seeley Lake
    recreation corridor, 134–37
Arnica, heart-leaf, 142
Arno, Matt, 120
Arno, Stephen, ix–xi
Arnold, Elizabeth, 107
Ash, mountain, 22
Aspen:
    Banff National Park, 166
    Eagle Lake Ranger District, 177,
        180–81
    habitat restoration, wildlife, 151, 152
    mixed fire regime, 22
    stand replacement fire regime, 25
Aster, 142

Bandelier National Monument, 59–64
Banff National Park, 162–66
Barrett, Steve, 159
Beale, Edward, 7
Beargrass, 158

Bears, grizzly, 166–68
Beaver Ridge, 173
Beetle, engraver, 82, 95–96
Beetles, bark:
    Banff National Park, 166
    Boise National Forest, 106
    Clearwater/Salmon River area, 196
    E Bar L Ranch, 113
    Greater Flagstaff Forests Partnership, 82
    historical fire regimes, knowledge
        from, 26
    pinyon/juniper woodlands, 58–59
    Rocking K Ranch, 120
    Seeley Lake recreation corridor, 137
Beetles, western pine, 91
Bidwell DFPZ timber sale, 183
Biodiversity, 11
Biomass energy, 176
Biswell, Harold, 10
Bitterbrush, 67
Bittercherry, 22
Bitterroot National Forest, 66–73, 117,
    154–59, 171, 198
Blacks Mountain Experimental Forest, 178
Blister rust, white pine, 168, 169–70
Blue Mountains, 97–101
Bob Marshall Wilderness, 33, 138, 141–43
Boise National Forest, 101–7
Bonney, Byron, 197, 199
Book of Fire, The (Cottrell), 39
Bradt, Bill, 115–17
British Columbia's Coast Range, 88–91

Brown-spot disease, 10
Buck Vegetation Management Project, 99–100
Budworm, 26, 94
Buffaloberry, 166
Bunchgrass, 120, 177
Bureau of Indian Affairs, xii
Burnt Fork Ranch, 114–17
Burr, Karen, 173
Byproducts of restoration forestry, 49–50, 204, 205–6

California Department of Forestry, 129
Calloway, Ray, 147
Campbell, Dave, 155, 157, 158
Canopy-closure requirements for sensitive wildlife species, 186–87
Caprio, Tony, 129, 130
Carbon dioxide, atmospheric, 57
Cascade Range, 26, 31, 91–97, 169
    see also Eagle Lake Ranger District
Casner Project in Boise National Forest, 104–6
Cedar, incense, 123
Challis National Forest, 171
Cheatgrass, 59
Chokecherry, 22
Chonka, Jerry, 150–53
Clark, William, 30
Clearcutting, 8, 76–77, 153, 155
Clearwater National Forest, 171, 173
Clearwater/Salmon River area
geography/vegetation, overview of, 188–89
impetus for restoring fire, 189–91
prescribed natural fires, 191–96
success, sustaining, 196–98
wildland-urban interface, 198–99
Clements, Frederic, 10
Coconino National Forest, 81
Colorado Division of Wildlife, 152
Comprehensive thinning, 186
Conifers, see specific tree type
Conservation easements, 11, 51
    see also Private conservation reserves

Cooperative Extension offices, state forestry, 51
Covington, Wally, 82
Creech, Kay, 115
Creech, Randy, 115
Crown fire hazard, 46
Currants, 22
Cut-to-length systems, 119

Daniels, Orville, 190
Deerlodge National Forest, 120
Defenders of Wildlife, 36
Defensible fuel profile zones (DFPZs), 178, 183
Dense forests representing unstable conditions/ecological imbalances, 178–79, 209–10
Deschutes National Forest, 92–94
Divoky, Dennis, 141
Dougherty, Margaret, 133
Dragonhead, 142
Duff accumulations, 32, 123, 145, 160

Eagle Lake Ranger District:
    aspen groves, restoration of, 180–81
    geography/vegetation, overview of, 175–76
    goals/strategies, restoration, 175
    history of forest management in, 176–80
    mixed-conifer/shrub communities, restoration of, 184–86
    pine, ponderosa, 181–84
    selection systems for maintaining forests, 186–87
    vegetation management objective, 179–80
Easements, conservation, 11, 51
    see also Private conservation reserves
E Bar L Ranch, 109–14
Ecological Restoration Institute, 83
Ecology revealing role of fire in forests, 8, 10, 26–28
Ecosystem-based management, 11, 111, 177
    see also Prescribed burning; Silviculture
Edminster, Carl, 83

Eklund, Ray, 104, 107
Elk, 155
Environmental issues, public interest in, 11
European approach, modifying a, 77–78
Even-aged forest management methods, xi, xii
Exploitation logging, 40, 41–42

"Fallacy of Passive Management, The" (Agee), 207
Federal funds for restoration forestry, 51
Fescue, Arizona, 86
Fiedler, Carl, xi–xiii
Financing restoration forestry projects, 49, 51
Fir, alpine, 26
Fir, Douglas, 22–26, 144–47, 151
    see also Private conservation reserves; Public lands, forest management on; Research/demonstration areas
Fir, white, 95–96, 123, 177, 184
"Fire/Fire Surrogate Studies," 130
Fireproofing homes/communities, 34
Fire regimes, see Historical listings; Lightning fires; Low-intensity disturbance regime; Prescribed burning; Underburns; Wildfires sweeping through forests of Western North America
Fireweed, 25, 142, 158
Firewise, 199
Firewise Forest Landscaping, 116–17
Firewood as a byproduct of restoration forestry, 49
Fireworks, 199
Flathead Indian Reservation, 80
Flathead National Forest/River, 138–43, 171
Forage, wildlife, 166
Forbs, 120
Forest Management Stewardship Fund, 113
Forestry, failure of traditional, 7–9
    see also Historical fire regimes, knowledge from
Forest Service, U.S. (USFS):
    Bitterroot National Forest, 154

Clearwater/Salmon River area, 189
easements, conservation, 51
ecosystem management, 177
Greater Flagstaff Forests Partnership, 83
Larch, western, 133
pine, whitebark, 173
prescribed fire, criticisms of, 33
roots of restoration forestry, 10, 11
stewardship authority, 99
suppression, fire, 8
Frank Church/River of No Return Wilderness (FC/RNRW), 190, 196
Frequent fires and understory fire regime, 16–17, 19
Friends of the Metolius, 97
Fruit-bearing shrubs, 22, 25
Fuels associated with historical fires, 31–32
Fulé, Pete, 81–82, 86
Fungus, Indian paint, 95

Geographic information systems (GIS), 126–27
Geological Survey, U.S., 133
Geranium bicknellii, 142
Gilliam, Jim, 89, 91
Glacier National Park, 138–41
Glide Project in Boise National Forest, 105
Goetz, Hank, 80, 110, 111
Gold mining in Boise National Forest, 102
Gooseberries, 22
Grasslands, nonnative species displacing native, 59
Gray, Robert, 89, 91
Grazing, disruptive influence of, 60–61, 177, 180
Grazing as a restoration tool, 118
Greater Flagstaff Forests Partnership (GFFP), 81–87
Grizzly bears, 166–68
Grove, Janet, 155–56
Gruell, George, 67
Gunnison National Forest, 150

Habitat restoration, wildlife, 150–53, 177
Haglund, Steve, xii
Hand-thinning, 105–6
Hardy, Colin, 159, 160
Harrington, Mick, 144
Harvey Mountain, 185
Hawthorn, 22
Helicopter yarding, 105
Hells Canyon Wilderness, 188
Herbs:
    Bob Marshall Wilderness, 142
    British Columbia's Coast Range, 89
    Rocking K Ranch, 120
    Sequoia and Kings Canyon National
        Park, 128
    stand replacement fire regime, 25
High-grade logging, 40, 41–42
Historical fire regimes, knowledge from:
    ecological knowledge, applying, 26–28
    mixed fire regime, 21–23
    overview, 14–15, 17
    stand replacement fire regime, 23–26
    understory fire regime, 15–21
Historical forest conditions, returning to:
    fuels, 31–32
    ignitions, 30–31
    overview, 29
    political/economic barriers, 33–35
    reality, sobering, 36
    scale of fires, 30
    structure, forest, 32–33
    wrong fire regime, restoring the, 35
Hog-fuel chips and power generation, 176
Hollyhock, 25
Huckleberry, 22, 142–43

Idaho Conservation League, 107
Identity crisis gripping forestry, 74
Ignitions, historical look at fire, 30–31
Indian paint fungus, 95
Infrastructure needed for restoration
        forestry, support, 205–7
Interior Department, U.S., 130
Intermediate silviculture treatments, 45

Intermountain Research Station, 69–70
Inventory data and restoration forestry, 44

Jacobs, Brian, 61
Johnson, Janet, 155–56
Johnson Brothers Contracting, 115
Joint Fire Science Program, 130
Journal of Forestry, 10, 46
Juniper trees, *see* Pinyon/Juniper woodlands

Keane, Bob, 170, 173
Keen, F. P., 10
Ketcham, Rebecca, 98
Kings Canyon National Park, 10
Koch, Elers, 66, 189–90

Labor costs for restoration forestry, 51
Land and Water Consulting, 118
Land ethic, 10
Landscape-scale fires, 30
Larch, western:
    Bob Marshall Wilderness, 138, 141–43
    Flathead River valley, 138–41
    Glacier National Park, 138–41
    old-growth grove, 143–48
    overview, 131–32
    Seeley Lake recreation corridor, 132–38
Lassen Volcanic National Park, 175
    see also Eagle Lake Ranger District
Late successional reserves (LSRs), 92–97
Legacy Program, 51
Legislation:
    Clean Air Act, 8
    Clean Water Act, 8–9
    Endangered Species Act (ESA) of 1973,
        97, 155
    Herger-Feinstein Quincy Library
        Group Forest Recovery Act, 178, 186
    Multiple Use Act of 1960, 154
    National Environmental Protection Act
        of 1969, 9, 191
    National Parks Act of 2000, 164
    Wilderness Act of 1964, 190
Leopold, A. Starker, 122

Leopold, Aldo, 10, 203
Lewis, Meriwether, 30
Lewis and Clark National Forest, 159
Lick Creek project (Bitterroot National
    Forest), xii, xiii, 66–73
Lightning fires:
    Banff National Park, 164
    Bob Marshall Wilderness, 143
    Clearwater/Salmon River area, 191–95
    Glacier National Park, 139
    historical fire regimes, knowledge
        from, 16
    pine, whitebark, 170–71, 173
    programs allowing return of, 33
    reality check concerning, 36
    returning historical ignitions, 30
    seedlings, propagating rust-resistant, 173
    Sequoia and Kings Canyon National
        Park, 122–23, 127
Lillooet First Nations, 89, 90
Lindbergh, Land, 110, 111
Little Belt Mountains, 159
Local vegetation/disturbance determining
    restoration strategy, 64
Logging techniques used for exploita-
    tion/timber management/restoration,
    40–43
Lolo National Forest, 117, 132–38, 171
Love, Tim, 138
Lovejoy, Stu, 155, 156, 158
Low-intensity disturbance regime:
    British Columbia's Coast Range, 89–90
    Cascade Range, 92
    Eagle Lake Ranger District, 182
    Lubrecht Experimental Forest, 74–75
Lubrecht Experimental Forest:
    aesthetic appeal, importance of, 80
    E Bar L Ranch, 110
    European approach, modifying a, 77–78
    identity crisis gripping forestry, 74
    implementing treatments, 78–79
    lessons learned, 79–81
    low-intensity disturbance regime, 74–75
    opposition to treatments in, 76–77

origins of, 73
overview of, xii–xiii, 11
problems, potential, 80–81
scar analysis, fire, 74–75
selection cutting, 75–79
Lupine, 158

Maladapted trees, 106
Mallard-Larkins Pioneer Area, 189
Manzanita, green-leaf, 94
Maple, mountain, 22, 25
McCache Vegetation Management
    Project, 93–94
McCaughey, Ward, 159, 160
McLeod, Milo, 134
Meadow areas, rejuvenating, 118
Mining in Boise National Forest, 102
Missoula Fire Sciences Laboratory, 143
Mistletoe, dwarf, 66, 95, 151, 152, 155
Mixed fire regime:
    historical fire regimes, knowledge from,
        21–23, 27
    pine, lodgepole, 149–50
    pinyon/juniper woodlands, 58
    traditional forestry, failure of, 8, 9
Monitoring and restoration forestry, 44
Moore, Bud, 190
Morrell timber sale in Seeley Lake recre-
    ation corridor, 136–37
Muir, John, 130
Mutch, Bob, 190, 198

National Fire Plan, 51, 105
National Park Service, U.S. (NPS), 33,
    124–25
National Public Radio, 107
Native Americans, fires started by:
    Banff National Park, 164
    British Columbia's Coast Range, 89, 90
    historical fire regime, knowledge
        from, 16
    returning historical ignitions, 30–31
    Seeley Lake recreation corridor, 133–34
Nature Conservancy, The, 36, 51, 111–13

Nez Perce National Forest, 193
Nitrogen released into soils, 72
Nonfire regimes, 15
Nonmerchantable thinning treatment, 185
Northern Arizona University (NAU),
    83–86
Northwest Forest Plan, 92–93, 97
Nutcracker, Clark's, 168–69

Oelig, Bill, 137
Owl, flammulated, 94
Owl, northern spotted, 92–94, 96

Parker, Tammy R., 83
Parks Canada, 166
Passive management in western forests,
    207–8
Payette National Forest, 193
Pengelly, Ian, 162, 165
Per-acre treatment costs, 50
Pfister, Bob, xii
Phacelia, 120
Phenology, 52
Piazza, Mike, 100
Pile burning, 145, 147
Pilot Stewardship Authority (2001), 105
Pinchot, Gifford, 9, 66, 121, 131
Pine, Jeffrey, 16, 184–85
Pine, lodgepole:
    Banff National Park, 162–66
    Bitterroot National Forest, 154–59
    commercial forests in Montana, 153–54
    habitat restoration, wildlife, 150–53
    Larch, codomination with western, 131
    mixed fire regime, 149–50
    roots of restoration forestry, 10
    stand replacement fires, 24, 26
    Tenderfoot Creek Experimental Forest,
        159–62
Pine, longleaf, 10
Pine, pinyon, *see* Pinyon/Juniper woodlands
Pine, ponderosa:
    Clearwater/Salmon River area, 196
    Eagle Lake Ranger District, 181–84
    fire resistant, 16

roots of restoration forestry, 10
suppression, fire, 23
    see also Private conservation reserves;
    Public lands, forest management on;
    Research/demonstration areas
Pine, sugar, 23
Pine, whitebark:
    blister rust, 168, 169–70
    competition and growth patterns, 169
    cone crops, 168–69
    grizzly bears and, 167
    keystone species, 167
    lightning fires, 170–71, 173
    models for studying factors responsible
        for decline of, 170
    prescribed burning, 171–73
    seed predators, 168–69
    Whitebark Pine Ecosystem Foundation,
        174
Pinegrass, 120, 142, 158
Pinyon/Juniper woodlands
    Anasazi people, 60
    Bandelier National Monument, 59–64
    classifying, 58
    expansion of, 57–58
    grazing changing fire regimes, 60–61
    local vegetation/disturbance determin-
        ing restoration strategy, 64
    reducing, restoration efforts aimed at, 59
    soil issues, 59, 61–63
    staple of Southwestern life, 57–58
Plan, a written restoration, 46–48
Plants, fire-dependent, 25
Plant vigor, improving, 120, 128, 142–43,
    179–80
Political/economic barriers to returning
    to historical fire conditions, 33–35
Potter, Bill, 80, 109–14
Potter, Ma, 73
Powell, John W., 30
Prescott National Forest, 203
Prescribed burning:
    Banff National Park, 162–66
    Blue Mountains, 100–101
    Bob Marshall Wilderness, 141–42

British Columbia's Coast Range, 90
Cascade Range, 95
Clearwater/Salmon River area, 191–96
criticisms of, 33
Eagle Lake Ranger District, 183–84, 187
E Bar L Ranch, 114
Glacier National Park, 139
habitat restoration, wildlife, 151–53
Larch, old-growth western, 147
Lick Creek demonstration area, 69,
    70–73
objectives/methods, choosing/
    considering, 39
overview, 36
phenology, 52
pine, whitebark, 170, 171–73
Sequoia and Kings Canyon National
    Park, 124–30
Sierra Nevada Forest Plan Amendment,
    179
Tenderfoot Creek Experimental Forest,
    160–62
Tolan Creek/Beaver-Woods projects,
    156–59
Wilderness Act of 1964, 190
Prescription process in restoration forestry,
    44–45, 83–86, 94
Prison labor and hand-thinning, 105–6
Private conservation reserves:
    Burnt Fork Ranch, 114–17
    E Bar L Ranch, 109–14
    overview, 108–9
    Rocking K Ranch, 117–20
Private lands, lack of awareness of restora-
    tion on, 11
Private property as a barrier to returning
    to historical fire conditions, 33–35
Professionals needed to design/implement
    restoration forestry, 206–7
Public lands, forest management on:
    Blue Mountains, 97–101
    Boise National Forest, 101–7
    British Columbia's Coast Range,
        88–91
    Cascade Range, 91–97

Pulpwood as a byproduct of restoration
    forestry, 49
Pyramid Mountain sawmill, 136

Ramirez, Kathy, 104, 107
Ranches with forestland, see Private
    conservation reserves
Raspberry, 120
Reagan, Ronald, 33
Regeneration cuttings, 45
Regulatory environment and restoration
    forestry, 204, 207–10
Research/demonstration areas:
    Greater Flagstaff Forests Partnership,
        81–87
    Lick Creek, 66–73
    Lubrecht Experimental Forest, 73–81
Restoration forestry:
    antagonistic views of, 12–13
    byproducts of, 49–50, 204, 205–6
    definitions/needs for, 2–3, 11–13, 203–5
    economic considerations, 5–6, 9, 33–35,
        48–52, 154
    exploitation and timber management
        compared to, 40–43
    financing, 49, 51
    fire hazard, treatment effects on, 45–46
    infrastructure is paramount, 205–7
    objectives/methods, choosing/
        considering, 39–40
    overview, 37
    plan, developing a management, 46–48
    prescription process, 44–45, 83–86, 94
    profiles of projects by forest type, 55–56
    regulatory environment that supports,
        207–10
    roots of, 9–11
    scheduling issues, 51–52
    skilled people/professionals needed for,
        206–7
    stewardship of native forests, 38–39
    technology available for, 50
    see also Historical listings; Prescribed
        burning; Silviculture; specific tree/
        forest type

Rickman, Tom, 177, 179, 182
Rocking K Ranch, 117–20
Rocky Mountain Elk Foundation, 36,
    51, 114
Rocky Mountain Research Station's Fire
    Science Laboratory, 133
Rocky Mountains, 26, 31
Root diseases, 95

Safety issues for restoration forestry, 52
Sala, Anna, 147
Salmon National Forest, 171
Salmon River, see Clearwater/Salmon
    River area
Sapphire Mountain Range, 114, 117
Sawtooth Wilderness, 189
Scar analysis, fire:
    British Columbia's Coast Range, 89
    Larch, western, 143–44
    Lubrecht Experimental Forest, 74–75
Seeley Lake recreation corridor, 133
    Tenderfoot Creek Experimental
        Forest, 159
Scheduling issues for restoration forestry,
    51–52
Schenck, Carl, 9
Seeley, Chuck, 115
Seeley Lake recreation corridor, 132–38
Selection cutting, see Silviculture
Selway-Bitterroot Wilderness, 11, 14
    see also Clearwater/Salmon River area
Sequoia and Kings Canyon National Park
    (SEKI):
    burns, restoration, 123–24, 126, 127
    constraints on prescribed burning, 126,
        129, 130
    coordination with other agencies, 129
    core areas, concentration on achieving
        goals in, 129–30
    debate over goals of the Park Service,
        124–25
    geographic information systems, 126–27
    panel of outside experts, 124–26
    Pierce fire in 1987, 128
    Pinchot, Gifford, 121

pioneer in use of prescribed/lightning
    fires, 122–23
prescribed burning, 124–30
seedlings, survival of sequoia, 123
visitors/neighbors, sharing management
    practices with, 128–29
Sequoia National Park, 10
Serviceberry, 22
Service contracts with embedded timber
    sales, 104–5
Shade-intolerant trees, 19, 22, 23
    see also Larch, western; Pine, ponderosa;
        Pine, whitebark
Sheep (bighorn), habitat restoration for,
    150–53
Shrubs:
    Banff National Park, 166
    Eagle Lake Ranger District, 177
    Lick Creek demonstration area, 67
    mixed fire regime, 22
    Rocking K Ranch, 120
    Sequoia and Kings Canyon National
        Park, 128
    stand replacement fire regime, 25
    see also specific shrub
Sierra Nevada Ecosystem Project, 179
Sierra Nevada Forest Plan Amendment, 179
Sierra Nevada ranges, 31
    see also Eagle Lake Ranger District
Silviculture:
    Blue Mountains, 99–101
    Boise National Forest, 104–7
    British Columbia's Coast Range, 90
    Burnt Fork Ranch, 115–17
    Cascade Range, 92, 94, 96–97
    defining, 39–40, 45
    Eagle Lake Ranger District, 181–87
    E Bar L Ranch, 111–13
    Greater Flagstaff Forests Partnership,
        83–86
    Larch, old-growth western, 145, 147
    Lick Creek demonstration area, 67–73
    Lubrecht Experimental Forest, 75–79
    pine, lodgepole, 153–54
    Rocking K Ranch, 119–20

roots of restoration forestry, 11
Seeley Lake recreation corridor, 134–38
Tenderfoot Creek Experimental Forest,
    160–62
Tolan Creek/Beaver-Woods projects,
    156–57
Slash, 66, 69, 71, 158
Smith River, 159
Smurfit-Stone Container Corporation, 115
Snags (standing dead trees), 8, 9, 71, 94, 96,
    153, 154
Snake River, 188
Snowberry, 120
Soil issues:
    Blue Mountains, 100
    Burnt Fork Ranch, 115–17
    clearcutting, 8
    Clearwater/Salmon River area, 196
    Lick Creek demonstration area, 72
    pinyon/juniper woodlands, 59, 61–63
    stand replacement fire regime, 25–26
    Tolan Creek/Beaver-Woods projects, 158
Southern Idaho Correctional Institution,
    105–6
Southwest Forest Alliance, 83, 85–86
Spanish explorers and pinyon/juniper
    woodlands, 60
Spread rate, 46
Sprouts, aspen, 120
Spruce, Engelmann, 26
Squirrels, pine, 168, 169
Stable/static forest, myth of the, 38–39,
    110–11
Stand replacement fire regime:
    Banff National Park, 163, 165–66
    Clearwater/Salmon River area, 188
    historical fire regime, knowledge from,
        23–27
    pine, lodgepole, 149
    pinyon/juniper woodlands, 58
    Tenderfoot Creek Experimental Forest,
        159
    Tolan Creek/Beaver-Woods projects,
        158
Stephenson, Nathan L., 129

Stern, Barry, 106
Stewardship, forest, 11, 38–39, 99–100,
    113, 118
Strip head-fire technique, 127, 152
Subalpine forests and stand replacement
    fire regime, 24
Suburban/commercial development
    threatening western forests, 204
Suppression, fire:
    Banff National Park, 166
    Bob Marshall Wilderness, 141
    British Columbia's Coast Range, 91
    Cascade Range, 96
    Clearwater/Salmon River area, 193–96
    Eagle Lake Ranger District, 177, 178,
        182, 185
    environmental regulations aiding, 97
    fireproofing homes/communities, 34
    forage, wildlife, 166
    Forest Service, primary mission of
        U.S., 8
    Glacier National Park, 139, 140
    hazards from a century of, 1–2, 29
    historical fire regime, knowledge from,
        22, 25, 26
    industry built up around, 8
    legislation easing way for, 8–9
    mixed fire regime, 22–23
    Northwest Forest Plan, 93
    pine, lodgepole, 150, 153
    pine, whitebark, 169
    pinyon/juniper woodlands, 58
    stand replacement fire regime, 25, 26
    Tolan Creek/Beaver-Woods projects,
        156
Survis, Paul, 100
Sweetvetch, 166

Tandy, Brian, 94–95
Targhee National Forest, 171
Taylor River Canyon, 150–53
Technology available for restoration
    forestry, 50
Tenderfoot Creek Experimental Forest,
    159–62

Thimbleberry, 22
Thomas, Craig, 115–17
Thomas, Jack W., 97, 207
Timber management, logging for, 42–43
Tolan Creek/Beaver-Woods projects, 155–59
Tomback, Diana, 169
Torching potential, 45–46
Traditional forestry, failure of, 7–9
    see also Historical fire regimes, knowledge from
Trout, Eagle Lake, 176
Trout Unlimited, 157

Udall, Stewart, 122
Underburns:
    Blue Mountains, 100
    Burnt Fork Ranch, 116–17
    Cascade Range, 92, 94
    Larch, old-growth western, 145, 147
    Lick Creek demonstration area, 67
    Rocking K Ranch, 119, 120
    Seeley Lake recreation corridor, 137
    Sequoia and Kings Canyon National Park, 123–24, 126, 127
Understory fire regime, 9, 15–21, 26–27, 67, 69
    see also Low-intensity disturbance regime; Underburns
Uneven-forest management methods, xii, 26–27
    see also Silviculture
University of Montana (UM), 69–70, 110, 112
    see also Lubrecht Experimental Forest

Vancouver Sun, 91
Vanhorn, Fred, 140
Variable retention harvesting, 9
Vazquez, Al, 177
Wallowa-Whitman National Forest, 99
Watson, Kay, 118
Watson, Max, 118
Weaver, Harold, 10

Whitebark Pine Ecosystem Foundation, 174
Whortleberry, 158
"Why prescribed fire must be implemented on the Boise National Forest" (Barbouletos, Morelan & Carroll), 101
Wilderness Society, The, 136
Wildfires sweeping through forests of Western North America:
    Anaconda (1999), 140
    B and B (2003), 92
    Biscuit, 208
    Bitterroot Complex, 208
    Boise National Forest, 102, 103
    Cache Mountain (2002), 96–97
    Canyon Creek (1998), 132
    Cerro Grande (2000), 82, 208
    Clear Creek (2000), 195–96
    Clearwater/Salmon River area, 189–90
    Cone (2002), 178
    Great Idaho (1910), 24, 189
    Kelowna (2003), 91
    Mineral-Primm (2003), 33
    Moose (2001), 139
    overview, 1, 19–21, 208–9
    Pierce (1987), 128
    Red Bench (1988), 138, 139
    Rodeo-Chediski (2002), 82, 208
    Savage Creek (1985), 193
    Wedge Canyon (2003), 140–41
    Wenatchee, 208
    White Cap (1973), 14
    Wilderness Complex (2000), 196
    Yellowstone National Park (1988), 132, 149, 198
Wildland fire use (WFU), 193–95, 197
Wildland-urban interface (WUI), 198–99
Willow, Scouler's, 25, 67
Wilson, Woodrow, 59
Wirt, Steve, 143
Wolves, 166
Woodland Restoration, Inc., 118–20
Woodpecker, white-headed, 94

Yellowstone National Park, 24, 32, 33, 149